Facing the Fires

Judaic Traditions in Literature, Music, and Art
Ken Frieden and Harold Bloom, *Series Editors*

A. B. Yehoshua and Bernard Horn.
Courtesy of Leslie Starobin

Facing the Fires

Conversations with A. B. Yehoshua

Bernard Horn

 Syracuse University Press

First Edition 1997
97 98 99 00 01 02   6 5 4 3 2 1

The paper used in this publication meets the minimum requirements of
American National Standard for Information Sciences—Permanence of Paper for
Printed Library Materials, ANSI Z39.48-1984. ∞™

Library of Congress Cataloging-in-Publication Data
Horn, Bernard.
    Facing the fires : conversations with A. B. Yehoshua / Bernard
Horn.
       p. cm. — (Judaic traditions in literature, music, and art)
    Includes bibliographical references and index.
    ISBN 0-8156-0493-9 (cloth : alk. paper)
    1. Yehoshua, Abraham B.—Interviews. 2. Authors, Israeli—
Interviews. I. Yehoshua, Abraham B. II. Title. III. Series.
PJ5054.Y42Z54 1997
892.4'36—dc21   97-10439

To my father, may his memory be a blessing,
a lover of Zion,
and my mother,
a scion of rabbis

Bernard Horn is professor of English at Framingham State College in Massachusetts, where he teaches American literature, mythology, Russian literature, technical writing, and seminars on Herman Melville, Norman Mailer, Toni Morrison, Genesis, and A. B. Yehoshua. A recipient of five fellowships from the National Endowment for the Humanities, he has published poems, as well as articles on Herman Melville, Norman Mailer, David Mamet, and the biblical Book of Numbers.

Contents

Acknowledgments

I wish to thank A. B. Yehoshua for his patience and good humor, for being more entertained than irritated by my persistence.

I have received support from several communities. Framingham State College has encouraged and supported me in this work. The Modern Language Association Discussion Group on Hebrew Literature accepted an outsider into its ranks; Warren Bargad was encouraging early on, and Naomi Sokoloff and Gilead Morahg helped my bibliographic investigations. The libraries of the Hebrew College in Boston and, especially, Brandeis University opened their collections to me; the staffs at both, especially James Rosenbloom at Brandeis, were consistently gracious and helpful. My congregation, Beth El of the Sudbury River Valley, and my rabbi, Lawrence Kushner, have blessed me with the chance to explore my identity as American Zionist, Jewish American, and American Jew. My students at both the college and the congregation have taught me as much as I have taught them.

I am indebted to many friends who have engaged me in an ongoing discussion over the years about Yehoshua and Israel, especially, Beverly Scott Gidron, Zeev Mehler, Shlomo Segev, Leslie Starobin, Barbara Harshav, Bob Lindenberg, Arnie and Lorel Zar-Kessler, and, particularly, Daniel Gidron and my son-in-law, Dan Avital, two devourers of Hebrew literature, who have been my resources in matters of the Hebrew language.

Two friends read this work in progress. Alan Feldman saw its possibilities from the very beginning and offered continuous insight and support.

Beverly Scott Gidron painstakingly read and reread (and reread) the manuscript with passion, commitment, and astuteness, alert to both style and substance.

I also wish to thank my brother, Merv, for putting up with more than his share of family responsibilities while this book crawled burdened toward completion.

My daughters, Gabi, Hedya, and Rebecca, Israeli Americans all, provided constant support and continue to overwhelm me by their creativity, integrity, beauty, and intelligence.

My wife, Linda, has been my companion on this voyage from the start: supporter, critic, artist, lover.

Author's Note

In Hebrew words, in general, the consonant *h* indicates both the Hebrew *heh* (as in *halachah*), pronounced as the English *h*, and the guttural Hebrew *het* (as in *haver* or Yitzhak), pronounced from the back of the palate. I use *ch* for the other guttural Hebrew letter, *chaf,* except when American usage has adopted the *kh* for the *chaf* (as in Molkho, the hero of *Five Seasons*) or the *ch* for the *het* as in Menachem.

Facing the Fires

Prologue
The Novelist as Citizen

The shadow of the intifada falls over these conversations. They begin on January 14, 1988, in Haifa, five weeks after the uprising began, and end on May 2, 1996, in Boston, three weeks before the election of Benjamin Netanyahu as Israeli prime minister awakened fears that the intifada may start up again.

The uprising started on December 8, 1987, when a truck driven by an Israeli civilian smashed into a car near the Jabaliya refugee camp in Gaza, killing four Arabs. Riots broke out immediately, and within a week rioting spread throughout the West Bank and Gaza and assumed the character of an intifada, or "awakening."

Five years of intifada were the catalyst for the series of remarkable events leading up to the Israeli elections of 1996: the Oslo negotiations and the handshake in Washington in 1993; the Israeli withdrawal from many of the towns and cities in the West Bank and Gaza in 1994 and 1995; the assassination of Yitzhak Rabin in 1995; the Palestinian elections and the change in the Palestinian covenant in 1996; and the intermittent terror atrocities by the enemies of peace. All of these events seemed to mark the end of the intifada as a unifying popular uprising of the Palestinian people.

These changes in Israel—and the cataclysmic changes in other parts of the world—have charted what seems to be nothing less than a sea change in history, a change so large that only the cunning of time will reveal its consequences and meaning. But A. B. Yehoshua, my conversa-

1

tion partner in this book, is no detached observer of history. On the contrary, he feels a moral obligation and a patriotic commitment to try to intervene and nudge his people to make the difficult decisions that bode best for their future. This commitment arises in part because of his acute awareness that he is present at the renaissance of his people. This commitment also defines where he diverges from the writer he admires most. For Tolstoy, in his fiction at least, is the great historical fatalist, while Yehoshua fits into the line of prophets, actively engaged in trying to transform history.

The intifada is unquestionably a political event of historic importance, but politics only scratches the surface of its importance to Yehoshua. His very best work by his own account is the fifth conversation of *Mr. Mani*, which was fashioned in part as a quiet response to the worst days of the intifada. He also links the intifada with the theme that, as I reflect back on these conversations, stands out most: identity and its discontents—this may not be the most important matter we talk about, but it is the one we talk about most often. For Yehoshua the intifada is the birth, or the rebirth, of the Palestinian people; it is a seminal event for the Palestinians in much the same way the Declaration of Independence is a seminal document for the American people. The intifada is, in sum, the belated collective act of self-creation of a Palestinian national identity. And Yehoshua's abiding preoccupation with Jewish identity in both Israel and the Diaspora makes him peculiarly sensitive to the identity of his nation's great modern antagonist.

Yehoshua's attitude toward the intifada reveals something of his character, for it is as a committed Zionist that he welcomes (in no simple way) the intifada in the same way that, as a Jew who does not believe in God, he fashions a radical interpretation of the Binding of Isaac. Zionist and Jew, he insists on his identification with a group whose identity markers and cherished values he tests and challenges: religion, morality, Zion, Holocaust, Diaspora. It is true that he tests these markers and beliefs in fiction, but unlike the United States (and this is one of the matters that most intrigues me as an American) the fact that his testing takes a literary form places him at the center, not the margins, of his culture.

Called Bulli by his friends, Yehoshua is a stocky man of sixty—he celebrated his birthday in December 1996—with a round gentle face, clearly a Jew of Sephardic origins. I asked him how he came to be called Bulli. "Bulli was a nickname that was given to me when I was thirteen by two beautiful girls in my class, and because I didn't want to carry the very heavy name Avraham, I preferred to be called Bulli, and this is how the name stuck to me. Now in the last few years I prefer the name Avraham but it is too late."

His most striking feature is his pair of deep-set dark eyes, which fasten fixedly and hold the glance of whomever he is talking to—a little longer than Americans are accustomed to—and are apt to glow with somber seriousness, twinkle with amusement, shine with perplexity, and sparkle with laughter, all in just a few moments of conversation. Passionate and exuberant in speech, he takes visible pleasure in sharing his enthusiasms. He gestures freely and sometimes stammers a bit and lisps as his words race to catch up to his thoughts. Occasionally, a French pronunciation or word will slip in, partly a product of four years in France in the mid-sixties as the general secretary of the World Union of Jewish Students. Even though I ought to have known better, my reading of his early stories and novels led me to expect a more brooding person than the ebullient, curious, and outgoing man I encountered, when I met him for the first time early in 1988. He lives in Haifa with his wife, Rivka, called Ika, a psychoanalyst and clinical psychologist at the Carmel Hospital in Haifa; they married in 1960. He has three children, a daughter, Sivan, 30, an art therapist, and two sons, Gidon, 26, in his first year at the university, and Nahum, 21, who has completed his basic training and is now an officer in the regular army.

Like his longtime friend, Amos Oz, he is one of the preeminent members of "the generation of the State," native Israelis who came of age after the birth of modern Israel in 1948 and emerged in the literary world as the *gal hadash,* or "new wave," in the 1960s. He has written six novels, three collections of short stories, several plays, and two fiercely polemical collections of essays, *Between Right and Right* (1980), which was published in English in 1981, and *The Wall and the Mountain* (1989), which has not yet appeared in English. At the same time a serious and a popular novelist, he is the most vigorous and intellectually adventurous defender of liberal Zionism in Israel. All six of his novels have been best-sellers in Israel: *The Lover* (1977, 1978 U.S.); *A Late Divorce* (1982, 1984 U.S.); *Molkho* (1987), published as *Five Seasons* in the United States in 1989; *Mr. Mani* (1990, 1992 U.S.); *The Return from India* (1994), published as *Open Heart* in the United States in 1996; and *Voyage to the End of the Millennium* (1997), which will be published in the United States in 1998. *Open Heart,* the most successful of all, sold more than a hundred thousand copies, one sale for every fifty inhabitants of the country. He was awarded the Brenner Prize in 1983, the Alterman Prize in 1986, and the Bialik Prize in 1988. He won the American Prize for the best Jewish book in 1990 and in 1993. In January 1991 *Mr. Mani* was the inaugural winner of the new Israeli Booker Prize, for the best Israeli book written in the previous two years, and in 1995 he received the highest literary honor in Israel, the Israel Prize, for the body of his work. All of the novels have been widely translated, *Mr. Mani,* for instance, appearing in twelve or thirteen languages.

Three of his works—*The Lover* and the novellas "Three Days and a Child" and "Early in the Summer of 1970"—have been made into theatrical movies; "Three Days and a Child" was the official Israeli entry at the 1967 Cannes Film Festival and garnered the best actor prize for Odded Kotler. *The Lover* and *A Late Divorce* have been dramatized and performed in Israeli theaters. If you talk to Israelis, you get the distinct impression that, aside from the ultraorthodox, everyone between eighteen and forty has read *The Lover;* it has been required reading for the comprehensive high school examinations for many years. All five of the conversations that make up *Mr. Mani* have been staged in Israel, a five-part television version was put on in the fall of 1996, and a radio actor gave a public reading in Frankfurt of the German translation of the second conversation, in which a charming and sinister German soldier talks to his fiercely nationalistic grandmother in 1944 during the German occupation of Crete. When I asked him how the German audience responded, he told me, "The reaction of the audience was very good. It was an audience of intellectuals." The novel was published in Germany in the fall of 1993.

He has been associated with the University of Haifa since 1967, first as dean of students and since 1972 as professor of comparative literature. He has been guest professor at Harvard (1977), the University of Chicago (1988), and Princeton (1992), and returned to the University of Chicago in the spring of 1997.

Though, with the singular exception of *Mr. Mani,* he has been loathe to talk about his work in his many public appearances, I suspect that his willingness to persist in these conversations for more than eight years is related to his many years as a literature professor. In that role, he and I are colleagues, chatting about the work of a writer one of us is something of a specialist in. In that role too, he displays a wide and passionate familiarity with world literature and American literature, and the conversations abound with allusions to some of his favorite non-Israeli writers, including Euripides, Molière, Racine, Tolstoy, Dostoyevsky, Chekhov, Mann, Woolf, Kafka, Babel, Faulkner, Marquez, Bellow, and Morrison.

In literary terms the conversations range freely over all four parameters of literary inquiry: the novel as formal artwork; the novel as "mirror up to nature," or cultural artifact; the novel as self-expression; the novel as creator and manipulator of its readers. He has been a rare bird over these eight years, willing to address these matters with patience and good humor. Consequently, the conversations give the reader a rare opportunity: the possibility to explore the work of a major literary artist through the prisms of all the things people talk about when they talk about literary art. Do his books represent human nature? Of course. Do his books represent Israeli reality? To a fault. Do his books manipulate his readers? Absolutely. Do his books express his private relationships and his ideology? Unquestionably. Are his novels about other novels? Certainly; as a matter of fact, they represent what Harold Bloom would label "strong readings" of Franz Kafka and William Faulkner, S. Y. Agnon and Leo Tolstoy. Obviously, this book would not exist without his cooperation over these many years. Of all his qualities, the most indispensable ones—it is impossible to imagine this book without them—are his willingness to direct the lens of an astute literature professor at his own writings and to participate in conversations about his work and his society with passion laced with a healthy dose of detachment and curiosity.

One of the strongest undercurrents is Yehoshua's complex relationship with books. In a long discussion of the Diaspora that took place while the secret peace negotiations were being held in Oslo in 1993, he challenged the very value of books and suggested that a Jew in the Diaspora leads only half a life as a Jew because of books. "He cannot live only with his Judaism on a bookshelf," Yehoshua insisted, "in which there are just ideas, while he lives in another reality, which is American, English, or whatever." This bookish identity contrasts with the density of an Israeli Jewish identity that is defined by language, material history, social structure, and, most important, the collective power to do good or evil and the collective moral responsibility that is the corollary of this power. On the other hand, in an illuminating and controversial diagnosis of the perils of peace in 1996, he not only argues for the importance of adding "Jewish" elements to Israeli identity but adds that "our Chateaux de la Loire, our Louvre, our Florence, our Michelangelo are texts." And in the rueful optimism that preceded the Israeli elections of 1996, he called for secular Israelis to make overtures to religious Zionists, the bitterest enemies of the peace camp, because they "work with the texts all the time—not as scholars, but in human dialogue with the texts."

With books looming as both an obstacle to an abundant Jewish identity in the Diaspora and an essential ingredient in Israel, I had the temerity to suggest to him once that his works belong on the same shelf as the traditional textual cathedrals that are the Jewish equivalent of material culture. He did not respond.

What precipitated these conversations was a letter. In the fall of 1987 I invited him, out of the blue, to speak at my congregation if he happened to be visiting the Boston area in the near future. I had been teaching his first two novels for years in general education literature classes to students who know virtually nothing about Israel, the Middle East, or Judaism. In that first letter I briefly described my students and mentioned that at the end of the spring semester more than half of them voted *The Lover* their favorite of the nine books they had read. I had no way of knowing how deep a chord that vote would sound in him. In Israel, although he is a novelist of love and desire and the profound impediments to human connection, he is often described and debated as if he were a purely ideological writer with only perfunctory interest in the rich soil of the human condition. For me, in contrast, what is always engaging about him and his work is his desire and ability to fuse idea and human character. In our discussion of the genesis of *Mr. Mani,* he made this desire quite clear. "I always respect the combination between something that is physical and something that is spiritual. I do not believe only in spiritual acts. I think that spiritual acts must demonstrate themselves physically."

The chapters that follow are conversations, really one long conversation, the vertebrae of which are the discussions of Yehoshua's fiction. The organization is not chronological but thematic, with the first and fifth chapters reflecting on the genesis and the implications of *Mr. Mani,* the fourth and most ambitious of his six novels. The conversations loop back from recent politics to the beginning of his literary career in chapter two and move on to his first two novels in chapter three and his third and fifth novels in chapter four, before returning to *Mr. Mani* and reaching out toward his sixth novel and the future in chapter five.

To supplement the body of the text, I have included an epilogue, which summarizes what has been written about Yehoshua in English, a chronology of the important dates that came up during the conversations, a list of his publications, a glossary of Hebrew words, and a bibliography of English-language criticism of his work.

1

The Novelist as Psychotherapist

Early in the winter of 1988, I was sitting across a coffee table from A. B. Yehoshua in his late mother-in-law's apartment overlooking the harbor in Haifa, the port city built on Mount Carmel in northern Israel. It was three weeks after she had died, having lived for a year in the silence brought on by a stroke. It was five weeks after the intifada had begun on December 8, 1987. "I'm extremely happy with the riots," he told me.

Four years later, in a phone conversation in January 1992, when I asked him whether he still felt that way, he said, "Unfortunately, yes, even though my son, Gidon, was one of the soldiers who had to struggle against the riots." Such provocative statements are Yehoshua's way of dramatizing an extremely serious point. "These riots are very important," he explained. "The Palestinians were so lazy, too cooperative, too silent. We cannot *give* them a state; they have to work for it. The riots are the only way for the Palestinians to present their problems to the Israelis and the world. If they don't demonstrate that they are fighting for their independence, they will be totally ignored."

This is not to say that he has ever been sentimental about the Palestinians. I asked him about the violence Palestinians were inflicting on themselves, especially in Gaza, the murders and mutilations of suspected informers. By the end of 1989, a third of the twenty-seven hundred attacks by Palestinians had been directed at fellow Arabs. He told me how disturbing he found "the killing the Palestinians are doing among themselves. It is really something that is abnormal, the brutality and the wildness with which they are killing their brothers."

7

We came back to this topic during another phone conversation one year later, in January 1993. He had just returned to Israel after spending the fall 1992 semester teaching at Princeton. I asked him about the effects of the increased violence of Palestinians against Israelis after Yitzhak Rabin took office in the summer of 1992. Hamas terrorists had murdered seven Israelis in just one week that December. "Does this affect your commitment to the peace camp in Israel?" I asked.

"On the contrary," he said, "this reinforces my thinking that we have to establish a leader and a government in the West Bank and Gaza to prevent the wild and savage actions that deteriorate the fabric of their own existence."

"It seems to me," I said, "that over the first five years of the intifada, it has changed from being a true mass movement to something much narrower ideologically and much more vicious." I mentioned the case of a woman who was axed to death in Gaza.

"About the intifada . . ." he began, gathering his thoughts. "My position is that—unfortunately, and I repeat, unfortunately—only the intifada could have pushed the Israelis to understand the despair and the terrible situation of the occupation of the territories. I agree that the intifada started as popular riots with no intention to kill Israelis. But it lasted for four years"—this was early in 1993—"and it didn't yield any results."

"No results at all?"

"Of course, there were *some* results: the fact is that the Israelis were ready, even under the Shamir government, to negotiate with the Palestinians in Madrid, although Shamir did not want to give them anything. At least there was a kind of a formula for the negotiations. This was the result of the intifada." The Madrid Conference, orchestrated by Secretary of State James Baker in the aftermath of the Gulf War, began in November 1991. At the conference, the Palestinian representative, Haidar Abd al-Shafi, a doctor from Gaza, indicated that the Palestinians were ready to compromise.

We came back to the intifada once again a few months later in the spring of 1993 in New York City. We were sitting in a crowded coffee shop on Madison Avenue, around the corner of the Frick Museum, with his wife, Ika, and my wife, Linda, who had lived in Israel from 1968 to 1978. We had two hours to kill before the museum would open. "The last time we spoke," I said, "you mainly talked about the effect of the intifada on the Israelis. What about the Palestinians?"

"I have to clarify something here. The intifada affected both sides. The intifada awakened the Palestinians from their sleep, and the fighting made them more moderate. While they were sleeping, they cooperated with the Israeli regime and waited for the great solution that would come in the Time of the Messiah, when all of Palestine would be transferred to their hands." His voice had taken on the rhythm of a sermon, and caught the attention of a man at the next table of the noisy coffee shop. We both smiled at the incongruity of it all, and he continued. "While they slept, they were also more hawkish. They were hawkish when they were not doing a thing."

"That's an interesting idea," I said. "What you're saying is that taking action made them more realistic."

"Yes. When they fought and they started to suffer, their suffering made them more moderate—as happened to the Israelis themselves and, earlier, to the Egyptians. It was only when the Egyptians suffered during the War of Attrition with Israel that they understood that they had to make peace with Israel. This is the result of a fight." The War of Attrition was a difficult period of sporadic, intense, and unresolved warfare between Israel and Egypt along the Suez Canal during 1969 and 1970.

"I take it that you're still referring to the first years of the intifada."

"Yes, the first stage of the intifada—that is, the popular, huge riots against Israel—was the awakening of the minds and the hearts of the Israelis to the reality of the Palestinians' problems, especially because the Israelis could no longer go on nature hikes in the occupied territories. The intifada established the green line." The "green line" is the pre-1967 border between Israel and what was then Jordanian territory; Israelis are great lovers of nature hikes and, in the years after the Six-Day War, they were particularly attracted to exploring the new terrain of the occupied territories. These trips had nourished the illusion that occupation (or even absorption) of the territories would cost Israel nothing, an illusion shattered when the intifada made all of the territories dangerous.

"So the intifada profoundly changed how Israelis thought and felt about the territories."

"But, unfortunately, this new thinking did not bring the final result, the separation of a Palestinian state and the recognition of the Palestinian right to self-determination. And this is the reason why, through despair, there is now—as we sit here in New York City waiting for the museum to open—the second terrible stage, of the suicidal killings of Israelis by gunmen, by men with knives and axes. I don't say that all these half-crazy people, these religious fanatics, support a two-state solution. Some of them are doing it totally from a kind of despairing exaltation. And this is why we have to retaliate and to respond to the killings in a harsh way. But this second stage also has given the Israelis another dose of the painful knowledge that there can be no solution other than separation. In a way, you know, all of this violence is the result of the slowness and the hesitations of the Rabin government, because the Rabin government has not gone as fast as it could in the negotiations."

"But at least," I said, feeling an obligation to defend Rabin; after all, he hadn't even been in office for a year. "At least Rabin's words are more promising than Shamir's. When they asked him about the terrible intensification of the violence, he did say that a political solution is the only answer to the problems."

"But there has been no substantive development in the political sense," he said slowly, emphasizing every word, "just the increase in violence. We have to enter negotiations. We have to speak to the PLO. It is very important that we speak to the PLO because the PLO is recognized by the Palestinian people as its representative, and we *cannot* choose to whom we will speak; they have to decide who is their representative."

"Many of my Israeli friends describe Feisal Husseini as a natural leader. They clearly would prefer him to Yasser Arafat."

"I don't know Feisal Husseini. He seems very good, but he's not the leader, and, I repeat, we can't choose their leadership. If there are people behind the scenes, bring them on stage and let them negotiate. To speak with someone when behind him is someone else is immoral and inefficient." And he returned to what was his theme during the spring of 1993. "In any case, I believe that Rabin has been very slow, that he must go fast, and that he must propose to the Palestinians, not just autonomy, but the final target of these negotiations, the self-determination of the Palestinian people—without that nothing will move! I think all the ministers have been very lazy and that they, in a way, have been asleep, and if they do not push Rabin to make a decision, they will miss the opportunity of this government for peace—of course, I don't believe that there is another solution for another government—so that all they would do is delay the situation."

"Can the United States do anything?" I asked.

"No. There is nothing for the Americans to do. It is only up to the State of Israel, the government of Israel. All the components of the solution are in their hands, and if they will move, there is a solution. The Palestinian problem is far more important than the Syrian border. The Syrian border can wait until the Palestinian problem is solved."

At the same moment, in May 1993, that Yehoshua was so critical of the Rabin government as we sat in that coffee shop in New York City, nearly four thousand miles away in Oslo, this same Rabin government was engaged in secret negotiations with the PLO. Nearly three years later, on February 24, 1996, I asked, "How did you feel when you found out that the Oslo talks were going on even as we spoke?" We were speaking by phone, he in Haifa, I in the United States. As we spoke we had no way of knowing that the next day would by marked by the first of the four Hamas and the Islamic Jihad suicide bombings of February 25, March 3, and March 4, 1996.

"Really," he said, happiness filling his voice, "I was so pleased with Oslo I. I did not know about the secret negotiations, and, as you know, I could not understand why Rabin and Peres were hesitating so much, because they did not have any other alternative. And then they did it! And I was totally surprised, not because of the move itself; the move was necessary, it was logical, and it *would* come, but that it was done secretly and it was done successfully! I was extremely happy and extremely moved." His joy was contagious, as if he had reimmersed himself into that time in 1993 and had pulled me in with him. "Oslo I," the Oslo Stage I agreement, is the interim self-government arrangement agreed to by Israel and the PLO in 1993 and 1994. "Oslo II" is the negotiating of a permanent relationship between Israel and the Palestinians to go into effect May 1999 through negotiations that were supposed to begin no later than May 1996.

"I remember so clearly," I said, "that as the information about the Oslo talks started coming out, late in the summer, how all of us, virtually everyone I know . . . do you know the Keats lines? . . . 'looked at each other with a wild surmise,' as if it were something of a miracle."

"I thought it was unbelievable, unbelievable! I once asked Rabin at a private meeting with him, 'Did you ever think that you could make such an important move and recognize the PLO by only one vote in the Knesset, not only *one* vote, but one *Arab* vote, not only one Arab vote, but *five* Arab votes? Did you ever think that this would be the only majority that you would have and that, nevertheless, you would get legitimacy from the people?' "

"What did he say?"

"He said, 'Never in my life did I believe that this could be possible.' And this *was* possible and this was the most important thing."

"And without the intifada . . ."

"Without the intifada we might still be waiting."

As he spoke about the Palestinians and the effect of the intifada on both their own sense of their identity and the Israeli view of them, my thoughts leapt to one of the several Joseph Manis who play central roles in Yehoshua's extraordinary fourth novel, *Mr. Mani,* which was greeted by universal critical acclaim in Israel and the United States, Alfred Kazin, for one, calling it "one of the most remarkable pieces of fiction I have ever read." During World War I, in 1918, this Joseph Mani, at the risk of his life, crosses from British-held Jerusalem behind the Turkish lines and travels from one Arab village to another, reading an Arabic translation of the brand-new Balfour Declaration to audiences of uncomprehending peasants and crying out to them, "Who are ye? Awake, before it is too late and the world is changed beyond recognition! Get ye an identity, and be quick!"

The scene in the novel and the comments about the intifada spring from the same sort of audacity, which is characteristic of Yehoshua's way of being in the world. Not too many Israelis, whatever their political views, were happy with the riots. And of those who were, still fewer are willing to express their happiness freely. But this casual audacity informs Yehoshua's activity as an actor in Israeli political reality and a creator of innovative and evocative fiction.

During our first conversation, in 1988, we got to talking about how well such fiction crossed international borders, especially in the light of the critical reception of his first three novels in the United States. Although the appraisal by critics in the United States has been very positive, he is not yet as widely known here as his compatriots, Amos Oz and Aharon Appelfeld. From the time his stories were published here in the 1970s, he has been hailed as a mighty artist of incantatory power, and reviewers have associated his name with the Nobel Prize in literature for twenty years. *The Lover,* his first novel, was greeted enthusiastically by such critics as Alfred Kazin and Robert Alter. *Five Seasons* and *A Late Divorce* were celebrated on the front page of the *New York Times Book Review* by Lore Segal and Harold Bloom, respectively, Segal comparing Yehoshua to Kafka, Bloom to Faulkner and Joyce.

I asked him whether he had met Harold Bloom. "Yes, I know Harold Bloom—he is really a madman, but also a genius."

"A genius . . ." I said.

"He wrote nice things about *A Late Divorce* in the *New York Times.*" We looked at each other, and then both of us burst into laughter.

"I've seen him lecture a couple of times," I said. "Sometimes I think he intentionally cultivates the image of a mad genius."

"I met him at Yale, and he really fascinated me because he seemed like a character coming right out of a Bellow novel."

I wondered whether he knew Robert Alter, a professor at Berkeley who had written about his early work quite sympathetically and had profoundly affected my understanding of biblical narrative and poetry.

"Uri Alter is a good scholar," he replied, referring to Alter by his Hebrew name. "He's really honest and decent. He follows the new critical methods, but he absorbs them in a far more reasonable way than the majority of critics, who just take the latest article, swallow it whole, and project it onto everything." This was Yehoshua speaking as professor of comparative literature at Haifa University. For the past few moments he had been giving me my first glimpse of one of his most unusual, intriguing, and endearing traits: the candor, humor, and intelligence he brings to discussions of other people's work and his own.

Yehoshua acknowledges that *Mr. Mani* is the most ambitious of his six novels, in scope, intellectual force, and moral energy. It is unquestionably a novel of astounding moral, mythological, and psychological ambition, and he was mildly surprised by its success—more than forty thousand copies since it came out in Israel in 1990—"even though," as he put it, "it is not a simple book." On a political level, it is Yehoshua's direct assault against the nationalists and religious fundamentalists in the war for the memory, hence the soul and future, of his nation. His way of engaging in this battle is to dive deeply into the historical and mythological past of the Jewish people. His purpose, he told me in that coffee shop in 1993, "is to understand the present." This is why he was so insistent when he said, "It is not an historical novel—even though it covers 150 years of history. If it were an historical novel, it would be totally different. The present is the key, the present is the target. I feel that Israel is now at a kind of crossroads, between war and peace, and I want very much to understand that crossroads."

There was pain and passion in his voice as he continued. "I wanted to understand why we keep repeating the same thing, why we keep repeating the same stupidity, why we cannot move." And the stakes are beyond calculation. If there is no peace settlement, he sees the danger of a new *shoah,* a new Holocaust. "There is a threat that in ten years there could be atomic terrorism in Israel and a new kind of *shoah,* and yet no one is thinking about it, as in the thirties no one was thinking about the *shoah* that would come in the forties." He paused to let his last words sink in. "So perhaps in ten years we will look back and say we had another option and we didn't take it, and this is what we have come to, this is the new disaster that has fallen on us."

It would be a mistake, however, to think of *Mr. Mani* as a novel of ideas. On the contrary, the way the collective past impinges on the collective present of the nation is profoundly tangled and rooted in the way the past inhabits each character psychologically. I asked him how he sees the relationship between the large ideas of the novel and the individual characters. "First of all—and it's the most important thing for me, before ideology, before Jewish history, before the crossroads of Jewish history, and all those big themes—first of all, the purpose of this novel is to try to explore the unconscious material that comes from fathers to sons and from our grandfathers and great-grandfathers to ourselves."

"That takes us beyond Freud," I said, "and the oversimplified psychological theories you give to Hagar Shiloh's mother, Yael." I was referring to the silent participant in the first conversation in the novel.

"Yes. In the Freudian scheme we continually work with our unconscious in the framework of one personality, one life. But here I wanted to examine the things that work inside us that come from an unknown— not something we repress, but things that we cannot know because we cannot know our great-grandfather, what he was feeling, and what are the things that work in us now that he transmitted to us without our knowledge."

The direction, like the direction of psychoanalysis, is from the present to the past. "You know that Ika is a psychoanalyst and she always tells me that her patients, even when they are in their forties or fifties, are far more preoccupied with their mothers and their fathers than with their children. We worry about our children, we are very much concerned with the fate of our children. But emotionally, when we think about ourselves, the real dialogue is not with our children. The real dialogue, the true dialogue, is with our parents. We are always obsessed with our parents. The dialogue with our parents is the deep dialogue inside our souls. So the true dialogue goes on in reverse, and this is the reason why the whole novel goes in reverse."

"Bernie," he asked me, "do you know something about your grandfathers?"

"I only know a few stories. Neither was alive when I was born. But I do feel a close kinship with my mother's father. My mother, who was with him when he was killed in a pogrom in 1919, told me many stories about him. What about you?"

"I know *something*, I know about one of them. The other was dead when I was born. So I do know something, but only vaguely; but my grandfather was still very important in the life of my father, and my father was very important for me. But what about the dialogue between the father of my grandfather and his father? I don't know anything. This is a total darkness and this darkness still works in the present. Some of our behavior, some of the inner course of our lives, is still inherited from our grandfathers or our great-grandfathers whom we know almost nothing about. And in the novel I wanted to shine some spots of light on this darkness, in order to discover and explore this darkness, the part of it that is still working inside us."

"How does this darkness work on us?"

"Perhaps I am a writer because my grandfather or the father of my grandfather had this imagination that was working in him and he transmitted it to me. Perhaps my ideological convictions come from a dispute between my father and my grandfather that I don't know anything about! So this is the structure of the novel. We have to go backwards in order to understand the present, individually and as a nation."

"When you say, 'We *have* to go backwards,'" I interjected, "you are speaking, not of choice, but of compulsions or obsessions. And *Mr. Mani* is rife with obsessions. But it occurs to me that there are obsessions and obsessions, some sane, some destructive. For instance, if Israel collectively or Gavriel Mani individually is in a profound crisis, it makes sense to be obsessed with getting to the bottom of the crisis until he finally understands it. At the same time an obsession may be deeply self-destructive."

"*Mr. Mani* is about obsessions that were self-destructive: the heroes in *Mr. Mani* are, I would say, directed by a very antique self-destruction, a murder, that is lying in their unconscious without their knowing it. Let me put it this way: what I wanted to do in *Mr. Mani* is to enlarge the psychoanalytic game, to transform the psychoanalytic forces inside the individual human psyche into intergenerational forces. A person can always discuss his interaction with his parents but, as I said, he cannot discuss his interaction with his grandfathers and with the fathers of his grandfathers and I wanted to enlarge the psychoanalytic scheme into a wider one and something that can be traced only in literature and not even in the deepest psychoanalytic process because the generations that are behind us are totally darkened for us."

"When I suggested before that you are going beyond Freud," I said, "I was also thinking of movement from the individual to the group."

"Yes," he said. "What psychoanalysis tries to do is to go slowly, slowly, in circles to find certain moments in the life of a person in which there were unsolved conflicts, in order to understand some of the neurosis and some of the disturbances of the present. So my feeling was to do psychoanalysis on a national level, and to try to see why we are in such a confusion now by understanding some of the elements of the past."

Yehoshua's interest in psychoanalysis goes beyond its psychological importance or its literary use. He is an eloquent defender of the moral weight of psychoanalysis. "In psychoanalysis, the work is done by the person himself. And this is its moral dignity, because psychoanalysis is not a magical force that comes and says, 'You have to do this. This is the explanation. This is the interpretation.' The work is done by the man himself. Liberty is preserved in this technique. There is something morally correct in this therapy because the man repairs himself—he just gets some guidelines, some signs, but there is no guru imposing himself on the person. He doesn't even see a face. The face is something behind a canopy, behind the sofa. He just hears a voice that directs him so that he can make this exploration better by himself."

And who is called on in *Mr. Mani* to do the equivalent of this psychoanalytical work? "It is the reader. The characters themselves don't know what is happening, but the reader, who has a kind of bird's-eye view, a vision of five generations, understands and explores the unconscious elements in the interactions between the generations."

"I was thinking about the readers and the structure in a slightly different way," I said. "By the time we get to the end of the novel, as readers, we've spent six hours, seven hours, a few days, deeply involved with these characters, all of whom would not exist if Avraham Mani had not done the extraordinary things he did at the end of the novel."

"Go on," he said, smiling.

"So," I continued, "we have a big stake in what Avraham Mani does, just simply as readers. If he shrinks from breaking the terrible taboos against incest and against murder at the end of the novel, all of those wonderful characters would not even exist. And that leads to a whole odd sense of destiny, of how we interpret fate and destiny."

"Yes," he chimed in, "and you don't read *Mr. Mani* in the innocent way you read a normal book in which you don't know what will happen in the future. In *Mr. Mani* you always know what will happen in the future . . . and you don't know. Because in each paragraph itself you don't know what will happen, and you read each paragraph as you read an ordinary book. But you know what will happen in the future because you have read the previous chapter. So it is, in a way, both kinds of reading at once, an ordinary reading in which you want to know what will happen on the next page and a reading in which you know very well the consequence of what is done now. You know the distant future, but you don't know the near future."

"Let me tell you an odd thing that happened as a result of this," I said. "I read Amos Elon's biography of Herzl right after I had finished *Mr. Mani,* and as I was reading the biography, I felt as if I were still reading *Mr. Mani,* and it was awful. I got to the last part of the biography at two in the morning and I couldn't put it down. I felt as if I were listening to Efrayim Shapiro describing the tragic-comic scenes at the Third Zionist Congress in 1899, and I desperately wanted all of the real historical people to listen to Herzl, as if my desire as a reader could change reality itself."

"That's exactly the feeling you should have," was Yehoshua's reply.

"But reading *Mr. Mani* also made me look at the present, at the current escalation of violence in a special way." This was 1993, and I was referring to the intensification of violence that spring, violence that seems almost mild now, in the wake of Baruch Goldstein's murder of praying Arabs in February 1994, Yigal Amir's murder of Rabin in November 1995, and the Hamas suicide bombings of February and March 1996. "As you said before," I continued, "in the middle years of the intifada, in 1990 or 1991, there was a real opportunity for peace that was lost, and part of me fears that once again we did not act in time, that it would have been better to have acted then, in 1990 or 1991, when there seems to have been more unity and moderation among the Palestinians."

"My feeling," Yehoshua said sadly, "is that every day it becomes more difficult, and every day the tissues become more torn. There is the brutality. But, in addition, there are some very good people among the Palestinians who are physically leaving because they are fed up—people whom we have many relationships with—and good relationships with—are despairing and leaving. And the most unsophisticated, fundamentalist part of the Palestinian people remain in the territories and have so many children. At the same time, there are more and more Israeli settlements in the territories, so more and more people will have to leave their houses when peace comes. So it does get more difficult the longer we wait. Listen: if Russia had moved to democracy ten years ago, let's say, it would be better for Russia than what is going on now."

Mr. Mani represents a convergence of all of Yehoshua's identities, as a son, father, and husband, as an ardent Zionist, and as a Jew—and as a literary artist. In fact, when readers pick up *Mr. Mani,* the first thing that is likely to strike them is the form itself. Yehoshua told me that it is "unique in form," and he's right. It was with a charming combination of enthusiasm and modesty that he confided, "I don't think something like it was ever created before, in terms of structure." The novel consists of five "conversations"—he calls them "missing or one-sided dialogues"—in which we hear one side of an extended conversation between two "conversation partners." Each of the five speakers has a vivid and unique voice. The silence of each listener forces us into an intimate and complicitous relationship in which we must, as Yehoshua put it, "invent and recreate the silent partner."

Each of the conversations takes place in a different setting and time, and the sequence is from present to past from a kibbutz in the Negev in 1982 to a hotel in Athens in 1848, with stops along the way at Crete in 1944, Jerusalem in 1918, and Auschwitz in 1899. And it continues, by allusion, all the way back to the mythic origins of the Jewish people in the biblical story of Abraham and Isaac. Each conversation is written in the Hebrew style of its time. If each of the conversations were written in the historical language of the speaker, the first conversation would be in Hebrew, the second in German, the third in English, the fourth in Yiddish, and the fifth in Ladino—and Yehoshua's Hebrew, as it moves backward through its own development, also gives the feel of each of these languages. The 1996 Israeli television version is told in the five "true" languages (with Hebrew subtitles), and the director's conception is to rotate through the conversations each night, giving ten minutes to each of the five conversations. When Yehoshua described the project to me in 1993, the five languages seemed to me to be a better idea than fragmenting the conversations. I said, "Including ten minutes from each section each night seems like the kind of Big Idea directors get sometimes and should discard. What do you think?"

He was much more open to the idea than I. "They made a pilot program. Two directors from Israeli television were very enthusiastic. I saw it myself. It was one hour long and it was very good. The final results will be ready in 1994." Two years later it still had not been completed, as if the production itself had caught the Mani-mania, and it was not shown until the fall of 1996.

I asked him to elaborate on the backward structure. "I wanted to understand two things," he explained, "what are the conflicts that threaten to destroy us and whether there is a way out. This is the reason why on the personal level and on the national level the direction is backwards in the service of the present."

Each of the conversations is about a different "Mr. Mani," so that by the time we are done, we know six generations of Manis quite intensely—only in the fifth conversation is a Mani one of the conversation partners. Each conversation is framed by a prologue and epilogue that contain capsule biographies of the partners; the Tolstoyan style of these, sympathetic to all parties, ironic, and detached, contrasts with the idiosyncratic, individualistic styles of the five speakers. It is as if he put Dostoevskian characters within a Tolstoyan frame; imagine an *Anna Karenina* composed as a series of variations on Levin's brother Nikolay.

He describes the novel as "a combination of my craft as a novelist and as a writer of short stories." As a novel, "the five chapters are tied together with one unity, one center in it." As stories, "each section is a separate one." The sharpness of focus and emotional power of each section attests to Yehoshua's mastery of the form of the short story, a mastery William Novak articulated for all Yehoshua's early readers as early as 1977. "Of his eight stories in English," Novak wrote in the *Village Voice* on April 25, "at least five are as good as anything that has appeared since 1945. Nobel prizes have been given for less." This sentiment returned fifteen years later as the conclusion of Ted Solotaroff's review of *Mr. Mani* in the *Nation*. The language is virtually identical: "The Nobel Prize has been given for less."

Given the scope, scale, and achievement of the novel, it comes as no surprise that *Mr. Mani* was received in Israel not only as a masterpiece but also as a significant cultural phenomenon. "It was received very well," he said, in his modest way. Many articles have been written about it, and a regular Mani industry has been thriving in Israel ever since its publication in 1990. By 1995 two collections of critical articles have been published, which contain between them no fewer than eighty articles. The first of these volumes, published in January 1992 by Haifa University, covers the initial response to the novel; the second, *In the Opposite Direction,* published three years later by Yehoshua's regular publisher, *Hakibbutz Hame'uhad,* consists of longer, fuller treatments of various aspects of the novel. "For the first time in my life," Yehoshua told me in 1993, "I was willing, after the book came out, to participate in readers' meetings and to speak publicly about the book."

"But you frequently give public lectures," I said.

"Yes, but for a long time I have not talked about *my own works* publicly. From time to time, I would give some examples from my work along with examples from others' works, but I felt that when I came to give a lecture, I should talk about general topics, about the problems of Hebrew literature, and so forth. But I have changed my custom and my habits with this book, and I don't think that I will ever do it again with any books I write in the future."

He was apologetic about this activity, but felt he had no choice. "I couldn't just publish it, and say, 'Read it, and take from it whatever you understand.' Because this was a unique book for me also, and I had to try to speak about it, to explain this book, because, in a certain way, I myself don't totally understand my book." He brushed aside my laughter. "Seriously. There are books in which you understand what you have done. Of course, critics can reveal something new, and there is some enlightenment that you can get from one article or another, but you know the framework. But for me, *Mr. Mani* is without an end, and I have a kind of disease with this book, a kind of mania, and I know that there are other people who also caught a mania with this book and they keep digging more and more in the book itself to see all the connections, all the structures." These activities went on in Hebrew in 1990 after the novel was published in Israel and resumed in 1992 in English in the United States, after the American version came out. The title of the seminal Hebrew essay on *Mr. Mani* by Professor Dan Miron, the dean of Israeli literary critics, gives a taste of the mania the book induces: "Behind Every Thought, There's Another Thought Hiding."

I asked him to give me an example of his own limited understanding of *Mr. Mani.* His favorite example has to do with the name itself. "I chose the name Mani," he explained, "because it is an Iraqi family name. I wanted to bring the family from Iraq—the place where Judaism started—when Abraham left his home in Iraq and came to Israel. It was important for me, at least theoretically, to dig back to the start of the Jewish people and the Jewish faith. I also liked the name's association with mania and Manicheism."

He laughed and then continued. "But after I finished the book, some critics came to me and said, 'Why did you choose the name Mani? Because it is *ma ani,* what am I.' You can imagine my reaction—writing a book for three or four years, all the time dealing with the word 'mani,' and it never crossed my mind, that Mani can be *ma ani,* what am I? And this is why I have again and again to reread this book, because I did not realize or I did not pay attention to the simplest things. And I admit that the critics were right and caught part of the reason for the name: not *mi ani,* but *ma ani:* not 'who am I,' but 'what am I.' "

The most remarkable thing about the Israeli reception is that the novel's importance was recognized as early as 1986, long before the novel was completed, let alone published—a time when Yehoshua had come to a dead end in the writing and was not at all sure he could leap the chasm between conception and execution. So it seemed likely that he would have interesting things to say about how and when he composed the novel.

When I raised with him this question of the book's composition, I had two pieces of information to go on. I had read the third conversation in English translation in the *Tel Aviv Review* in 1988, so it was not hard to figure out that, though it is his fourth novel, he had started *Mr. Mani* before he began working on *Five Seasons,* his third, which was published in Israel in 1987. I also recognized that he had tried the form of *Mr. Mani,* the one-sided dialogue before, in one of the chapters of his second novel, *A Late Divorce,* published in 1982.

"You're right," he said. "I took the scheme, the patent, from the fifth chapter of *A Late Divorce.* I was very much attracted to the one-sided dialogue, and the reaction to this genre was a very positive one, in the context of the general reaction to the novel." His first two novels are both constructed as a series of interior monologues, and "they are very much in the present," he told me. "What I wanted to do was to expand what I was exploring in *The Lover* and *A Late Divorce* by going back in time."

He started *Mr. Mani* in 1983, a year after the death of his father, Ya'akov Yehoshua. "I worked on it between October 1983 and October 1984. In that year I planned the whole novel. I had the novel's entire scheme in my mind. I knew it would go from present to past, and I knew there would be five conversations and that the conversations would be only one-sided. I even knew the five settings. And I wrote the third conversation, 'Jerusalem, Palestine, 7 A.M. Wednesday, April 10, 1918,' which is the pillar of the novel."

Then he got stuck. "I started the other conversations and I stopped. I started the second one, I started the fourth one, and I could not go on.

I wrote three or four pages and I stopped. I couldn't go on. And this is why I stopped writing this novel. In 1984 I started to write a completely different kind of novel, *Five Seasons.*"

Five Seasons was published in 1987 in Israel and two years later in the United States. Named *Molkho* in Hebrew for the name of the main character, this novel represented a sharp turn inward for Yehoshua. "In this book," he said, "I picked a very personal subject, a very intimate question of what happens to a man of fifty after the death of his wife. I tried to penetrate in the slowest and most detailed way his movement after her death." He takes up this sort of private subject again in his fifth novel, *Open Heart.*

I asked him how he got back to work on *Mr. Mani.* "In March 1986 I published the third conversation in *Politika,* a political magazine in Israel, just as an experiment. And immediately there were such vivid reactions! I have to mention Dan Miron." Miron had written a short piece about the third conversation just two months after the conversation was published. "Almost immediately, Miron wrote a special article about this chapter, saying, 'It is very important that Mr. Yehoshua continue to write this novel because it is a very important one.'" The article, "M'shulash Mavti'ah" (A promising triangle), appeared in the magazine *Ha'olam Hazeh* on April 2, 1986. "And—without my having written anything about the novel—he said very clever things about the composition of the whole novel. Later that month, the Haifa Municipal Theatre staged this chapter as a monodrama performed by a marvelous actor, and again there was a great reaction."

But Yehoshua did not come back to the actual writing of *Mr. Mani* until after he had completed *Five Seasons.* "In June or July of 1988 I again started to write and two years afterwards, more or less, it was published. The order in which I wrote the conversations was: number three was the first, then number four, then number five, and then I returned to number two, and the last one I wrote was number one."

I was also interested in the immediate sources of the central themes and images of the novel. I had read his play *Possessions,* a comic play, hilarious and painful in spots, which depicts the aftermath of a man's death, how it affects his wife, his married son, and his married daughter, as the mother liquidates her apartment before she moves into a retirement home. I told him that I felt that this play and *Five Seasons* and *Mr. Mani* made it clear that he had been reflecting hard about death, especially the death of parents and spouses, for a long time. Knowing Yehoshua's profound kinship with Faulkner, in the back of my mind was Faulkner's famous statement that the root of *The Sound and the Fury* was "the picture of the little girl's muddy drawers, climbing that tree to look in the parlor window." For the play, as well as the two novels, it seemed to me that a death must have played the same role for Yehoshua as the image of the "little girl's muddy drawers" had played for Faulkner.

"I wrote *Possessions,*" he told me, "after *A Late Divorce.* This was just after the death of my father. It is a very autobiographical play."

"Exactly when did he die?" I asked.

"In December 1982 after an illness of about three weeks; he had liver cancer. It was quite painful. He was always in the hospital, and I was far away. I had to keep going to Jerusalem. It was not good because I could not stay; I was working in Haifa and I could not stay with him all day. We all participated, my sister coming from Tel Aviv, my mother, and myself. But, Bernie, you know this very well"—he was referring to the illness of my father, who had suffered a massive stroke in 1977 during his only visit to Israel—"you know that even coming twice a week or even three times a week to Jerusalem—it was not enough. I felt a certain guilt."

"And *Possessions* was written immediately afterwards," I said.

"Yes," he said, "and it was staged. It was *not* a success. There was a lot of criticism of the production. Mainly, I think, because the direction was not good. The decor was lousy. And even though there were good actors in it, there was also some miscasting. Now the Cameri Theatre wants to put it on again because it felt that the play did not get the production it deserved. But I think that I myself have to rework the play a little. I read it again because you asked about it, and I laughed so much because the situations are funny in a way, but there is something missing emotionally in the play. Anyhow, this was the first blow, I would say, a kind of a comic response to the death in my family. Afterwards I started to write *Mr. Mani.*"

"Was there an equally direct relationship between your father's death and the writing of *Mr. Mani?*"

"I think the seed, the idea, of this book was born in one day. From time to time a book is created over many, many years, and it grows up slowly, organically. And when you ask yourself, when was the key discovered, when did you get the formula of the book, you realize that you got the formula little by little and corrected it from time to time and you cannot catch the moment when you finally got the seed of the book. But *Mr. Mani* was created from one moment, and over one night I knew the whole structure of the book. The conception of this book was given to me and I couldn't get rid of it."

"So there was an obsessive quality in the book from the very moment of its conception."

"Yes. And in a certain way it was a burden for me, because the conception was so strong that I could not elaborate, I could not change it, and I had to be totally dominated by this structure and by this conception."

"And that moment was . . ."

"The day in which this conception was born in me was the day of the funeral of my father. I always connect the two events, one to another—I don't know if it was actually on the same day—but I believe that the conception came from the death of my father. Freud said that the day of the funeral of his father is the most important day of a man's life. I don't know if it was the most important day of my life, but it was an important day, not because it revealed something totally different or because something changed in my relationship with my father. I had a very good relationship with him. He gave me a lot of freedom, and this was very important for me—I would say emotional and ideological freedom. In a certain way, he admired me; I was far stronger than he. But I followed some of his spiritual ideas concerning the relations between Jews and Arabs."

"You were saying that something *did* happen on the day of his funeral . . ." I said.

"I found that I could for the first time connect myself to a past that until that day I had been totally alienated from, or at least I had always tried to keep a distance from."

This new relationship with the past was profoundly connected with his father. "My father was a native of Jerusalem. He was fourth generation in Jerusalem. He was an orientalist by profession; he had finished his M.A. in Oriental studies and worked for the government on Arab problems and Moslem problems. He knew Arabic very well and worked closely with the Arabs, and he was far more realistic vis-à-vis the Arabs than I. He knew their language and he could understand their inner codes. But after the death of his parents, he felt such nostalgia for his parents that he started to go and meet with other Sephardic people in Jerusalem and try to reconstruct the life of the Sephardic community in Jerusalem at the end of the nineteenth and the beginning of the twentieth century. He would go to talk to old people and try to hear stories from them and accumulate story after story about Sephardic Jerusalem at the end of the nineteenth century—feeling that the past was disappearing, that nothing would be left of it."

"This attempt to recapture the past goes on all the time, in literature and in life. What made your father's activity special?"

"Yes, this process of people going back to their childhood or going back to their communities in order to reconstruct and to preserve what was lost is very usual. It is done in many, many places. But here in Israel, it was a little bit unique because the remnant of this Sephardic life was nearby, in Jerusalem. There are people who go back to their little village in eastern Europe. But for my father the past was nearby, and he felt that if he would not reconstruct it or at least preserve it, all this past will *seem*, at least to the young generation and to other generations, something miserable, lost, and totally unimportant. The remnant of this past was nearby. If a person speaks about the little village in eastern Europe, no one can judge what had happened there and what had not happened there. It is totally destroyed and totally far away. But the Sephardic life of Jerusalem especially was a reality that was deteriorating and degenerating all the time, and he wanted, in order to keep its dignity, to speak of what actually happened and to record and preserve the fame or at least some values of this past. And he did this in many, many books."

"How did you react?"

"When he gave me these books, I always read them with half a heart. I didn't have much patience again and again to dig and to plunge into this nostalgia about how good the people were then, how warm were the relationships between people. I don't like nostalgia. I don't believe in nostalgia. I don't like it that people always say, when the past is behind them, that the past is nice and the present is always gloomy and unimportant. I don't like this way of returning to the past. The fact that he did this all the time made me feel as if he were complaining about his life, or that I did not satisfy him enough, or that his home was so gloomy for him and that this return to the past was his way of escaping from the present. And this was especially true because of the burning political situation in the late seventies and early eighties, when Menachem Begin was at the peak of his power, and all the discussions that we were always reading about in the press—about the new political movement, the new political position. I saw all his nostalgia as an escape from making decisions about the present political scene, which I was living in with all my heart. And this was my relationship to his writing, and he was writing a lot."

Yehoshua had been remarkably candid about his father's reaction to his own works at the Brenner Prize award ceremony on March 7, 1983. In his acceptance speech, "Brenner's Wife—as Metaphor," he quoted some words of writer Haim Be'er that, Yehoshua acknowledged, caught "so exactly my father's embarrassment in relation to my writing." A few years earlier Ya'akov Yehoshua had been showing Be'er around Jerusalem and during their conversations Ya'akov Yehoshua had spoken of his son's stories. Be'er wrote, "I averted my eyes from the sad and sober man straying lost and confused among the lines written by his son, innocent of any trace of the folklore, free of any hint or allusion to the colorful world of his parents with all of its tastes and smells."

Yehoshua had given this speech just two and a half months after his father's funeral. "What you seem to be saying," I observed, "is that everything changed for you at the funeral."

"On the day of the funeral." His tone was precise and sad. "After he died, I did not know where he would be buried. I had just left Sanhedria, the Jerusalem neighborhood where the body was lying and where the memorial service was held. And then the *hevrah kadishah*, the burial society, said to me, 'Follow our car.' I did not know which cemetery we were going to, and they said only that it is a special cemetery. And we followed their car, and we found ourselves going to an old cemetery on the Mount of Olives. This was more or less in the same area where Begin was buried, only Begin was buried a little bit higher up. It was a very old, neglected, abandoned Sephardic cemetery, in which a lot, a lot of the *matzevot* . . . I don't recall the English word . . ."

"Gravestones."

"Yes, the gravestones were in ruins—it was not a functioning cemetery anymore. There my father had found the two graves of his parents, which had not been used because they died during the years that Jerusalem was divided [the nineteen years from 1948 to 1967 when East Jerusalem was under the control of Jordan and it was impossible for Jews to visit these sites]. "And he took the old graveyards of his parents and he was buried there. For the first time I understood the meaning of the expression that we hear all the time when we study the Bible. You know the expression *shachav im avotav*, to lie with his fathers; every chapter of the Book of Kings ends with 'and he was lying with his fathers.' "

"*Shachav* has sexual connotations," I said.

"Yes, *shachav*, lie, is a very sexual word; *shachav* is to do a sexual act. And to lie with your fathers has a kind of sexual meaning; you are binding yourself to your father sexually. And the fact that my father, there, in the old yard of his father and grandfather, the graveyard of the old Sephardic community, in a deserted place that is not functioning anymore, that he was lying there—made me pay attention. It was one of those bright days in which you can see all of Jerusalem clear in front of you, and at that moment I think something was happening in my heart, to see that the nostalgia, the research into the past was not just a kind of intellectual thing, but something that ended physically."

For Yehoshua, this was the key, the connection between the physical and the intellectual. "I always respect the combination between something that is physical and spiritual. I do not believe only in spiritual acts. I think that spiritual acts must demonstrate themselves physically. And the fact that this was the combination of his longing for the past, his research into the past, and putting himself in a quite deserted cemetery, a destroyed and broken cemetery, and lying there: for me it was a kind of revelation —and I even had a kind of a smile on my face when I was watching the ceremony, the painful ceremony. I think that in that moment the seed of *Mr. Mani* came to my mind, and, as you know, the description of this cemetery is detailed in the first chapter and it is also, in a way, in the last chapter in the monologue of Avraham Mani."

That old and abandoned Sephardic cemetery on the Mount of Olives is only one instance of the way *Mr. Mani* is saturated with Jerusalem, the real historical and living Jerusalem, not the Jerusalem of nationalist fantasy, nor the Jerusalem of fundamentalist frenzy, but a dense, lived-in, fascinating city—like Joyce's Dublin or Kafka's Prague. This immersion in his capital city is not surprising, considering that Yehoshua is a fifth-generation Jerusalemite with a father so preoccupied with the city. What is surprising, especially to a non-Israeli, is that Yehoshua left Jerusalem and has not lived there in nearly thirty years.

"Jerusalem is becoming impossible, impossible!" he told me. "People complain all the time about my leaving Jerusalem. 'How could you be a traitor and leave Jerusalem?' they say." His voice rises in mockery. "And, more and more, I am so happy that I do not live there. I have so much conflict about Jerusalem. It has become for me the main obstacle to peace, this city, the place from which the destruction of Israel could come."

I asked him whether he thinks of *Mr. Mani* as an answer to these complaints that he has abandoned his city. "I'm proud in a certain way that I could bring Jerusalem *live* to this novel, even through the nineteenth century," was his modest answer. "And this, of course, was done with the help of my father and the little details of Jerusalem he worked on. And I think it helped me so much that I at least could write the third conversation very freely, just through the material that he gave me. He always used to say to me, when I was a little skeptical about all of those nostalgic memories about turn-of-the-century Jerusalem, when I was a little fed up with it, he would say to me, 'Don't worry, you will use this material, one day you will use this material, I'm sure, and the best thing that you will write, you will write after my death.' "

"He said that!?"

"Yes, this is what he said, and I think in a certain way *Five Seasons* and *Mr. Mani* are much better than my first two novels. My feeling was that my father gave me his material—you know the book is dedicated to him —and afterwards, of course, I had to do some exploring on my own for the fourth conversation and the fifth one."

I wondered whether it was easier to reflect on Jerusalem from the detached heights of Haifa. "I think so," he said. "Also, I could at least escape from the total confrontation of an historical novel because all the people in the novel who come to Jerusalem and tell their stories are visitors, so they see it from a visitor's point of view. I took many of the facts from many friends; I read books to get the atmosphere and the details, because there were so many details that I had no way of knowing, for example, that the road from Jaffa to Jerusalem in 1848 was only a very small and narrow path in which two horses could not go side by side but had to follow each other. And there was not one carriage in Israel at this time. All these details I had to work for, and there were so many remarks afterwards, after the book was published. So many people wrote to me to correct here, to correct there. And I have to say that as the book went through its first nine editions, there were corrections in each one."

"Anyhow," he concluded, nodding his head and pursing his lips, "this was the book of Jerusalem." I asked him about the relationship between this literary and historical immersion in Jerusalem and his political exasperation with the city.

"As you know," he said, "I have had a strong ideological opposition to Jerusalem ever since 1967, and especially in the late 1970s and the beginning of the 1980s when the American Jews were coming and playing with the Old City, as if it all were a kind of sacred toy. But afterwards, the intifada started and Jerusalem was again cut into two parts by the Arabs who were saying, 'We are here also. Please. We are not a nonexisting entity. We are here. We are a living people. You cannot just impose upon us and take our houses, and push us here and there, you have to consider us. We are people, we have been living here for hundreds of years, so you have to take us into account.' " He was speaking with quiet intensity now.

"The fact is that now, in 1993, Jews cannot go everywhere in the Old City. I cannot go to my father's grave by myself, and when I must go, I can go only in daylight and I must make sure that there are people there because it has become dangerous. So *Mr. Mani* has given me a way to see Jerusalem, and, yes, I've become a little bit reconciled with Jerusalem in the last years."

I saw how the intifada has, for Yehoshua, exposed the dangerous self-deception behind the fantasy of a "Greater" Jerusalem. I said, "Your emotional reconciliation with the city doesn't seem to have diminished your political opposition to the notion of a Greater Jerusalem."

"You're right about my opposition to this Greater Jerusalem. The fact is that there must also be a political solution to Jerusalem. I wrote a very long article about how to realize this solution, how to divide Jerusalem into two capitals. The Old City would be totally without any national sovereignty but only under religious sovereignty, and I also proposed to build a new temple, a Jewish temple alongside the El Aqsa Mosque of today, in order that the Jews would have more than this *kotel,* more than this bare, destroyed wall. They would have a temple of their own, and all this would be under a comprehensive interfaith authority, a kind of Vatican, and a lot of money would be invested there. This proposal got a lot of responses from many, many people—even right-wing people quite agreed, and the article was also published in the foreign press."

"I only mention this article," he continued, "because I think that the intifada put a stop to this hypocritical attitude of Israel: 'Jerusalem is finished! It's Jewish. It will always be Jewish. The capital of Israel!'—his voice has assumed a derisive sing-song intonation, like that of Jackie Mason doing one of his Jewish turns. "But now Jerusalem is returning to the negotiating table, and even the United States doesn't recognize all of Jerusalem as the capital of Israel."

When we talked in 1996, I asked him about Congress's decision in 1995 to move the United States embassy to Jerusalem. I noted that "many Americans in the peace camp believe the pressure to make the move now was instigated by members of Likud and their supporters in order to disrupt the peace process."

"Never mind about that," he said. "Congress's decision to move the embassy to Jerusalem is right. They have to move the embassy to Jerusalem; it's the capital of Israel. This doesn't mean America recognizes the unification of Jerusalem. The embassy has to be in West Jerusalem as the capital of Israel. But what will be the size of Jerusalem? What parts of Jerusalem will be included in the capital of Israel and what parts will not be included? That is the business of the negotiations between Israel and the Palestinians. But part of Jerusalem, of course, always will be and always was the capital of Israel. And it's very important to me."

"In other words," I couldn't resist saying, "you can take Bulli out of Jerusalem, but you can't take Jerusalem out of Bulli." He laughed. "You are totally right to say that. Jerusalem is in my blood. And of course there is not one novel or one story in which Jerusalem is not present. Jerusalem is a kernel and a permanent component in my being. And this is the reason why here, in *Mr. Mani*, I dealt with Jerusalem in a most complete way, and I think that now I am somewhat liberated and I can tell myself I have done all my duty to Jerusalem. But God knows if it will last."

But *Mr. Mani* does not limit itself to the city that is the mythological center of the Jewish people in physical space. As Abraham Heschel and many others have observed, space is far less central than time in the sacred imagination of Jews. So it is not surprising that Yehoshua also meditates on the temporal center of his people by retelling the central story, the primary myth of the Jewish people, the story of the sacrifice of Isaac, whose setting is exactly in the heart of the Old City of Jerusalem, on Mount Moriah, the site of both the ancient Jewish temple and the Dome of the Rock. According to Jewish and Moslem tradition, both were built on the *even shetiyyah,* the "rock from which the world was woven," "the foundation rock" of the whole world, where Mohammed rose to heaven during his Night Journey and where Isaac was bound for the slaughter.

This myth has haunted Yehoshua's fiction long before *Mr. Mani,* including two of the greatest of his novellas, "Three Days and a Child" and "Early in the Summer of 1970"—even though he had dismissed an oversimplified application of the myth to Israeli reality in *Between Right and Right,* writing, for example, "Here the situation was in no way that of an all-knowing, believing father sending his passive son off to the slaughter." I also had felt the theme reverberating as a vital but subdued undercurrent earlier, as we spoke about the relationship between *Mr. Mani* and his father's nostalgic writings about Jerusalem. But never in his earlier writings had he dealt with this theme so fully and so brilliantly—so I asked him to talk about it.

"You are right to bring up the myth of the sacrifice of Isaac," he began, slowly. "It is the basic myth, I think, in most of my work. But in

Mr. Mani it was given full expression. First I must give you my interpretation of the myth itself, the biblical story of the sacrifice of Isaac. As you know, I am not a believer in God and I cannot just say, 'And God said to Abraham.' "

"So, for you, it is not God who gives the orders, but human beings."

"Yes. I have to explain the whole story through the personalities of Abraham and Isaac and their relationship. I cannot accept an interpretation that comes from God." He was weighing his words carefully, and his eyes fixed on mine, with an attentiveness that felt preternatural.

"So what is Abraham up to? Why does he take his son to Mount Moriah, try to kill him, say at the last minute, 'No, God told me you will not be killed,' and then take an animal instead of his son? My feeling is that Abraham thinks like this: 'I believe in God, I have invented this monotheism, this one God that will be for the whole world. But I don't know whether my son will continue. I have reached this intellectual understanding. But I am not at all sure that my son will walk after me and follow my work. How can I guarantee that this idea will not end up as a caprice of mine which will be forgotten and lost? How will I ensure that a whole people and a whole family will follow my thinking?'

"So he takes Isaac to the mountain and he puts on a kind of a play for him. He takes hold of Isaac and says to him, 'I'm going to kill you.' And, at the last moment, he says, 'No! I am not going to kill you, because God said to me I should not kill you!' From then on, Isaac knows that he owes his life to this God. He doesn't perhaps believe in him intellectually, perhaps he doesn't understand all the aspects, all the components of God's existence, perhaps he cannot identify intellectually with Abraham. But he is now committed existentially to this God."

"Whether Isaac believes in Him or not."

"Yes. And this is the reason why Abraham puts on this play for Isaac: in order to link him in a very existential way, in his soul, to this God. 'If you believe or you don't believe, you have to know that you owe your life to him, because if not for him, I would have killed you, if he were not there, even just in my mind, I would have killed you.' The problem is not even whether this God exists or does not exist. 'He exists for *me*' is what Abraham says to his son. And since God exists for Abraham, Abraham has to guarantee that all of us will continue to believe in this God by committing Isaac to him existentially."

He pauses, looking at me as if expecting a question, and when I say nothing, he continues. "This, I think, is the whole story of the Jewish

people." He believes that Jews throughout their history have been addicted to the figure of Isaac. "The problem is," he continues, speaking so
quietly and slowly that I have to lean closer to hear him clearly, "that from
time to time the knife penetrates. The Jewish people puts itself into a
dangerous situation—for example, the Holocaust—and afterwards, at the
last moment, says, *'But* God is going to save me, *but* God is going to give
an order to save me.' But we cannot always control the hand that is
holding the knife. Abraham could control the hand, and at the last moment—you should read the description again—at the very last moment,
he stops and says, 'No!' But this last moment cannot always be realized.
From time to time, the last moment is too *late,* and the knife is already *down."* We are both silent for fifteen or twenty seconds before he
continues.

"This myth is so important for me and important for the Jewish
people, and I believe this is how you can explain Abraham morally. This
is, in my opinion, the only explanation for his deed: that he is playing with
death in order to commit his son to his belief. Not for one minute did it
cross his mind that he would kill his son. This is the only way I can justify
all these things, because if there were a God, and if Abraham thought that
this God told him to kill his son for this God, that is the most terrible of
all the terrible things that can be imagined."

My mind was filling with some of the implications of this interpretation of the binding of Isaac. For one thing, I was thinking of his father's
prediction that "the best thing you will write, you will write after my
death," at the very moment that Yehoshua was concluding his analysis:
"But, I repeat again, this myth, I believe, directs the history of the Jewish
people, and from my explanation I have also composed this novel." Without spelling out the details of the stunning and disturbing variation on
the Abraham and Isaac story at the climax of *Mr. Mani,* it is enough to
say that the principal characters are Avraham Mani and his son and that
the setting is at Mount Moriah in the Old City of Jerusalem. As Abraham
the patriarch threatens but does not take his son's life to assure the continuation of his tribe and his religion, so Avraham Mani breaks the taboos
against both incest and murder to assure the continuation of his tribe and
his religion.

2

The Beginnings of a Literary Career

Our talk of Jerusalem reminded me that my first encounter with Yehoshua and his ideas was in two articles by Saul Bellow that appeared in the *New Yorker* in 1976 and were published later that year as the book *To Jerusalem and Back*. What captured my attention was a statement Bellow quoted from *Unease in Zion,* a collection of interviews with Israeli intellectuals, edited by Ehud Ben Ezer. Yehoshua's words about the push and pull between artists' public responsibility as citizens and their private responsibility to their personal creative visions made it clear to me that Israeli artists occupy a creative planet a galaxy away from the planet inhabited by American writers. "You are insistently summoned to solidarity," Yehoshua had said, "summoned from within yourself rather than by any external compulsion, because you live from one newscast to the next, and it becomes a solidarity that is technical, automatic from the standpoint of its emotional reaction, because by now you are completely built to react that way and to live in tension. Your emotional reactions to any piece of news about an Israeli casualty, a plane shot down, are predetermined. . . .Hence the lack of solitude, the inability to be alone in the spiritual sense and to arrive at a life of intellectual creativity."

In our first conversation, back in 1988, I asked him whether that visit was the first time he had met Bellow. "No, he was here a couple of years before that for discussions with Israeli writers, and I met him then."

Yehoshua has great admiration for Saul Bellow's work, and he helped organize a celebration in Bellow's honor in Israel in 1987.

"Is *Herzog* your favorite Bellow novel?" I asked.

"Yes," he said brimming with enthusiasm. "I think it is a marvelous book, because the character is a real one and all the philosophy and all the ideas and all the wonderful thinking, all of it goes along with the character with esthetic correctness. Herzog is not just a hanger for the ideas, he is a real character. Also, the book looks upon a certain aspect of America that I love very much, the intellectual urban kind of craziness, and it also is optimistic. I think it's a very successful book, a very wonderful book."

Because of this friendship with Bellow, Yehoshua served for a time as something of a token leftist in American neoconservative circles. He had been a guest professor at the University of Chicago at the Ollin Center, which was led by Allan Bloom, who died in October 1992, four years after this conversation. "The famous Allen Bloom," Yehoshua had said. "I don't know how you reacted to *The Closing of the American Mind,* but I think he never recovered from the trauma of Cornell in the sixties, when he was locked in a building, and so on."

I wondered how he came to know Bloom. "They invited me to a conference around 1985," he said. "Bellow organized a small conference in Vermont for ten writers from all over the world. This was my first confrontation with the Right, the center Right, in America. I, of course, am very leftist because I'm a socialist in my thinking and they were quite amused. There was Milosz, the Nobel Prize winner, and Bellow, and there was Sinyavsky, the hawkish Soviet writer, and I kept pushing certain leftist positions, in my way."

"You had no allies?"

"No."

"They didn't invite Kundera or . . ."

"No. No allies at all. The meeting was in a hotel, and Bloom brought some of his best students from the University of Chicago, and this was the first time I encountered students with short hair, the Reaganites, who actually admired Ronald Reagan." His inflection had pulled me right into his old astonishment. "Those Reaganites!" He shook his head and smiled. "The last time I had been in America for a long time—it was for eight or nine months—was in 1969. I remember the barefoot beautiful girls in Iowa, and the drugs, and all those things."

Clearly a committed leftist, Yehoshua is one of the intellectual leaders of Peace Now and has sometimes been described in the United States as one of the founders of the organization. I asked him to clear that up. "I was not one of the founders of Peace Now," he said. "Peace Now was founded in 1978 and 1979 by army officers who sent letters to Menachem

Begin after Sadat started his peace initiative. About a hundred active officers and reserve officers in the army sent these letters. They created the
Peace Now movement."

In any event, he has been active in the peace camp in Israel for many
years, writing newspaper articles. He even participated in some of the
Labor Party's activities until the campaign for the June 1992 elections
that brought Yitzhak Rabin to power. A month before the elections, he
and Amos Oz shifted their support to Meretz, an alliance of three leftist
parties, Ratz, Mapam, and Shinui. When I asked him about the change,
just before the elections, he said, "It was a natural thing. There are now
enough doves in the Labor Party, and our job there was complete. Amos
and I feel more at home in Meretz, because of its clarity and because we
agree with its main policies, so it's natural that we join them."

I knew that he and Amos Oz had known each other for a long time,
that Yehoshua, in fact, had been Amos Oz's group leader in Jerusalem
when they were young. When I asked him about that, he was amused. "I
was not Amos Oz's group leader," he replied. "I was the leader of some
of the people who studied with him in school. He had already left school
and joined Kibbutz Hulda. He came once or twice to the activities that I
held on Shabbat, so I saw him then only briefly. But I know him only
from the Hebrew University. Before that, there weren't any real relations
between us. But there is also the very strange fact that we were born in
the same quarter of Jerusalem—the house where I was born and the
house where he was born were separated by only forty or fifty yards in
Kerem Avraham, the neighborhood where Gavriel lives in *Mr. Mani.*"

He is casually explicit about his politics, and has been for many years.
"I am for a Palestinian state, of course, and for giving back even East
Jerusalem," he told me in 1988. "I am for the limit."

Eight years later, in February 1996, I asked him to reflect back on the
remarkable events that began in the Oslo talks in 1993. "It seems to me,"
I said, "that 1993 is as important a year in Israeli history as any since
1948. Do you agree, or am I exaggerating?"

"I don't think that you are exaggerating too much when you say that
1993 was as important as 1948. If you are asking me to speak about
what was important during Israel's fifty years, I would say that the most
important event, of course, was the creation of the state in 1948. The
Six-Day War was extremely important, and perhaps now, as you say, we
can add the recognition of the PLO, of the Palestinians. But that's not
quite right, you know, because in 1948 we already recognized them."

"So how *would* you appraise 1993?"

"It's really just a repair of the mistake that we made after 1967. So it's not a new phase. As I said, you must not forget that in 1948 Israel recognized the Palestinian people and recognized their right to have a state of their own. And for the first nineteen years of the state, we recognized that the territories do not belong to us. So this is not really a major step, like the others. 1948 was a major step. The regression and the opening up of the whole issue again after the Six-Day War was a major step."

"How important was the murder of Rabin?" I asked. He had written an article for *Tikkun* (January/February 1996), in which he described Rabin as an older, wiser friend, "responsible for getting his comrades out of the circle of war to the horizon of peace."

"You say that the prime minister was murdered. Yes, he was murdered, and it's a sad moment. But after Kennedy was murdered, would you say that 1963 was the most important year of American history because Kennedy was murdered? And there was an attempt to murder Reagan, and there was an attempt to murder de Gaulle. This is normal. And I expected that someone would like to strike at Rabin. The truth is, I expected far more violence against this government concerning the Oslo I and the Oslo II agreements."

"And the Palestinian elections?" I asked.

"The Palestinian elections are wonderful. I was so happy that day to see them having elections. It's very important, not only for the Palestinians but also for us, and it's also very important for the Arab world. It's the first time that really free elections have been held. And we must do everything we can to make sure that democracy will be established firmly in the Palestinian state; we have to interfere, if necessary, in order that democracy will prevail. And as someone has said, never in history have two democracies gone to war against each other. So democracy is the most wonderful guarantee that we really will have peace."

I told him on the day of the Rabin murder that I happened to be with many of our friends because it was the day of my youngest daughter's fourteenth birthday and also the opening reception of an exhibit of my wife's paintings in Boston. "All of us assumed, when we first heard the news of the murder, that it was done by a religious American immigrant —which somehow made it more understandable. It felt so different from the assassination of John Kennedy."

"Yes, it was. The assassination of Rabin was an ideological murder. It came in the midst of an ideological debate. It was very different from the killing of Kennedy because Kennedy's killer came from a dark hole, and people felt lost afterwards. We know who he is, this killer, and all of the religious Right started doing a *heshbon nefesh*, an accounting of the soul, about their responsibility."

"This was also true of religious leaders in the U.S.," I said.

"It is very important that it was a religious murder. I was not in Israel when it happened. I was in Turkey, and I got the news from my son, who called me in the hotel to tell me that Rabin had been murdered. I said, 'By a religious man.' He said, 'Yes.' "

"For us, in America, the fact that he was an Israeli made it harder to swallow."

"Ah! You didn't understand what kind of Israeli. To me, the fact that he is Yemenite added another drop of poison to the hatred that he felt for Rabin. He struck at Rabin not only from the hatred that came from the right-wing religious movement but also from the hatred directed from the Yemenite community as part of the East-West, Oriental-European conflict. So it was not by chance that this was a Yemenite, given all the problems of the Yemenite community in Israel and the violence coming from that community. So this added another drop of poison. I would not say that it came about only because he is a Yemenite, but only that the fact that he is Yemenite gave him another push towards the murder."

I also wanted to know about the settlers. I reminded him of my pet theory "that the settlers reproduce the condition of Jews in the Diaspora just a few kilometers from the place that is the alternative to the Diaspora."

"You want to know about the settlers. Well, the settlers are becoming good boys, and, remember, I never wanted to make them into demons. Of course, some of them *are* demons, but after Oslo I, they behaved quite correctly. Their demonstrations were relatively mild—people can always complain, but their demonstrations were not so terrible. The most important thing is that the majority of the people have accepted what they should have accepted a long time ago."

"Even though Rabin's majority in the Knesset was so slim."

"Yes. You know, when Nixon began his solution to Vietnam, the American people felt that it was reasonable. What did they think? That they could stay in Vietnam forever? And afterwards, after 1974, everyone said, 'Yes we thought this all along, we knew in 1968 that we don't belong in Vietnam.' It is the same thing with the French people in Algeria.

Afterward, when the right mood comes, all is forgotten, all the mistakes are forgotten."

I asked him whether he's had any direct contact with Shimon Peres lately. "No, I haven't had much contact with him. And I really don't want to have contact with him. He is doing his job. He's prime minister. I had two private contacts in small parties with Yitzhak Rabin before he died. But that's all. I don't want to have any more contact with politicians. The major task has been accomplished. The breakthrough has been achieved. And, anyway, I am incapable of giving political advice. I can only give ideological advice, and they have accepted my ideology, so they have graduated from my school. I don't want these pupils anymore."

Early in 1993, in the aftermath of a series of Hamas attacks that had claimed seven Israeli lives in one week in December 1992, I had asked him, "Do you have any fears about the Islamic fundamentalists?"

"Of course, I do," he'd said. "The fundamentalists are what they are, infecting the whole Middle East. But we invited this kind of movement upon ourselves. My belief is that there still are enough moderate forces among the Palestinians that if we were to give them a sound solution, even some of the Hamas people would join in and come to compromise with the Israelis. They are ready for compromise. Afterwards, there may be internal problems with Hamas and other elements. But it will be up to the Palestinian leadership, and they will do whatever they wish. We see the same thing in many Arab countries, in Algeria, in Egypt: secular re-gimes fighting Hamas, and the secular leaders will have to fight Hamas in the Palestinian state also."

"So your basic position is unchanged."

"Yes, if you ask me what is my position towards all that is happening, it is the same position. The killing is, of course, unnecessary because we can negotiate. But the problem is: what is Israel's offer? And I repeat again —it's already twenty-seven years that I have been saying this: the only possibility is the separation between the territories and Israel, the self-determination of the Palestinians, giving them the right to determine their own fate (whether they want to do it with Jordan or without Jordan is up to them), the demilitarization of the Palestinian state, and the return to the Palestinians of the sovereignty over the territories that were occupied during the Six-Day War."

"And Israeli security?"

"Of course, there must also be security measures." There was impa-tience in his voice—he had said this many times. "But the only security measures that have to be taken in the territories are to guarantee that the territories won't be used as a base for further attacks against Israel."

From the first time we spoke in 1988, he has expressed his concern with the human aftermath of a peace settlement. "When there will be peace with the Palestinians, there will have to be a lot of connection in order to warm this peace," he said in 1988. "If Israelis think that they can just get rid of them by giving them a state, they will not be happy because there will be a lot of connection between the two states. Palestinians work here, and there will be open borders. So a lot of energy will have to be invested in warming the peace, not just peace and get rid of them."

He is equally direct about the Israeli settlements in the West Bank and Gaza. During a visit to the United States in the spring of 1992, before the 1992 elections in Israel and the United States that brought Rabin and Clinton to power, he told me how important it was to him to make a moral case to Americans to support the American policy of putting pressure on the Shamir government to stop building settlements in the territories. We were sitting across the street from Harvard University in a hotel lobby that looked like a Disney version of a Renaissance courtyard. "I know that you and many other Americans may not support Bush for many reasons, for his domestic policies and so forth. But we in the peace camp support the Bush and Baker policy of linking the loan guarantees to the settlement policy." I shrugged, noncommittally.

"Listen," he said, "I need an image to get Americans to support Bush's policy morally. I am going to say that the occupied territories are Israel's drugs, that they are addicted to the territories. Do you think that's a good idea?"

"Yes," I said, but I suggested he pick a more specific drug. "Call it Israel's crack cocaine, or Israel's crack, and American audiences will get the point." He smiled in agreement.

His public activities had taken on a personal intensity and immediacy because of the shadow the intifada cast on the military service of both of his sons, Gidon and Nahum. Gidon's ended in January 1992, and Nahum's began in April 1993. When I spoke to him early in April 1993, he was distracted, being preoccupied with Nahum, who had been mobilized to the army just a week before.

His worry prompted me to remember two other phone calls almost exactly one year apart, the first of which took place in January 1991, just a few days after the beginning of the Gulf War. "I think I am pushed by the fact that Gidon is in the army," he had said. "Ika has been waking me up at night full of worry, full of anxiety, and telling me, 'Do something. You have to work harder. We cannot let it continue like this.' So I can say that, the fact that I am a father intensely stimulated my activity as a public figure and writer in the peace camp."

One year later, in January 1992, I happened to call just a couple of days after Gidon's release from the army. I remember Yehoshua bubbling over with the pleasure and relief of having Gidon home again. Oddly enough, it was that happy occasion that engraved a harsh truth on my mind, that in contrast to all the Americans I know, Israelis count their lives by wars and military service. I realized that Yehoshua's military service had not come up during the course of any of our conversations. I hadn't asked and he hadn't volunteered any information about it. So I asked him, "When did you serve in the army?"

"From 1954 to 1957, for two and a half years; this was the length of military service then."

"What was it like?"

"It was a very bizarre kind of army service. It was divided into two parts. One part was totally nothing. I was a Leader in the Boy Scouts. I was a civilian. I wasn't in the army at all. It was quite lovely because discipline was not strict and I was with intellectuals coming from all over the country, who, like me, had been group leaders in the youth move-ment. But the other part, thirteen months long, was among the toughest service I have ever heard about. The eight months of basic training to become a paratrooper were very, very tough, the conditions were horrible, and it was a time when discipline in the army was quite severe. Afterwards, I took part in difficult military action, battles against Jordan, which took me across the border three times. I also participated in the Sinai campaign in 1956 and in the occupation of Sinai that followed."

Perhaps it is the fact of war and the fact of terrorism that is behind the stark difference I have detected between the pragmatism of the Israeli peace camp and the sentimentality and naiveté of many Americans who consider themselves their allies. Yehoshua is a case in point. Though he has been an eloquent spokesperson for the peace camp for many years, he is not, by any stretch of the imagination, a pacifist, as he made clear during that phone conversation of January 1991, a conversation that was cut short by an incoming SCUD missile. "I can understand those Palestinians who emotionally at least try to identify with Saddam Hussein," he said, "but it is very dangerous for them to identify with him because they are mis-seeing their real interest. Their interest is with the moderates, with

Saudi Arabia, with Egypt, with the rich Arab countries. Saddam Hussein will not help them at all.''

About the war itself, he was emphatic: "I'm *totally* for the war that America has declared against Iraq, and I think that all the peace demonstrations in America are immoral, immoral"—he was adamant about this —"because if they think that Saddam Hussein should be permitted to conquer a country like Kuwait, it means that they are for establishing disorder in the world and giving permission to pirates to take over other countries. America has to know that being left alone as the only policeman in the world and the only authority in the world, it has to take more responsibility in order to prevent the world from deteriorating into a chaos that, with the spread of nuclear and chemical and biological weapons, can be extremely dangerous.'' I found it fascinating to hear a leading citizen of a friendly foreign country speak of the United States this way, at the same time as many American politicians were chanting a familiar litany that "the United States should not be the world's policeman.''

Yehoshua understands full well the part that national political and economic interest played in the American decision to go to war. "We know that America would not come to help a country like, let's say, Cambodia if it were conquered by Vietnam or Chad if it were conquered by Kenya. We know that there is also economic interest because of the oil, but the fact that there is also interest does not exclude the fact that this is a just war, and that America *has* to do it and will do it, I believe, quickly and effectively.'' In these very early days of the Gulf War, it was striking that Yehoshua was much more assured about the final outcome of the war than were many American military experts who were busy overestimating the military prowess of Iraq.

As these last comments make clear, Yehoshua's passion for politics does not stop at the borders of Israel. But Israel remains his abiding concern, and the citizens of Israel have made the sort of political demands on Yehoshua and the other major Israeli writers that are typical everywhere but here, in the United States. This demand to enter the political arena has only intensified in the decade since the invasion of Lebanon in 1982. "I remember about two weeks after the Palestinian uprising had started,'' Yehoshua told me during his visit in the spring of 1992. "It was just a couple of weeks before you and I had spoken for the first time. I had not said anything—I didn't know what to say. The uprising was expected; many of us in the peace camp had spoken about it for many years, and yet there were people who were angry at us. Amos Oz and Yoram Kaniuk and others told me that people were angry at us: Why didn't we speak immediately? Why didn't we immediately go on the radio? As if we were responsible and had the moral responsibility to respond."

I wondered how this came to pass. "Even before the 1982 war in Lebanon, and emphatically afterwards," he explained, "literature has filled the ideological vacuum that has been created since the late seventies."

"What created the vacuum?" I asked.

"In Israel, until then," he said, "politics and politicians were always escorted by an ideology. Ben-Gurion, for example, did not act by himself; when he acted, he was always surrounded by the labor Zionist ideology that gave him feedback about what he was doing. There was never a politician in the American sense; generally, in America, in the presidential elections, you don't see a debate about ideology but a debate about candidates as people—Jesse Jackson seemed to be an exception to this. Each American candidate says, 'I am better, I will do more, I have more experience.' In general, Americans don't vote about some proposition, but about someone's personality. In Israel, there always had been an ideological debate, but by the late seventies, the ideology was completely destroyed."

"And who destroyed ideology?"

"The two figures who destroyed it were Golda Meir and Moshe Dayan—especially Dayan who presented himself so much as an anti-ideological person, as a pragmatist who would find the best solutions for the problems that come. But not according to ideology. This is why he could shift himself easily from one position to another"—even, for instance, joining Begin's Likud government as foreign minister in 1977, after many years of leadership in the Labor coalition.

As a reader of American literature, I found the connection between pragmatic politics and ideological literature an exotic phenomenon, and I told him so. "Yes," he said, "here literature has, in a way, replaced ideological interpretation. This is the reason why there has been such an increase of book buying in Israel in recent years. No one was able to explain why suddenly so many people started buying books. The truth is that they buy books, not just for esthetic pleasure, but they also refer themselves to literature to get some explanation for the difficulties we are facing."

"This is a heavy burden for literature," I said.

"Yes, this gives a lot of responsibility to literature, and we feel ourselves responsible and, from time to time, even scared by the responsibility and the demands the public makes on us." He is clear about the dangers and the attraction of this intimacy between the writers and their society, as he had indicated in the statement Bellow had quoted in *To Jerusalem and Back,* and he referred to Hayim Nahman Bialik, the greatest Hebrew poet of modern times, to make his point. "If whenever you are writing, you see the eyes of the nation looking at you, you become scared. Bialik, for example, stopped writing for thirty years because of this situation. If you have such social responsibility, you cannot act naturally and spontaneously in your writing. Nonetheless, I think Israeli writers can be quite satisfied by the response they have from the public." He smiled sardonically. "Perhaps American writers envy us for this, because they are so isolated and lonely in their writing." Before Meretz published its list of candidates for the June 1992 elections, there even were rumors circulating in the press that he and Amos Oz would be candidates for the Knesset in the new peace camp alliance. When I asked him about that during his visit to the States in 1992, he laughed. "No, no. They think writers and artists are too much prima donnas to be active in politics."

One of the most fascinating things about his profound participation in his nation's current ideological debate is that it would have astonished anyone who had only been exposed to Yehoshua's earliest work, as would his direct and symphonic engagement with history in *Mr. Mani.* Yehoshua himself is the first to admit this, as the opening words of *Between Right and Right* make clear. "If fifteen years ago," he wrote in 1980, "someone had told me that one day I would publish a collection of essays about Zionism, I would have dismissed him with an indulgent smile. At that time I considered Zionism a closed book. It had proven itself, made itself clear politically and historically, and had been acknowledged by most of humankind. Since the Six-Day War, however, we have come to realize that questions we thought decided were not decided—not for us and not for the outside world; that matters which for us were simple and straightforward were not all that simple and straightforward."

When we follow the trajectory of his career from *The Death of an Old Man* (1962), his first collection of stories, to *Voyage to the End of the Millennium* (1997), we can see a development that began as literary rebellion but has flourished as an intense, nuanced, sometimes visionary and lyrical, often comic or grotesque exploration of the most difficult human implications of the social reality he inhabits. When he himself reflects on the stages of his literary career, beginning with the stories in *The Death of an Old Man,* through his early novels, *The Lover* and *A Late Divorce,* up to his later works, *Five Seasons, Mr. Mani, Open Heart,* and *Voyage to the End of the Millenium,* he tends to describe them in terms of his affinity with three other writers: Franz Kafka, William Faulkner, and S. Y. Agnon. The apparent anomaly on this short list is Faulkner; and Yehoshua has learned at least as much from the American southerner as from his greatest Israeli predecessor and the Czech Jew.

When Yehoshua began writing his stories in the late fifties, the literary scene was dominated by the writers of the "Palmach generation," which is what the Israelis call the generation of the War of Independence; they include such figures as S. Yizhar, Moshe Shamir, Benjamin Tammuz, and Aharon Megged, who are virtually unknown in the United States. "It's amazing!" he said, leaning forward in his armchair, during our first conversation in 1988. "Forty years after their main experience as writers in the late forties and the beginning of the fifties, even though their literary techniques have changed, they still have the same attitude towards the collective as the authority, as the context you have to refer to all the time, even if you struggle against it." This is not to say that these writers march in lockstep support of the values represented by the secular Zionism of the Labor Party. "No," Yehoshua said, "the writers reacted with acceptance, rebellion, nostalgia, ignorance, or indifference, but they all knew what the context was."

"The majority of them were from eastern European families, secular and socialist in their orientation," he explained. "This was the classical Israeli Hebrew writer." Their aim "was to speak about whole society" and they were confident in their ability "to really dominate the panoramic scene." The masterpiece of this generation was Yizhar's *The Days of Ziklag,* published in 1958, which Hillel Hailkin, who translated three of Yehoshua's novels, is translating into English and which Yehoshua still regards as *"the* great Israeli novel."

Not until thirty-four years later, in 1992, did Yizhar publish another novel, *Mikdamot.* I asked Yehoshua what he thought of the new novel and whether his generalization about the Palmach generation applied to this new novel. "Yizhar's new book is a wonderful phenomenon," he said. "I just bought it, and I like it very much. What I can see in just skimming the pages is that it's Yizhar." The pleasure and enthusiasm in his voice were contagious. "Of course, it's Yizhar! He did not produce something new, he did not go on to a new element. But who cares? It is the good old Yizhar. He is a real writer, and I enjoy his writing very much."

Whatever pleasure he takes now in Yizhar's work, what was crucial for

Yehoshua and for other writers of the generation of the state at the start of their careers was to resist the pull of collective solidarity as the context for fiction. In his own struggle against the collective, he seized on Kafka and his fables—and, to a lesser extent, the Kafkaesque side of Agnon—as a way of creating fictional worlds at a distant remove from the Israeli reality. "I started," he said, "as a kind of surrealistic writer. In the stories I published in magazines in the 1950s, I wanted first of all to detach myself from the collective experience of the Palmach generation. In the fifties, when I and other young writers had to identify our character as writers, we felt we had to detach ourselves from this very intensive collective experience which we had not participated in, because we were youngsters during the War of Independence, and we thought that this collective experience could strangle our breasts."

At first glance, it may seem curious that a man who was to become one of the fiercest and most original spokesmen for left-wing Zionism should have gone for literary inspiration to a writer many regard as the archetypal alienated Diaspora Jew. But if we imagine ourselves in Yehoshua's shoes in the late fifties, we could not invent a more violent antidote to the realistic, panoramic, socially committed fiction of the Palmach generation than Kafka's fables of isolated mortals who struggle frantically in a universe designed to afflict and confuse them.

Still fascinated with Kafka, Yehoshua was delighted to describe a television interview with Kafka's Hebrew teacher. "Kafka wanted to come to Israel. He even applied to one of the kibbutzim, and he said, I wouldn't be able to work physically, but I could be in the accounting department, or something like that. His Hebrew teacher spoke in Hebrew about him, about how he was studying Hebrew. She was a very nice person, younger than he, and their relationship as Hebrew teacher and pupil was fascinating. Kafka is always universal, always relevant. For example, the situation of waiting for the Gulf War to start on the fifteenth of January 1991 was a Kafkaesque situation."

The visionary parables, disorienting and suggestively allegorical, which Yehoshua described to me as "a kind of surrealistic writing, very Kafkaesque, completely out of time and space," were collected in his first book, *The Death of the Old Man* in 1962. His most recent collection in English, *The Continuing Silence of a Poet,* which includes four stories from that collection ("Flood Tide," "Galia's Wedding," "The Last Commander," and "The Yatir Evening Express") was first published in England in 1988 by Peter Halban and is available in the States as a Penguin

Paperback. Three of these four are also included in his earlier American collections, *Three Days and a Child* (1970) and *Early in the Summer of 1970* (1977). What is remarkable is that, now, more than thirty years later, he remains in easy emotional touch with the force of his rebellion. "I couldn't even give Israeli names to the heroes. This was a very violent act necessary to separate myself from the Palmach generation."

"The Last Commander" looks ahead with remarkable foresight— long before even the Six-Day War of 1967—at the totalitarian temptation, so manifest in contemporary Israel in the late Meir Kahane, Baruch Goldstein, Yigal Amir, and their cohorts. It is an account of a company of veterans subjected to the blaze and glare of the desert sun when they are called up for summer military exercises. The only choices available for an isolated army unit are totalitarian energy or utter chaos. But when I suggested a kind of prophetic political quality to this story, he would not hear of it. His ultimate concern in this story was human alienation, and, as Robert Alter puts it in *Defenses of the Imagination*, "the strain of maintaining the disciplines of civilization in an utterly indifferent cosmos." Such a strain twists and turns more ambiguously in "Flood Tide," the best—and least allegorical—story in his first collection, which bubbles with the Kafkaesque broth of detachment, sadism, masochism, guilt, and the irresistible power of repressed feelings.

I told Yehoshua that, as I read "Flood Tide," I had the uncanny sense that it was haunted by Kafka's "The Penal Colony." "Yes, yes," he said, bursting into laughter. "But I didn't know 'The Penal Colony' when I wrote 'Flood Tide.' I knew some of his other stories; I knew 'The Metamorphosis' quite well. But 'The Penal Colony' I didn't know at all. I so identified with Kafka that I absorbed some of his stories that I hadn't even read."

In the novellas Yehoshua wrote during the fifteen years after *The Death of an Old Man* was published in 1962, he abandoned allegory for a symbolically charged and subtle realism, although the Kafka presence remains a constant. "Little by little," he told me, "this surrealistic writing gave way to more symbolic writing. This symbolic writing dealt with some of the questions of the existence of human beings in Israel and some of the national problems, through stories in which the reality was quite thin and the narration itself was very, very much dominated by the symbolic structure."

Beginning with these relatively realistic stories, all of Yehoshua's fiction—including *Mr. Mani* and *Open Heart*—are filled with human beings who live right at the membrane between their inner worlds and objective reality. This semipermeable boundary is the psychological terrain in such short masterpieces of this period as "Three Days and a Child" and "Early in the Summer of 1970," and Yehoshua explored this terrain in the last conversation of *Mr. Mani,* probably his greatest artistic accomplishment to date, as well as in the unexpected mutability of identity that infects Benjy Rubin in India in *Open Heart.* As he explores this tricky and deadly terrain, the inner lives of his characters burn with an insomniac and hallucinatory incandescence that resembles such Kafka stories as "The Judgment."

The Israeli reality Yehoshua depicts in these stories is inhabited by isolated and rootless intellectuals who long for intimacy and suffer the pain of isolation. Alienated from the Zionist enterprise of the previous generation and frustrated in work and love, they are given to mysterious eruptions of repressed emotion, sometimes in acts of gratuitous destructiveness, occasionally in moments of violent intimacy. It is a reality that represents the nightmarish underside of the old Zionist dream of a land of bright sunshine, new forests, self-confidence, and hope. As readers, we respond with our eyes wide open in both judgment and sympathy because of the Chekhovian mixture of compassion and detachment that is Yehoshua's characteristic tone. Every one of the stories is remarkable; these are the stories William Novak was so taken with in 1977. One, "Three Days and a Child," written in 1965, is the first in which one these alienated and murderous heroes—Dov is his name—manages to change, to break through the wall of his isolation into intimacy; the agency is the spontaneous love of a child that Dov has unwittingly nurtured by telling the child a story. A second, earlier story, "Facing the Forests," partly because of extraliterary matters, has become the most well known story in modern Israeli literature.

Written in 1962, "Facing the Forests" tells of a frustrated and ineffectual graduate student who hires on as a forest ranger, a "fire watcher," to guard a young Jewish National Fund forest. He takes the job to find the solitude everyone thinks he needs to produce a scholarly masterpiece about "some dark issue buried within the subject" of the Crusades. With the fire watcher's complicity, an old mute Arab caretaker sets the forest ablaze—his tongue had been cut out and he lets the flames speak for him. As the fire watcher stands in his observation post watching the fire, "wild excitement sweeps him, rapture. He is happy."

Afterward, in the bare landscape of the burnt out forest, the ruins of the old Arab's village reappear. During the story, first the Israelis and then the trees themselves are linked to the Crusaders. At the end of the story, while the ruined Arab village is "born anew . . . as all things past and buried," it seems for a moment "as though the forest had never burnt down but had simply pulled up its roots and gone off on a journey, far off on a journey, far off to sea."

From the time it was published, political interpretation and critical controversy have swirled around the story in Israel. This response is not at all surprising, given the graduate student's rapt pleasure at the destruction of the single most familiar image of the self-confident Zionist enterprise. Looking back, Yehoshua describes it simply as a story "in which the hidden Palestinian problem was explored though a symbolic story about a student who pushes or helps the silent Arab worker set the fire in the forest in order to discover the ruins of the Arab village that was there." The village emerges from the burnt forest like the return of the repressed.

But even more subversive than the fire is Yehoshua's evocation of the Crusades. At the heart of the prickly Israeli identity and the fury at Palestinian attempts to question their legitimacy is their insistence that they are not Crusaders, that they are a people who have come home for good. With the drastic increase in forest fires after the intifada broke out, the story has returned to the Israeli public consciousness with a vengeance.

In 1988 the *New York Times Magazine* ran a profile of Anton Shammas, the Arab-Israeli author of *Arabesques*. Shammas is a friend and an intellectual adversary of Yehoshua. In late 1985 Shammas had written, "A monoracial, mononational state as established by the Law of Return is, in my view, the racist aspect of the Proclamation of Independence . . . on the surface of it, it promised 'complete social and political equality' for all; yet, it turns out . . . that the only democracy in the Middle East is dying. . . . What is to be done? Establish the State of Israel . . . a united Israeli nation in which some are of a Palestinian Arab ethnic origin." Yehoshua had responded, "I am saying to Anton Shammas: if you want your full identity, if you want to live in a state that has a Palestinian character, with a genuine Palestinian culture, arise, take your belongings, and extract yourself one hundred yards eastward, into the Palestinian state that would dwell alongside Israel."

At the same time, Yehoshua has nothing but praise for *Arabesques*. "It is a fine novel," Yehoshua told me. "His Hebrew is so sophisticated, I have to look up ten words on some pages. He has the same way with language as Conrad and Nabokov." When Shammas was asked, during the summer of 1988, about the increase in the number of fires, he immediately began talking about "Facing the Forests." "It is part of the Israeli psyche," he said. He predicted that the story "will be discussed now, in connection with the fires. Columnists will quote from it. And people will speak of Yehoshua as a prophet. And what can you say? He did write the story twenty-six years ago!"

Yehoshua acknowledged that many newspapers had discussed the story in 1988. "They saw my story as a kind of prophecy written in the sixties concerning the present situation. Of course, the story is much more complex than the political message and it really talks about the way in which the alienated, the ones on the fringe, and the opponents of society take advantage of its repressions in order to destroy it. In any case, the newspapers busied themselves so much with this story that I thought that soon they would accuse me of giving the Arabs the idea to burn forests."

By 1996 he was not very much interested in the prophetic quality of "Facing the Forests." When it came up again, he conceded, "Yes, it was in a certain way prophetic about the Palestinian problem, but you didn't have to be prophetic to know that the Palestinian problem was repressed in the 1960s and that one day it would come out. When the story was written it was not interpreted on its political level."

"But rather as a story of disillusionment and alienation."

"Yes. It was only later that it was interpreted too much on the political level. And I hope when peace will come the story will return back to its own dimension and its own atmosphere."

The alienated graduate student of "Facing the Forests" resembles the principal characters in the other five novellas of the sixties and early seventies. Isolated, impotent, and smoldering, they look at the fires burning in others before they suddenly and gratuitously burst into flames themselves. These stories, with their emphasis on alienated outsiders, continue the literary rebellion against the secular, socialist, Zionist norms of the Palmach generation. Ironically, the achievements by Yehoshua, Amos Oz, and the other new wave writers continued the fragmentation of the political and cultural center, at least in its literary dimension, as this generation of the State assumed a central place in the literary life of the nation. And it is possible to see Yehoshua himself, in a fuller sense, as someone who faces all of the implications of both the forests and the fires, as someone who is wholly committed to the deepest intentions of the Zionist endeavor and philosophy and, at the same time, acutely alert to the throng of raging forces, internal and external, that threaten to destroy it all.

In all of Yehoshua's novellas, the characters' isolation is so intense and their interaction with others so problematic that it is not surprising Yehoshua did not complete his first novel until 1977, a full fifteen years after his first collection of stories. "I moved very slowly to the novel," he told me. "It took me a long time." Nor, is it surprising, given his assessment of the condition of Israeli culture, that *The Lover* and *A Late Divorce*, his first two novels, took the form they did.

3

William Faulkner in Haifa

When Yehoshua talks about his slow movement, his andante, from the stories and novellas to the novels, he describes two paths. The first was the theater. "I also wrote plays," he told me during our first conversation, in 1988. "Three or four were staged here in Israel, and it was the stage through which I moved from the short stories to the novel." The two most well known of these early plays are *A Night in May*, set just before the outbreak of the Six-Day War in 1967, and *Last Treatments*, written in 1973. In their dramatic form, they resemble Pinter's *The Birthday Party* and *The Homecoming*. "I wanted to get out from under the first person, the 'I,' the one character who dominated the short story, and move to other characters without putting all the extra stuff around them. I just let them speak, and from these speeches came the novel."

The second, and most important, path was shaped by his reading of William Faulkner. By the time Yehoshua started writing *The Lover* in the mid-seventies, history had caught up with his stories, and fire watchers had moved from the edge of a self-confident, integrated culture to the center of a disintegrating one. "Reality here is so diverse and there is no controlled center anymore," he said. "And if I really wanted to reflect the diverse reality of Israel in my novel, I had to take into account that there are different points of view. And this is the reason why the technique of Faulkner was so helpful when I was trying to find my way in composing *The Lover*. I like the monologue technique so much. It is a kaleidoscope through which different people with different points of view can be seen."

The example of Faulkner's interior monologues solved more than the personal literary question of finding an appropriate form for his special breed of "isolatoes." What makes this clear is the sudden and pervasive presence of Faulkner in many Israeli writers besides Yehoshua. "In the 1970s a whole lot of Israeli literature began to use the Faulknerian method of multiple voices in the novels," he explained. "This technique was used in *The Lover,* in *A Late Divorce,* in Amos Oz's *The Black Box,* in *The Smile of the Lamb* by David Grossman, in some books by Binyamin Tammuz, and in many others. Multiple voices dominated the novel and reality was not represented by one voice."

"What explains this sudden rush to Faulkner?"

"By the 1970s the majority of the works of Faulkner were translated into Hebrew, and many Israeli writers encountered them for the first time." But this is not the only reason. Equally important, the monologue provided a form to mirror what Yehoshua described as "the gradual crumbling of the center of national values and cultural experience," a process that only intensified in the eighties. The political expression of this center, the secular Zionism of the Labor party, had held sway since the early part of the twentieth century, long before the establishment of the State of Israel. "Because the ideological center of Israel was dismantling itself," he explained, "we felt that we didn't have the possibility of really representing the Israeli society through an authoritative, controlling, single voice."

"This was true for all of you?"

"Yes, we felt that if you really want to represent Israeli reality in the 1970s—and this was our starting point—you have to bring it to the reader through different voices. There was no authority anymore as there had been in the 1950s and the 1960s, when the ideological center was ruled by certain people."

"And you, yourself, were part of this change."

"Of course!" he said. "In the 1970s, when I started to write my novels, I felt incapable of taking the controlling position and responsibility of an omniscient narrator who can really control the novel and speak on behalf of one hero. In Israel all you have to do is take a walk Friday afternoon in Jerusalem and pick seven or ten people in the street and ask each of them, what is your political program, what is your cultural program: you would find huge gaps, unbelievable distances between people who had been walking on the same pavement just an hour before. One speaks of a secular liberal kind of a state, like England or Norway, and sitting right next to him you would find another who speaks about destroying the mosque in Jerusalem and building a new temple there and waiting for the Messiah. Some believe in a new Hebraic kind of nation with no connection to the Diaspora. Others speak only of their feeling as Jews, see their stay in Israel only as a junket, would move to America immediately, and, in one month, forget all about Israel."

The influence of Faulkner, especially the Faulkner of *The Sound and the Fury,* on the form of *The Lover* and *A Late Divorce* has been noted by most of Yehoshua's critics. But Yehoshua's familiarity with and appreciation of Faulkner goes far beyond his formal and thematic use of the interior monologue as a way of responding to the many wildly heterogeneous voices that were clamoring to have their say in Israeli society. "I really admire Faulkner very much," he told me. Leaning forward in his chair, he could hardly contain his enthusiasm. "I don't know how much you appreciate Faulkner . . ." His voice trailed off, and he looked at me expectantly. Soon we were talking about the flexibility and delicacy of the internal monologue as a technique.

"Even if you take *Light in August,*" he said. "I am teaching that now, you know. It is not composed as ordered monologues, like *The Sound and the Fury,* but interior monologues keep coming all the time."

"As they do in parts of *Go Down Moses,*" I chimed in, and soon we were comparing notes about the unity of *Go Down Moses,* particularly, "The Bear," which, I told him, "has become an independent set piece in the United States, excerpted from the rest of the book and studied separately, as if it weren't part of the fabric of the novel. A lot of American students only read 'The Bear.' "

" 'The Bear'!" he said, doubly surprised, by the fact that it is studied separately and by the fact that "The Bear" is where many Americans begin —and often end—their reading of Faulkner. As our talk about Faulkner grew passionate, I got the impression that Yehoshua, for some reason, felt relieved by my familiarity with the story. " 'The Bear' is quite difficult," he said. "It's not so easy. But there are wonderful things there." He paused, looked a little pensive, and added, "You know, Bernie, when I speak to Americans about Faulkner—I don't know, perhaps I'm wrong— they don't know about him, they don't appreciate how important he is as a writer." He is completely perplexed by this phenomenon. "Hemingway they know about, but not Faulkner. And he is so much more important than Hemingway, beyond any comparison. He is the best American writer." All I could do was agree emphatically.

In a curious way, I felt as if I had passed some secret test, and when he continued, his tone became intimate, as if he were confiding in me. "Speak to South Americans or African writers or in Europe," he said, "or even in eastern Europe today, and you will find—I think the prime minister of Hungary is the translator of Faulkner into Hungarian!—people outside America appreciate Faulkner far more than Americans. For many, many writers, he is the most important writer of the twentieth century, far more than the others. He combines so many elements. And especially for those who are struggling with myth, with the application of myth to the world and life—he is one of the most distinguished examples."

"And the novel you admire most is *The Sound and the Fury?*"

"Yes. It is, in my view, the most important novel written in this century."

"And we in the last war lost a lover." Thus begins the first monologue of *The Lover.* The voice is that of Adam, the owner of a successful garage in Haifa, another in Yehoshua's choir of fire watchers; Adam's monologues provide the spine of the novel. The way the voices cycle through the novel has more in common formally with *As I Lay Dying* than with *The Sound and the Fury.* Set in the aftermath of the 1973 Yom Kippur War, the story is carried along by the monologues of five additional characters, all of whom are isolated from one another, all of whom are also lovers of one sort or another: Asya, Adam's wife, whose monologues are dreams; Dafi, Adam and Asya's teenage daughter; Na'im, an Israeli Arab teenager who works in Adam's garage; Gabriel, Asya's young lover, who has returned to Israel from abroad; and Veducha, Gabriel's old grandmother, who begins in a coma and whose illness has brought Gabriel back to Israel.

The Lover is not the only one of his novels in which virtually every character is a lover. In fact, the novel's title is emblematic of one of Yehoshua's preoccupations throughout his career, a preoccupation that grounds all the allegorical, ideological, and symbolic excursions that fly through his fiction in the primary human relationship, love. His books are inhabited by characters who both yearn and fear the move from isolation to connection; their whole identities are at stake in their desire for connection. And so the books are crowded with love in all of its variations and variability: young love, old love; love between lovers, between parents and children, and between siblings; incestuous and adoring love; liberating, destructive, and self-destructive love, consummated and unconsummated, fulfilled or thwarted, mad and reasonable, wild and subdued.

Consequently, it comes as no surprise that in Yehoshua's first full-length exploration of love he weaves a complex narrative that rotates among the six lovers' voices. Only Gabriel speaks once, and his monologue is the longest of the novel. "Was Gabriel's monologue also the seed of the novel?" I asked Yehoshua during his visit to the States in 1992.

"Yes, *The Lover* was started by the idea of the monologue of Gabriel. This was written first and this was the pillar of the novel."

"As the third conversation is the pillar of *Mr. Mani.*"

"Yes. After the Yom Kippur War there was all this news about missing people, as you had in Vietnam, because it was the first time in our military history that we had the problem of missing people. Because of the nature of the war in which the first two days were a total *balagan* [confusion, mess], a lot of people disappeared. So the disappearances were something new. There were even ads in the newspaper from parents who said, 'Has anyone seen my son? He has been seen here, he has last been seen there,' and so on. From this situation came the idea that one of the missing persons deserted by his own choice, which meant that he was not a true missing person, that he was a fake missing person. And this was my idea about Gabriel, how he escaped the war. I knew that there would be other characters, and they came one by one. I knew that there would be a family, that it would be a husband who is searching."

"What about Na'im?"

"It took me quite a long time to bring in Na'im. He was brought in later on. Afterwards Veducha was brought, and then all the six were gathered, and then it moved along."

I, along with my students and many other readers, was very much taken with his description of Veducha's awakening from her coma. "Do you remember what influenced your thinking about Veducha?"

"You mean the unconscious woman—how she came from unconsciousness to consciousness. I'm not sure exactly where it came from, but there was some connection with my old grandmother, a Sephardic woman, who, in her last years, was gradually losing her consciousness. I think something came from that. This old Sephardic woman losing her mind is also related to Haddaya." Haddaya is the old rabbi who is the silent conversation partner in the fifth conversation of *Mr. Mani.*

In many ways, Adam is the most interesting character in the book. His isolation and his yearning are perhaps the strongest. "What has always struck me about him," I said, "is that he is in many ways the most moral character in the book, and he also does the worst thing that anyone does in the book. After all, he does seduce his daughter's best friend. How do you think about him now?"

"Well, I identify with some of his deeds . . ."

"Such as loving to drive at night." We both laughed.

"Yes. But Adam was pretending to play a kind of a god, in the way in which he could even provide a lover for his wife! But my feeling was that this, in a way, was his morality because he thought that he could not satisfy his wife. And if I think in general of families in traditional marriages in which one of the partners, let's say the husband, takes a lover, it often seems that the other partner pushes him, or doesn't satisfy him, or permits him to do so. My feeling was that Adam did a kind of moral thing to bring a lover to his wife, from his point of view and from the point of view of their relationship. But he never, of course, understood what he is doing to his daughter, what he is doing to his whole environment, what he is doing to himself—and what he is doing to the lover himself. So, finally, the great love he feels for his wife enables him to bring her a lover. But the way in which he dominated the lover, the way in which he doesn't understand his wife—it's a very complex kind of situation—you cannot just speak about it only in terms of his being a moral person." This theme of a man, a husband or a lover, misunderstanding his wife or his lover and the self-deception and self-destruction that can accompany this misunderstanding receives full expression in *Open Heart*, Yehoshua's fifth novel.

To an American reader, this brief discussion does not suggest a novel that would naturally provoke ideological and political interpretation, even though the relationships between Jewish and Arab Israelis is a recurrent concern for the characters of the novel. This was evident back in 1987, when I taught the novel in a freshman general education course to three dozen students who knew virtually nothing about Israel or the politics of the Middle East. The students loved it: at the end of the semester when I asked them which of the ten books of the course they would most recommend to a friend, more than half chose *The Lover*. This result was remarkable enough to me that I asked them why. It turned out that they were interested in the blossoming young love between Dafi and Na'im. They were confused and then enthralled by Yehoshua's remarkable representation of Veducha's coma. They were puzzled by the novel's strange oscillation between sleep and insomnia. They were moved and disturbed by Adam: his isolation, his driven search for his wife's lover, and the moral contradictions in his character. They were fascinated by Gabriel's comic and surrealistic adventures in and around the war front, for me, one of the most marvelous stretches of narrative in contemporary literature.

When I described my students' response to the novel, Yehoshua burst into laughter, and before I had a chance to speak, he resorted to one of his favorite metaphors about literature to explain his laughter, and it was only after taking an extended loop through this metaphor that he came back to my unspoken question. "I see world literature as a forest," he said. This literary forest consists of trees and the ground they grow out of, and each tree has roots, foliage, and a trunk. "The ground is the human condition. The roots of every literature are deep in this ground."

My puzzled look must have been obvious. "Just bear with me for a few moments," he said, a broad smile covering his face. "The foliage represents literary technique, and like foliage, literary technique is more or less the same everywhere. When Joyce invented stream of consciousness, immediately this technique was adopted by other literatures without any difficulty. Or if you examine the kind of dialogue that existed in Greek drama, you would not notice *so* much difference between this dialogue and the dialogue of Racine or Molière."

"Okay," I said. "But what in this scheme allows for the possibility of uniqueness of American literature or Israeli literature or any other national literature?"

"If you really want to think about the specialty of every national literature, you must identify the trunk. The trunk represents the special nature of every literature. Every national literature has its own special way of selecting what it needs from the ground that is the common human condition and the foliage that is the technique and literary expression. In English literature, for instance—and you can see it clearly in detective stories—the trunk is always composed of the question of liberty and class. How are you identified by your class and still have the liberty to move to other classes? What are the borders between classes? In France, the question is always the relationship between the sexes. You understand the world by understanding the relationship between a man and a woman. In Germany, it is always the struggle of a romantic, grotesque, and aggressive rebel against an inner order and discipline. In America, one of the leading themes is the success or failure of the individual on the open border of the society which always challenges or threatens the individual."

As he spoke I kept trying to figure out what this elaborate metaphor had to do with his delight at my students' responses to *The Lover.* Suddenly, I caught on. "What you are saying is that, in Israel, because literature has been filling the ideological vacuum, critics have become preoccupied with one 'trunk,' political interpretation." And the pleasure he derived from my students reflects his intermittent wish to run away to a climate in which people read his novels to explore the human condition, not as coded interpretations of the latest political upheavals in Israel.

"This," he explained, "is the advantage I get from translations. You are not the only person teaching *The Lover* in America." We both laughed. "One day a woman from the Technological Institute of Illinois told me she was teaching *The Lover.*" He was in Chicago at the time, as a guest professor at Allan Bloom's Ollin Center. "She invited me to meet the class. 'Who is in the class?' I asked. They were like your classes. There is not one Jew there. She said, 'We are spending two weeks on the novel and they don't know anything about Israel.' So I went. And I was so pleased to meet with ten people who know nothing about Israel, nothing about the Palestinians, ten people who, like your students, were treating my novel mainly as a love affair between boy and girl. I was so pleased I wanted to record the class and play the tape to my critics at home who say I do not deal with human beings but only with ideas."

I brought up his tree metaphor. "So in America, we are free to deal with the ground, the soil," I said.

"Yes. I've always said that I was dealing with the soil. But the critics and the country itself are so much involved in ideological problems they don't see the human condition that is in the novels. But this I think is always true, even in a novel like *Anna Karenina.* You have to give some time to a novel, to leave its immediate political and ideological context and to see if there are some values from the human condition."

In the pages of *The Lover,* Yehoshua provided neither an explicit statement of his diagnosis of his culture nor an acknowledgment of his Faulknerian artistic response. Five years later, in *A Late Divorce,* he did, and the epigraphs to the first two chapters of the novel provide a kind of shorthand for what Yehoshua is about in his first two novels, one epigraph for art, one for politics. The first epigraph, a formal acknowledgment of Faulkner's presence, comes from Quentin Compson's monologue in *The Sound and the Fury:* "Benjy knew it when Da Muddy died. He cried. He smell hit. He smell hit." The second epigraph, the single most succinct key to what Yehoshua was thinking then about his society, comes from Yeats's "The Second Coming," arguably the greatest short poem of the twentieth century: "Things fall apart; the center cannot hold;/Mere anarchy is loosed upon the world."

In Yehoshua's second novel, the transformation of American materials and forms into the Israeli reality is complete. As his central theme, Yehoshua, like Faulkner, focuses on the devastating repercussions on a family of stunted parental love. Like Faulkner, Yehoshua follows the interior monologue pattern of one character per day, all of them members of one family. Like Faulkner, Yehoshua uses a traditional myth and a modern myth based on Freud as counterpoint to the human pathos of the disintegrating family.

Unlike Faulkner, however, Yehoshua creates an unfolding story in the present that connects the monologues as each character carries the story one day forward in time. The action is triggered when Yehuda Kaminka, who had emigrated from Israel to the United States, returns from abroad to secure a divorce from his schizophrenic wife so that he may marry his young and pregnant American lover. The nine days of his sojourn in Israel are narrated by Kaminka's family, all of whom, except Yael, his daughter, are eccentric, difficult, or troubled.

I was attracted to the voice of Yael. "Maybe it says something about me," I said, "but I felt that the voice that was strongly yours was the voice of Yael."

"Yael's," he said. "Yes."

"It was a relief to get to it. It reminded me of Oz's *A Perfect Peace,* when we get to Srulik."

"Yes, like Srulik, she is the more normal one, with a certain patience. And compassion. And not so aggressive."

Yehoshua's fundamental achievement in the novel is to bring the whole Kaminka brood vitally to life, while they manage, at the same time, to carry the story forward monologue by monologue toward its grotesque and disastrous conclusion. He accomplishes this double purpose with such grace, with so seamless an art, that both method and story seem inevitable. "When people ask me who is the real hero of the nine characters of *A Late Divorce,*" he explained to me, "I tell them that the hero is the space that is caught between the characters. This is the real hero. The hero is nobody among them, but only the air, the space that is caught between them."

The emotional variety is enormous. Typical episodes include a formal divorce scene that gradually tumbles into crazy hilarity and a family conversation that bursts into a terrible moment of grotesque pathos when Asa, Kaminka's son, suddenly reverts to his childhood habit of striking and slapping himself. In poetic prose, Yehoshua captures the dreamlike terror and courage of Mrs. Kaminka's ferocious internal struggle as her madness gradually rises and threatens to envelop her. In realistic dialogue, he catches the lovely moment when a resistant client breaks through his resistance, realizes for the first time that psychotherapy is work, and begins in earnest the work that is therapy. In the fifth chapter, Yehoshua introduces a new form, a one-sided dialogue, which he will exploit elaborately in the five conversations of *Mr. Mani.*

The psychological and moral complexity is equally impressive. Every one of the characters accumulates richness and opacity as the story unfolds and each one stands more revealed. The most opaque is Kaminka himself, a hard-nosed, self-centered patriarch, who is particularly mysterious in the sequence of increasingly bizarre actions that get him in the "dreadful mess" that closes the novel. I know several readers, including some real admirers of Yehoshua and *A Late Divorce,* who find Kaminka's behavior at the end—and the whole climax of the novel—somewhat unsatisfying because they find Kaminka's behavior insufficiently motivated, hence enigmatic. Characteristically, Yehoshua does not make it easy to sort out Kaminka's motives and his rationalizations from the deepest sources of his character. This restraint on Yehoshua's part demonstrates both his confidence and his adventurousness: he risks allowing his marvelous novel to collapse at the very last moment.

I do not wish to completely give away the end of the novel for those who have not yet read it, but the art of making Kaminka's actions unexpected yet plausible shows Yehoshua at the height of his powers—he gives us everything we need to figure things out and manipulates us so skillfully that we do not figure it out too soon. The most reliable authority on Kaminka turns out to be his estranged and mad wife! Yehoshua makes it clear that when Mrs. Kaminka is mad, she is very mad, but when she is lucid, she is the most lucid and perceptive member of the family—particularly when it comes to her husband. To underline the accuracy of her appraisal and indicate that she really does get under the rock of Kaminka's reasons, Yehoshua throws in yet another pointed epigraph, this one from a poem by Montale, at the head of Kaminka's chapter: "I still am haunted by the knowledge that,/whether separate or apart, we are one thing."

When I pressed him about the artistic riskiness of trusting to an epigraph and the insight of a madwoman, he said, "I don't know what you mean by 'artistic risk.' But I have to tell you that a couple of years ago *A Late Divorce* was republished in a new edition, *The Divorce Cantata,* which included the original tenth chapter that is the monologue of the family dog, Horatio." This chapter, "The Last Night," was cut when the novel was first published and appeared for the first time in the Hebrew magazine *Siman Qri'ah,* in December 1990. "This is a very amusing kind of chapter in which the dog gives a monologue and speaks about literary matters. He does literary criticism in a very ironic way. He argues with *me* about this form of monologue." *The Divorce Cantata* includes this chapter, "The Last Day." "But I repeat," he said, "I don't know what you mean by artistic risk."

It finally became clear to me that what I saw as risk was something he took for granted, namely, that writers must respect their readers enough to demand that they participate in creating the meaning of the stories. This applies to the "spaces" between the characters in *The Lover* and *A Late Divorce* and culminates in the one-sided dialogues of *Mr. Mani* and the spaces between the characters and the readers in *Five Seasons* and *Open Heart*. I asked him whether he knew the Nabokov one-liner in *Lectures on Russian Literature:* "Of all the characters that a great artist creates, his readers are the best." "That's wonderful," he said. "I will use it immediately. That is really wonderful."

The sense of the artist as master manipulator is crucial to Yehoshua. When I asked him to say more about Kaminka, he described a course he was teaching at Haifa University. "I am now giving a seminar," he said, "about the moral map of the literary text. Very fascinating, to look upon a story, not from psychology or sociology, but just to enter the moral map: What is the attitude of this hero? What is the attitude of the writer towards the hero? What is your attitude as a reader? And all kinds of complications come up. The class becomes very lively, because when you touch morality, people wake up immediately because it touches them directly." He could have been giving a lesson in how to read any of his fiction.

I realized that though I had not thought in terms of a "moral map," the approach was familiar. "I never thought of it the way you said it," I said, "but that's exactly what I've been trying to do in my own teaching." I started to tell him about what I've been doing with a remarkable very short story by Isaac Babel, "Crossing into Poland." He looked puzzled.

"It's the first story in *Red Cavalry*. It's also called "Crossing the Zebruch." I pronounced the river's name in two syllables.

His eyes lit up. " 'Crossing the Zbrukh,' yes. 'Crossing the Zbrukh'! It's only two pages long!"

"I spend two weeks on it, and I have the students stop after every paragraph, and I ask then what they see, what they feel, what attitude do the characters have, what is the attitude of the author, and so forth. And what we talk about finally is morality." The story presents a moment of stunning and unlikely moral awakening, which Babel prepares with audacity and subtlety. After panoramic and sensual descriptions of a nurturing, disturbing, and beautiful landscape and the aftermath of a battle, a young soldier, full of nothing but contempt and disgust for the faceless Jewish inhabitants, describes the ravaged and filthy house where he is being billeted. One of the Jews is a young pregnant woman, whose last words end the story and force the young soldier and the reader to see everything in the glare of totally unexpected moral illumination.

"It's a wonderful story," Yehoshua said. Given his own propensity for subtle and sneaky endings, I wasn't surprised by his delight. "How it goes from the cosmic plane to the child's tragedy, and all the moral things that are in the dirty room there, with the woman! The movement from the general to the private and to the single fact!"

We both were smiling broadly. "You know, Bernie, I don't know how old you are, but I'm already fifty-one. . . ." This whole discussion took place during our first conversation, in January 1988.

"I'm forty-three."

"Eight years are important at this age. But when you are approaching your fifties, when I reached that age, I started to speak about morality and things that I never had thought to speak about. It is fascinating to see how moral attitudes are changed through the literary method."

He had been teaching Euripides's *Alcestis,* in which Alcestis offers to die in place of her husband, Admetus, the main character of the story, who begins the play in supreme innocence, believing himself exempt from mortality and all the other constraints that define the human condition. During the play, he is confronted by a series of characters who, with increasingly sharp definition, illuminate his unconsciousness and ignorance, until, finally, learning from his silent wife's bravery and love, he comes, through suffering, to mortal wisdom and mortal humility. "I showed them how the literary manipulation of the text by the writer moves the reader from a hostile attitude towards a certain hero to a more comprehensive attitude, and how moral attitudes are changed from the beginning until the end through the literary technique."

This concern with morality and literary craft finds its practical application in Yehoshua's presentation of all the characters of *A Late Divorce,* especially Kaminka. But the portrayal of moral complexity is only part of the artistic story of this novel. There is also myth. To counterpoint the psychological, emotional, and moral richness potential in the interior monologue form, Yehoshua, like Faulkner, uses mythological structures.

"Yes," he repeated, "Faulkner is important to me because of how he combines myth and history."

Like Faulkner too, Yehoshua uses two myths to structure his story, a traditional myth and a contemporary one. His traditional story is the Jewish spring festival, Passover, which celebrates the Exodus, the liberation of the Jewish people from slavery in Egypt and the beginning of the Jewish nation. I asked him to compare his use of Passover with Faulkner's use of Easter week in *The Sound and the Fury*. "You're right to compare it to Faulkner," he said, "and I've always admitted that *The Sound and the Fury* had a great influence on *A Late Divorce*. I think that generally the time of festivities, the holidays and the festivals, are always, for Christians, for Muslims, for Jews, for everyone, concentrations of the personal neurosis as well as the general national neurosis, and it always makes for some stress, because more is demanded of people, to be something else, to participate in the collective activity of the festivals. So the festivals—the *hagim*, in Hebrew—always symbolize a crossroads, a very, very emotional crossroads, and this is the reason that, during the *hagim*—this is what Ika tells me—more and more people come to mental hospitals, to escape some of the emotional burden and stress that they are suffering. Of course, Faulkner used the Easter holiday very brilliantly in *The Sound and the Fury*." In his spring story, Yehoshua even throws a new Moses into the story in the form of a three-year-old stutterer born in America.

Yehoshua's contemporary myth, like Faulkner's, comes from Freud. But while Faulkner imported Freud's theory of the id, ego, superego, and libido into *The Sound and the Fury*, Yehoshua uses a psychohistorical myth of his own invention, which is rooted in psychoanalytical thinking. Both Yehoshua and Faulkner ground their novels in a realistic depiction of the disintegration of a family. But while Faulkner uses the Freudian material as a psychological allegory to illuminate the inner life of the family, Yehoshua uses his Freudian material as a psychohistorical allegory to move from the family to history. To put it baldly, in *The Sound and the Fury*, Quentin Compson (as ego) is destroyed because he cannot mediate between the unrestrained desire for Caddy (as libido) represented by Benjy (as id) and the ferocious repression of that desire by Jason (as superego). Yehoshua's psychohistorical myth, which he presents in *Between Right and Right*, the passionate polemic that was published in 1980, answers the question of the Diaspora, which he considers "the most important and profound question a Jew must pose to himself when trying to probe the essence of the Jewish people."

To explain the persistence of the Diaspora (*golah*, "exile," in He-brew), Yehoshua proposes a Freudian family romance among God (the father), the land of Israel (the mother), and the Jewish people (the child). Instead of "the proper and harmonious balance in the consciousness of the people between the father and the mother, between God and the homeland," he argues, the Diaspora is a "neurotic solution" in which a jealous, repressive, and dominant father-God permits the children of Israel to satisfy their natural desire for mother-homeland by "longing" for a "distant" and "remote" being, the child's mother transformed totally into the wife of a jealous father.

One consequence of the different uses of Freud in the two novels is the significant tonal difference between the predominantly tragic quality in *The Sound and the Fury* and the decidedly tragic-comic mix in *A Late Divorce*. Faulkner's use of the Freudian model as myth is nontemporal and fatalistic, leaving little hope for transformation or liberation from the terrible burdens of the family's history. Yehoshua's historical use of Freud-ian theory, in contrast, is less fatalistic and leaves the characters open to a possibility of change, even though the novel's ending is grim. This is clearest in the male characters. While Kaminka himself ends in a mad self-destructive swamp, two of the unpromising males of the next genera-tion show glimmers of hope. The brash and sarcastic son-in-law, Kedmi, feels responsibility to his family, loves his son, and even manages to wax poetic about Haifa for a moment. Tsvi, the selfish son, is caught, not in monologue, but in dialogue with his psychotherapist, at the instant he catches his very first glimpse of his deepest fears and desires.

Many critics have detected traces of Yehoshua's psychohistorical the-ory not only in *A Late Divorce* but also in *The Lover*. In both novels an intrusive Israeli émigré (a *yored*, "one who goes down," the derogatory Israeli word for an émigré from Israel, as opposed to an *oleh*, "one who goes up," an immigrant to Israel; the nouns are *yeridah* and *aliyah*) re-turns from the Diaspora and destabilizes the balanced forces of a family, which is to be recognized as both a literal family and a microcosm of the society. In both, a partly conscious woman—Veducha in *The Lover* and Naomi in *A Late Divorce*—acts the role of the homeland. Indeed, one of the refrains of Kaminka's monologue is "homeland will you ever be a homeland." Israeli readers tend to seize on these historical elements and read the works as purely ideological allegory, and Yehoshua concedes the element of truth in these interpretations. "I'm not saying the family is a symbol for Israel," he said, "but there is a layer of allegory. Like Kaminka who gives up his responsibilities and goes to America, Jews who leave Israel for America are escaping from their responsibilities. Or you, you know . . ."

"Me?"

"Yes, you wound up taking Linda, who was an *olah hadasha,* a new immigrant, away from Israel and back to America, which was not a good thing."

But I was still thinking about the layer of allegory in his novels, and the tendency in Israel to allegorize his novels entirely. The difficulty with such wholesale allegorical interpretation arises when it entirely supplants the human force of the work. No one would dream of saying that Joyce's *Ulysses* is about the *Odyssey* or that *The Sound and the Fury* is about Christ or Freud or, for that matter, that Eliot's *The Wasteland* is about the Fisher King or that Pound's *Cantos* are about Dante.

As Joyce, Faulkner, Eliot, and Pound seized on structural and ironic uses of myth in the wake of cultural disintegration they saw in World War I, so too does Yehoshua find mythological structures relevant to his young society, which seems to have lived through hundreds of years in its forty-nine years of existence as a modern state. The uses are similar: to emphasize the distance from some ideal, to use the story to illuminate some large historical or psychological forces, and to heighten the intensity of our emotional and intellectual response to the characters and their story.

4

"Normal" Novels for a "Normal" Time

In the years after *A Late Divorce*'s publication in 1982, the cultural fragmentation in Israel has, according to Yehoshua, only intensified. Accordingly, we might have expected his third novel to retain the kaleidoscopic form of the first two novels, a form, in fact, like that of *Mr. Mani,* his fourth novel. So I was not at all surprised when Yehoshua told me that the conception and design of *Mr. Mani* sprang directly from *A Late Divorce,* specifically Rafael's one-sided dialogue in the fifth chapter, "Thursday Night." What is surprising is the detour he took once his first round of work on *Mr. Mani* ground to a halt in 1984 after a full year's effort.

The product of this detour was *Five Seasons,* begun in 1984, published in 1987 in Israel and two years later in the United States. Named *Molkho* in Hebrew for the name of the main character, this novel represents a sharp turn inward for Yehoshua. Told by an omniscient narrator in the third person, Molkho's story moves through five seasons, beginning with the death of his wife in autumn, continuing with his relationships with four different women, one for each season, until the year comes around to a second autumn, a season of renewed vitality for the novel's humble hero.

Seven years after *Five Seasons* (and four years after *Mr. Mani*), Yehoshua completed a second relatively straightforward novel of love, *Open Heart,* published in Israel in 1994 and in the United States in 1996. Narrated almost entirely in the first person, the novel follows two years in the life of Dr. Benjamin Rubin, an ambitious, stable, and rational young

66

hospital resident, whose life and identity are plunged into wild chaos after he travels to India with Lazar, the hospital director, and Lazar's wife, Dori, to rescue their sick daughter, Einat, who had fallen ill. Entranced by the mystery of India, falling into an illicit and impossible love for Dori, marrying Einat's friend, Michaela, along the way, Benjy finds every one of his identities—as doctor, lover, and son; as husband and father; as individual human being—up for grabs, as the novel moves inexorably from falling in love, to fulfillment and betrayal, to despair, until Benjy finds himself hovering at the dizzy edge of suicide and rebirth. The Hebrew title of the novel, *HaShivah me-Hodu* (The Return from India) gives a taste of the richness of the novel. The title alludes not only to E. M. Forster's *A Passage to India* but also, in a play on words, to Shiva the Destroyer, the Indian God of destruction and rebirth: that is, "The Destruction and Rebirth from India." The English title, *Open Heart,* has some similar valence, for it refers both to the way Benjy's heart is opened by his encounter with India and to the open heart surgery that is one of the climactic and stunning scenes of the novel.

Formally speaking, the place of *Five Seasons* in Yehoshua's career took one slant when I thought about it in 1990, when *Mr. Mani* was published, and another when I look back from 1997. In 1990 *Five Seasons* seemed something of a detour in form because three of the four novels published by 1990 were multivoiced. But seven years later, especially if we include his sixth novel in this calculation, his fiction has become predominantly single-voiced, either told by a narrator in the third person, like *Five Seasons* and *Voyage to the End of the Millennium* or told by the main character in the first person, like *Open Heart.* The trend toward narrative integration is even more evident considering that *Mr. Mani* was conceived and begun before *Five Seasons.* Another way to look at it is that beginning with *Five Seasons* in 1987, he has been alternating between predominantly personal novels of private morality and identity, like *Five Seasons* and *Open Heart,* and novels that more directly address ideological and cultural issues, like *Mr. Mani* and *Voyage to the End of the Millennium.*

Five Seasons is dedicated to the memory of Hanna, a colleague of Yehoshua's wife, Ika. Hanna died of cancer in 1984. I asked him to talk about the relationship between her death and the novel. "We were very close to her," he said. "And I think perhaps that some of our emotion came from the fact that she died when we were in the United States, just for one week, for the promotion of *A Late Divorce.* I remember that we called Israel from Boston, and it was then that we learned of her death.

So Ika cut short the trip and returned home. Afterwards—the funeral had already taken place—Ika sat with Hanna's husband who told her all the details of the last hours, the last days of her life. Afterwards, Ika told me his stories. While I was writing the opening chapter of the novel, I had forgotten what Ika had told me and I thought it was all fantasy. I hadn't realized that the details in the first chapter of *Five Seasons* were so accurate, but she assured me that this was the case, so, finally, I have to admit that most of the material was based upon what Ika had told me about Hanna's husband. And this is the way the novel began, from this departure point about the death. But afterwards, all the other material was my own."

He saw his work on *Five Seasons* as a respite from the political debate. "I was so relieved to say to myself, 'I stop history. I'm not concerned with ideology. There is nothing political in it.' " But the novel's critical reception was another story. "When I published it, immediately there were articles saying this is a symbol of this, this is a symbol of that, and I could not escape." Written in the third person, though Molkho's point of view dominates, *Five Seasons* represents for him, "a completely different kind of writing. It was the first novel in which I returned to a more classical form. I felt I had to take control again and be more than just a medium for the characters. I wanted to look at them and examine them and not just let them speak. I think *Five Seasons* is my first real, 'classical' novel."

When I tried to press him on the relationship between *Five Seasons* and Israeli society, at first he was blunt. "In this book I was trying to detach myself entirely from the immediate political scene." It struck me that detachment too is a kind of response to fragmentation, and I suggested how easy it is, at least in retrospect, to see his third and fourth novels as oddly complementary responses to the crisis faced by Israeli writers in the mid-eighties: *Five Seasons,* an indirect, private, and, in Yehoshua's term, "classical" response, while *Mr. Mani* is confrontational, public, and boldly inventive. Both novels go back to the past in the service of the present; in *Five Seasons* the journey to the past is individual, inward, and regressive and the outcome is personal liberation, while in *Mr. Mani* the journey back is collective and outward and the outcome is collective illumination. Both represent a change from novels that only mirror a fragmented society to novels that, in different ways, respond to that fragmentation.

"Of course," he said, "Molkho is the anti-Mani, the total anti-Mani. No two books are so opposed to each other, by the characters, by the way they are structured. *Five Seasons* is a narrative, slow, present, ironic, without any of those dialogues, prologues, and epilogues, not historical, very limited in time and space. Nonetheless, the two novels are very much linked together. Elements that are not in *Five Seasons* are in *Mani,* and elements that are not in *Mani* are in *Five Seasons.* I think it is very important, this inner connection between *Five Seasons* and *Mr. Mani;* the fact is that they come from the same human organism even though they are the two most different books one can imagine." The richness of these inner connections has already resulted in one critical Hebrew monograph, Avraham Balaban's *Mar Molkho* (1992), the title of which is a witty hybrid of the Hebrew titles of the two novels, *Molkho* and *Mar Mani.* But, at the moment, I was more interested in the variety in his work, so I asked him about the differences between the two novels.

"There are two sorts of writers," he said. "Some, like Joyce and Proust and Faulkner, or, here in Israel, Aharon Appelfeld, create a world for themselves, with values, a code, and characters, and in all of their work, they dig deeply into this world."

"Do you know Appelfeld?"

"Of course! We were at university together. We started out together! I remember when he read me his first story. You know, it took a lot of guts for him to stay with his subject, and I respect very much his commitment to the world he created in his imagination and his literary way of dealing with the Holocaust. People would say, 'Enough with the Holocaust, already!' But he ignored them. And rightly so. He opened up whole new possibilities by dealing with the relationships between the Jews themselves and not only the relations between Germans and Jews."

"But you don't count yourself among the writers who create a world," I said.

"No. I am among the writers of subject, like Bellow or like Dostoevsky. And such writers face a real difficulty because the traditional subjects do not exist anymore."

It seemed to me that this question of literary subject was behind the complementary relationship between *Five Seasons* and *Mr. Mani,* both the differences between the two novels and the similarities. To get a more specific handle on the two novels, I asked Yehoshua to spell out in more detail his diagnosis of the cultural crisis faced by Israeli writers since the early 1980s. I thought it was important to have a fuller understanding of the cultural and literary context of the two novels, and, as usual, he gave me more than I had bargained for. When he described this context to me, he singled out four features for special emphasis: the loss of war as a literary subject and theme; the renewed preoccupation with Jewish identity as a theme; the increasing pluralism in Israeli life; and the problems with language. We discussed these issues during his visit to the United States in 1990, during his book tour for *Mr. Mani.*

"War gave Israeli literature a great subject," he said. "War makes it possible to balance your spiritual concerns with a real subject drawn from life. It provides a mine of dramatic situations: the mixing of classes, the struggle between superiors and inferiors, family relations and the relations with the enemy, and so on. If you want to kill a hero, for example, all you have to do is begin three months before a war. If a Danish writer wants to kill his hero, he has to prepare him for committing suicide, and I can tell you that it's extremely difficult to make a hero commit suicide in a reliable way." Though I didn't know it at the time, suicide would return as a theme in our later discussions of *Mr. Mani* and *Open Heart.*

He estimates that 50 to 60 percent of all Israeli literature deals with conflict. "In fact," he continued, smiling, "when Menachem Begin was making peace, we were a little suspicious, but he had mercy on us and gave us the Lebanon War of 1982." Now, he believes, because the political debate is too sharp, war has outlived its usefulness as a literary subject. "Before the Lebanon War," he said, "Israeli literature had escaped becoming a *literateur engagé* because the writers were engaged as citizens and as soldiers and so did not have to be engaged as writers. But that is no longer true."

When I asked him for an example from his earlier work, he referred to one of his best stories. "In 1970 I wrote a novella, 'Early in the Summer of 1970.' I don't know how much you know about the War of Attrition, but those were some of the toughest days for Israel, and peace was not in our hands." The War of Attrition, much less familiar outside Israel than the other wars, took place between Israel and Egypt along the Suez Canal during 1969 and 1970.

The story revolves around the moment when a traditional Bible teacher receives word that his son has been killed during his tour of duty in the army. The son had been called up just after his return from the United States via India, seeming to bring "some new gospel, tidings of a revolution, of some wonderful reality wonderful and unknown." Narrated entirely from the old teacher's point of view, the story captures the old man's struggle to find meaning in his son's death and his own life, as the biblical story of Abraham and Isaac reverberates in the background.

Although politics plays only a subdued role in the story, the present implications of the old man's politics have profound consequences on purely literary matters. In 1970 Yehoshua had no difficulty imagining the old man from the inside. "I could see the points, the stance, the attitudes of the old man . . . I could do justice to the old man." But twenty years with no progress toward peace had sharp literary consequences. "Now, twenty years later," he said, "I would put him in only to caricature him as responsible for the War in Lebanon, the deception of the Yom Kippur War, the refusal to recognize the Palestinian problem, and so on. And I would use my literature as an instrument in the political debate."

Yehoshua's response in 1990 to the old teacher he created resembles closely how his friend, Amos Oz, reacted to the world of the Orthodox eastern European Jews in 1982. "Nor can you afford yourself a measure of secret admiration for the incredible vitality of this Judaism," Oz wrote in *In the Land of Israel,* "for as it grows and swells, it threatens your own spiritual existence and eats away at the roots of your own world, prepared to inherit it all when you and your kind have gone."

This response also helps explain Yehoshua's feelings about Philip Roth. He feels troubled by Roth's characterization of the West Bank settlers in *The Counterlife.* "This is too near to me," he said. "I wouldn't dare write about the settlement of the occupied territories. I don't dare because I don't know it. I have to be inside. And he, the way in which he is doing it . . ." Yehoshua's implication was that Roth has the freedom to be evenhanded, even sympathetic in his portrayal of settlers only because Roth, unlike Yehoshua or any other Israeli, has nothing at all at stake.

By 1996 his feelings about Roth had only intensified. When I brought up *Operation Shylock,* I did ask about the Diasporism notion Roth plays with: that for the survival of the Jewish people, the Jews should leave Israel for Europe. "But what I'm much more interested in," I said, "is getting your reaction to the remarkable moment in the book when Roth throws himself entirely into the imagination of Demjanjuk, and releases the exhilarating pleasure of power and evil." Roth's diving in contrasts so sharply with the insinuating and Iago-ish way Yehoshua allows Egon Bruner, the German soldier who speaks to his grandmother in the second conversation of *Mr. Mani,* to infiltrate the imaginations of his poor, innocent complicitous readers. But Yehoshua wanted no part of Roth.

"I have not read *Operation Shylock* and I don't want to read it," he said. "What I got from the book when I took a look at it disgusts me so! Such an allegorical metaphor with the Shin Bet and so on—it's as if I tried to write about the United States and the CIA and Moscow and things like that! I just don't like it. I don't think that anyone in Israel liked this book. Nobody wants to know anything about it. The truth of course is that the Diaspora will come to Israel, not Israel to the Diaspora."

"Where do you think the notion of Diasporism came from?"

"It is related to ancient times, when we really thought that Israel would be destroyed by something terrible. But now, after the peace process has begun and especially after the renewed recognition of the Arabs by Israel, I think that the old dark prophecies given by the Jews of the Diaspora are not valid anymore."

In 1990 Yehoshua was not at all happy about the way his political response to the Lebanon War had restricted his imaginative freedom. But what annoyed him much more is the theme that seems to be emerging, or reemerging, as war loses its literary viability. What he saw and deplored vehemently was the reappearance in Israeli literature of an old worn-out theme, Jewish identity. This reappearance, he believes, is the second feature of the cultural crisis of the 1980s. Referring again to his forest metaphor, in which the soil represents the human condition, the foliage represents literary technique, and the trunk represents what is national about a national literature, he defines the main Jewish trunk over the last two hundred years as "identity."

"With the Jews," he said emphatically, "it is always a question of identity: In what sense am I Jewish? In what sense am I too Jewish? How can I be less Jewish? How will I keep my identity? Identity and the tuning of identity, the movement of identity: this is one of the main concerns of Jewish literature." As I thought about the accuracy of this assessment, I recalled a joke Jackie Mason tells about the old woman who comes up to him after his one-man show. "You're too Jewish," she says, in a heavy Jewish accent. "Why can't you talk like a regular person, like me."

Yehoshua's explanation for this is straightforward. "Because we are, on one hand, afraid of losing our identity and, on the other, we are afraid of having so much Jewish identity that we would lose our other identity, American or French or whatever. So playing with identity is a major Jewish preoccupation." A major preoccupation, that is, for Diaspora Jews. "When Israel was formed, we believed that Israel would be free of this question, and we would not speak any more about the borders of identity, but only the content of identity."

"But that seemed to be the case for many years," I said.

"Unfortunately, in these last years," he said, "we are returning to the question of the borders of identity and not the content of identity. I always hoped that we would get rid of the classical Jewish question of the tuning of the fine points of identity. But during the last few years, there has been a return to the borders of identity through the Holocaust question, the Israeli-Arab question, and the question of *yeridah,* of emigration from Israel. There are many novels about the prototype of the *yored* [the 'one who goes down,'] about the 'here' and the 'there' and the fact that Israelis are still Israelis when they go 'there.' This may give new elements that can enrich Israeli literature, but I can say personally that I deplore the returning of this question of the tuning of Jewish identity."

Other issues of Israeli identity were at the center of Yehoshua's extended debate with Anton Shammas. Shammas had argued that "Israeli" means citizenship only, while Yehoshua considers "Israeli" citizenship and identity, and Yehoshua has been criticized by some liberal academics for being too much an "essentialist" on this issue of identity. "When I say 'Israeli,' " he said, "I mean 'Jewish.' Israeli identity is not opposed to Jewish identity. On the contrary, Israeli identity is the strongest aspect of Jewish identity." Ideally, then, Jewish identity would not be the strongest aspect of Israeli identity.

"I know you believe the new Russian immigration proves you were right in your debate with Shammas," I said.

"Yes. The Russian immigration is, of course, wonderful. It was unexpected, and it reinforces Israel's sense of security. Unfortunately, it also provided a very dangerous weapon for the right wing to think that, from the point of view of demography, they can overcome the Arabs, even if Israel absorbs all of the West Bank. Of course, what the Right does not want to admit is that the permanent solution to the demographic issue is the establishment of a Palestinian state."

"But how do these demographic issues connect with your debate with Shammas?"

"I believe that after the Russian immigration, which was so large and so completely unexpected, Shammas cannot say any longer that Zionism is not relevant and that the Law of Return has to be abolished. This new immigration makes it very clear that I was right when I said that the Law of Return is eternal, that it is the moral basis of the state, and that we cannot give it up. The new immigration shows that the basic assumption and the basic conception of Zionism are still valid and are continuing to work as usual." His voice grew quiet as he continued. "But, at the same time, I can understand that it can't be easy for Israeli Arabs to see this wild and large immigration coming to Israel and perhaps even taking away their jobs. It is very dangerous and very frustrating for them, and I can identify with their feelings, and this is the reason why I want peace so much and why I want to establish and reinforce civil rights in Israel. But their situation is not easy at all."

Yehoshua's comments about Israeli Arabs and the *yored*, the West Bank settlers, and the loss of war as a theme are all connected with the third feature of the crumbling cultural center he emphasized in 1990. "This," he said, "is the new feeling of a great pluralism. The different places, social classes, and religious attitudes always existed, but they were shrouded by the conflict." He singled out two pieces of this pluralism for special emphasis: the Palestinians and the Oriental Jews, who are those Sephardic Jews who emigrated to Israel from North Africa and Asia after 1948.

His point about both groups is the same. The "one positive thing" Yehoshua concedes to the Likud governments of Begin and Shamir is that they gave the Oriental Jews "a sense of homeland, partnership, and belonging. They were silent for a long time. Now they are beginning to discover themselves." The consequences for literature are direct. "The Oriental Jew is becoming too specific, too shaped by himself, so that in order to describe him, you must penetrate deep inside him and understand him from the inside, and the people most capable of doing that are the Oriental Jews themselves."

The same is true of the Palestinians. Yehoshua recalled his creation of Na'im, one of the six narrators of *The Lover*. "I was trying to create an Arab hero in the seventies. And I believed then that I could really describe an Arab from inside. Of course, I was very careful. I took a child, a boy about fourteen or fifteen, and he had some love of Hebrew literature; this was a way I could relate myself to him. I thought I had described him, not in a sentimental way, not in a romantic way, but in a realistic way. If you would ask me to do again the same thing, to describe an Arab today, I would not be able to do it anymore. As Shammas's novel makes clear, they are becoming so special, so complicated, so unique in their existence that I would not be able to speak in behalf of them as I did in *The Lover*."

The Israeli Arabs represent a brand-new element in Jewish history. "It is an amazing, amazing development because we have to encounter the fact that now, for the first time in Jewish history, a minority is penetrating deep into our culture. We are not a people that loves to expose ourselves to the others. We know that generally those who dig deep in our culture do not favor the Jews, and there was always the thought that there was some anti-Semitic reason for doing it. But here the Arabs are doing it because they are obliged to, because they are entering universities —and they are not going into computer science, they are not going into physics."

"What *do* they study?" I asked.

"Most of them are studying Bible and Hebrew language and Hebrew literature, and they are starting to reveal our secrets. Think of Irving Howe and Alfred Kazin and Isaiah Berlin, great critics of Anglo-American literature, that came—or their parents came—from Poland or Russia fifty or sixty years ago, and by now they have mastered and are judging the whole of English literature."

"But Howe and Kazin and the others were first-generation Americans and Berlin moved to England as a child, while the Arabs have been in Israel for hundreds of years."

"Yes, but they have entered into our culture and our language only recently. And, though this may surprise you, I can foresee that someone with a name like Mohammed abu Yusef will be the Isaiah Berlin or the Dan Miron of Israeli literature in the twenty-first century." His wish may come true sooner than he thinks—one of the most interesting recent articles on *Mr. Mani,* published in a special number of the *Michigan Quarterly Review,* was written by Mohammed Saddiq, who teaches at Berkeley.

The moral consequences of this phenomenon fascinate Yehoshua. "This is a completely new dimension in Jewish history and very embarrassing. Speaking on television in perfect Hebrew, I mean really perfect Hebrew, they even try to strike at us with the language. They quote verses from our own sources and use these sources to teach us some lessons from our legacy to show us how wrong we are and how we are betraying our own past and our own spiritual values by doing to them what we are doing."

As the case of the old teacher in "Early in the Summer of 1970" suggests, Yehoshua found the cultural reality intruding into his literary possibilities. "I cannot describe Arabs, because I am in such an ambivalent relationship with them. On one hand, I feel so guilty because of what we have done to them in the last years that, if I would try to describe them, I would immediately try to make concessions because of my guilt. On the other hand, I am so angry about their stubbornness and their refusal to progress towards peace. So between the anger and guilt, I would not be clean enough to take an Arab personality and character and to describe him in a kind of objective way."

Whether the topic was the old religious Zionist, the Oriental Jews, or the Palestinians, Yehoshua kept circling back to the same fundamental point. Each kind of individual in Israel "is becoming so unique, so specific in its elements that, you can't dominate them the way our writers used to dominate the panoramic scene in the earlier texts." When I asked him about the artistic and human cost of these constraints, he conceded that "it's not good that you cannot put yourself into these characters any-more." He insisted, however, that his "duty is to create good literature, not just to take on a task and to do something for society. I will be judged only by how reliable and how serious I was as a writer, and not by my pretensions or my good intentions as a special thinker." He then drew an analogy to Faulkner.

"I admire, for example, how Faulkner describes blacks," he said. "Perhaps the most wonderful hero of twentieth-century literature in America is Dilsey, the old servant woman in *The Sound and the Fury*. Look how deeply he can represent blacks in his writing without making a sentimental picture, without making a romantic picture."

"But there's much more to her than that."

"Of course. She provides strong insights into the entire group of black Americans without losing her connection with white Americans, and, without losing her black American uniqueness, she is a reliable narra-tor of what goes on within the white Americans at the center of the story. And readers feel solidarity and intimacy with her, whether they are white or black, and understand the whole society and the metaphysical world through her."

"I would ask you," he said to me, "whether there is a white writing about black Americans in recent years and whether there is a serious black hero in recent white writing. I think no more. Because the blacks have become so specific that only the blacks can do it."

The new pluralism in Israel makes other literary demands as well. "We have to find new heroes if we want to survive," Yehoshua said. "We cannot count anymore on using the old stereotypical Zionist heroes that used to fill Israeli literature."

The extraordinary and aggressive heterogeneity of Israel, as well as its youth, accents the importance of the last feature of the cultural crisis, literary language. The difficulties involved in the creation of a flexible literary prose represent a convergence of several well-known factors, and some not so well known outside Israel. As a normal, living language, Yehoshua said, Hebrew "was nearly dead one hundred years ago." For the previous two thousand years, it had lived as a written language charged with religious and traditional meanings. A poetic tradition that exploited the traditional sources of the language was alive and well, but the "first prose novel was written only in the nineteenth century."

"What about theater?" I asked.

"Theater?" he laughed. "Theater was simply dim-witted."

Meanwhile, everyday colloquial language "has decreased its vocabulary and lost its connection with high and traditional sources." At the same time, the force of American English threatens contemporary Hebrew even more strongly than it does many other languages because "Israel and America have such close relations." The importance of English should not be underestimated. As a matter of fact, Yehoshua believes, "the strength of America comes first of all from English."

I wasn't surprised to find Yehoshua also alert to the moral dimension of language, especially with respect to the occupation and the intifada. I told him that one of my right-wing relatives had exploded when I referred to the territories as "occupied territories," rather than "administered territories." "He accused me of demagoguery," I said.

"Yes," he said. "Many Hebrew words were used in special ways for the language of occupation. Even if a boy of eight is killed, you do not say, 'A child was killed'; you say, 'A young man was killed.' There is also the question of 'natives' or 'local people' demonstrating rather than 'Palestinians,' or 'murdered' instead of 'killed'—this whole range of words was used to protect people from facing the reality. There was also, as you said, the question of the 'occupied territories' vis-à-vis 'Judea and Samaria.' The whole question of language used as a political weapon to avoid things or to emphasize things, this whole question is in itself a very interesting phenomenon."

"What do you see as your role as a writer when it comes to this whole business of the politics of language?"

"One of the tasks of the writer," he said, "is always to clean language, to make it again vital, to bring in new words. Here's another example. After the Six-Day War, there was a war of words about the liberation of the land. But you cannot liberate a land; you can only liberate a people. So one of the tasks of writers is to make people more sensitive to the language."

In literature, Israeli writers have faced the formidable task of creating a "flexible language, a language that can penetrate to all the layers of the society, all the layers of expression," and, according to Yehoshua, they have succeeded. The roll call is quite remarkable: Yehoshua, Amos Oz, Aharon Appelfeld, David Grossman, Batya Gur, Shulamith Hareven, Amalia Kahana-Carmon, Yoram Kaniuk, Yitzhak Orpaz, Yaakov Shabtai, Meir Shalev, and many others. Yehoshua gives much of the credit for the creation of a flexible language to playwright Hanoch Levine, who forged a poetic theatrical language from Israeli slang, Yiddish, and even some English—an accomplishment somewhat analogous to the special brand of American English in David Mamet's plays. The development of rich and flexible prose was delayed, Yehoshua believes, "because we had good subjects, especially, war. The subjects compensated for the lack of new invention in the language, of new stylistic kinds of prose."

In summary, then, four features define the transformed and fragmented cultural and literary landscape for Yehoshua: war; identity; pluralism; language. Although Yehoshua's first two novels, *The Lover* and *A Late Divorce,* mirror, or represent, the cultural fragmentation, *Five Seasons, Mr. Mani,* and *Open Heart* represent responses to the same phenomenon. *Five Seasons* and *Open Heart* respond by stepping back from extravagant confrontation with the four issues. It is as if Yehoshua had to gird his personal resources in *Five Seasons* to prepare for the comprehensive and direct confrontation in *Mr. Mani.* Or, in retrospect, it is as if he bracketed his most confrontational novel with two relatively "classical" works, much the same way that the priestly writers in Exodus bracketed the golden calf rebellion on one side with detailed instructions for the building of the tabernacle and on the other side with the implementation of these instructions. The three novels are linked in different ways. Between *Five Seasons* and *Mr. Mani* and between *Mr. Mani* and *Open Heart,* the bonds are thematic, in contrast to both formal and thematic ties between *Five Seasons* and *Open Heart.*

When it comes to the new pluralism and the problems of forging a literary language, Yehoshua's personal response in *Five Seasons, Mr. Mani,* and *Open Heart* is pretty straightforward. When I tried to apply his generalizations to his work in February 1996, I suggested that "in *Five Seasons* and *Mr. Mani,* you seemed to be taking your observations about pluralism to heart and diving in—like Anton Shammas and such Oriental Jewish novelists as Amnon Shamosh and Eli Amir—plunging deep into your own special turf, that of a fifth-generation Sephardic Jerusalemite." This trend has been noted by many of Yehoshua's critics.

"Yes," he said. "I felt I could no longer dominate a text with the kind of figure that represents the Israeli in general or the Ashkenazi Israeli of the center in general. And this was my way of approaching reality: little by little I discovered the Sephardic element that I had repressed a little and didn't want to touch in my early writings. I discovered the Sephardic element in my own identity and tried to use it as a way to penetrate through to my human soul and to the Jewish experience through my own biography. And I think this is the way I came first to *Five Seasons* and then to *Mr. Mani* itself." Roughly speaking, Sephardic Jews originate in the Mediterranean basin and Asia, while Ashkenazi Jews come from western, northern, and eastern Europe. Yehoshua discusses his relationship with his Sephardic past in an essay, "Remembrance of Sephardic Things Past," included in the anthology of his father's essays published in 1987 and in Yehoshua's second essay collection, *The Wall and the Mountain* (1989), which has not yet been published in English.

I was also interested in what the acknowledgment of his Sephardic roots meant to him personally. "Of course," he said, "it is also a return to some of my own sources and to the possibility of being courageous and admitting to some of my sources." The diving in to his sources in his fiction took two steps. *Five Seasons* is a personal contemporary look at his sources, a kind of preliminary testing of the waters, before the comprehensive historical plunge taken in *Mr. Mani*. Like Yehoshua, Molkho, the Levantine hero of *Five Seasons,* comes from a line of Sephardic Jerusalemites; like his creator, too, Molkho has abandoned Jerusalem for Haifa. But unlike Yehoshua, Molkho is utterly removed from politics and ideology and has little concern with history. The novel excludes almost everything, save the personal. In *Mr. Mani* Yehoshua tries to exclude nothing. "In *Mr. Mani,*" he said, "I very much wanted to understand this Sephardic element—Sephardic not in the sense of the Oriental Jew, but in the sense of a Sephardic Jerusalemite of the nineteenth century—the part his identity plays in the general boiling of Israeli identity." I found it noteworthy that he yields to the pressure of pluralism in both *Five Seasons* and *Mr. Mani* only in the subject and theme. In structure, however, both novels are brilliantly experimental in dramatically contrasting ways.

In language, too, the three novels provide complementary responses to the challenge of creating a new literary language. *Five Seasons* and *Open Heart* unobtrusively provide cross-sections of the possibilities of contemporary Hebrew. The language is full, various, and flexible, as Molkho moves gracefully through real and remembered landscapes and cityscapes and through the conversational worlds of sophisticated intellectuals and diplomats, government bureaucrats, and common people of a variety of ages and ethnic identities. In *Open Heart* the language expands still further to include the languages of medicine and physics and India, but I also felt a change in the characterization. I said, "Although I would say that the characters in both novels are specific and individualized, they are even more specific in *Open Heart* than in *Five Seasons.* Do you agree?"

"Yes," he said. "The characters in *Open Heart* are more specific and less symbolic. In the case of Molkho, his origin, his connection to the fact that he is Sephardic and not Ashkenazi, this gives him more a symbolic flavor. And, in fact, something that frightened me in *Open Heart* is that for the first time I was writing something with no double levels, but only one level, and I was worried that I was losing something in my writing."

"But there *is* a second level to the language of *Open Heart,*" I said. I was referring to the second voice, a dreamlike, poetic voice, in the third person, that addresses many of the themes of the novel metaphorically in a string of intermittent prologues printed in italics. I told him I especially like the "wild moments when images from this other voice break through the boundary between this voice and Benjy's voice." The example I mentioned was "the image of the young girl, the thin bespectacled man, and the refrigerator" that closes part 1 of *Open Heart.*

"I'm happy that you liked it," he said, "because there were people who did not like it, they were disturbed by this voice. I myself was a little bit hesitant about using this voice. I wanted to take abstract elements, like mystery, like death, like marriage, like love, like falling in love, and try to concretize them into winged figures, as in the old plays of the Middle Ages. Of course, afterwards, I wanted to connect the bits—only very, very few and very small bits of these lyric introductions—into the text, in order to make connections so that this voice wouldn't be totally separated. It was already separated by the italics and by the figures of speech and the words, but I didn't want it to be totally separated from the text. I have to say that thus far I am not totally convinced that this was a success. I don't know. There are different reactions. There are those who did not know what to do with these passages and were very critical about them. There were those who were very much impressed by them. There were those who said that they first skipped these paragraphs and then, when they returned to the book, first tried to read them separately, reading all the introductions as one big piece. I feel that I still have work to do about this kind of mixture between different codes. I've always known that when you are mixing two different codes it's very dangerous. And this is why finally I did not include the monologue of the dog in *A Late Divorce,* and I prefer the original version without the dog."

"Did you come up with this second voice entirely on your own?" I asked. "Or were you influenced by something you've read. I've never seen anything quite like it."

"I took the idea from an Italian book called *The Serpent;* that's where I found this method." He was referring to the 1966 novel *Il Serpente* by Luigi Malerba, which was published in the United States in 1968. "But all of *The Serpent* was a kind of dreamy book, so that the short dreamy introductions were not so different in style from the rest of the book as they are in my book. But I continue to question myself about this voice. In any case, it represents only 2 or 3 percent of the book, so it does not disturb it too much."

"Let me be a little more specific," I said. "I was puzzled and engaged by the voice. I was thinking that in a way it's a surrealistic variation of the omniscient voice in *War and Peace* that presents Tolstoy's philosophy of history. Here, the second voice provides an internal, dreamlike landscape where the themes of the novel come to life in a fatalistic way, as opposed to personal psychology in Benjy's voice that has a possibility of liberation, of not succumbing to fatalism. But for me as a reader what happens at the end of the novel, when Benjy breaks into that other voice, made it all worthwhile. Here, finally, he not only begins to transform himself as a character, he even manages to break, by a sudden act of will, the narrative convention, the 'code,' which you had created for the novel: two sharply contrasting voices, that touch each other only rarely and tenuously."

"As I said, I had many problems about this other voice in *Open Heart.* The small amount of negative criticism the novel received was directed mostly at this, even though it represents so little of the novel. There were people who could not find anything bad to say about the novel. 'It is magnificent!' they said. But I was suspicious. 'But you have some criticism?' I said. 'Yes, we are critical of this voice.' So I was quite upset."

"But not everyone was critical?"

"No. There were some who were very much enchanted by this other voice. And I myself am now in a *teku* position." *Teku* is a talmudic term for a stalemate, or an undecided question, that will be resolved, according to tradition, only by the prophet Elijah when he comes to herald the messianic age. "I don't know if I was right about it; I could have elaborated it more skillfully, but I was too lazy, I was afraid of this voice, so I did not develop it. So it stayed in the novel undeveloped, in an immature way. Still, in general, your explanation of it is very good." He broke into laughter. "But I would have to carry you along with the book, so that you will be with every reader that is reading this book and explain why you don't find those paragraphs disturbing."

"Well," I smiled too. "I *do* find it disturbing and also finally satisfying. But I have a question for you from India that has to do with that mysterious pair of large birds you use as an allegorical image of marriage in the dream voice." My daughter and son-in-law had just called from Varanasi and reported that the city matched the description in the book quite well—my son-in-law had devoured *Open Heart* in Hebrew when it was published in 1994. Except, that is, for one detail. In describing the Ganges, Benjy observes "that while one bank was teeming with people and activity, densely strewn with ghats and temples, the opposite bank was empty and abandoned, with not a house or human figure to be seen, evaporating into the void of the sky as if all that crowded holiness dissolved in the middle of the river and turned into nothingness." My daughter told me that the opposite bank was not empty, that there were many vultures there. With those mysterious birds of prey on my mind—those "mysterious and rather myopic" creatures that enter the novel immediately upon Benjy's return from India to Israel—I asked Yehoshua, "Did you know that the opposite bank of the Ganges at Varanasi is full of vultures?"

"What?" he said. "That's the first I've heard of them. Is that true?"

"Yes. Gabi just told me about them."

After a pause, he said, "That's strange, that's very strange."

As our discussion of the two voices makes clear (and the brief passage I quoted suggests, even in translation), the ambition and expressive ability of Yehoshua's language have grown in amplitude and subtlety. The emotion, both the humor and the sadness, is richer and mellower and more sustained in *Five Seasons* and *Open Heart* than in the first two novels—with less of the tour de force bravura that characterizes some of the most memorable passages of the earlier novels.

The tour de force quality returns with a vengeance in *Mr. Mani*. Not only is each of the five speakers characterized vividly and individually by a unique personal style, at the same time each is also typical of a time, a place, an ethnic identity. In addition, each section is written in the Hebrew of its time. So Yehoshua manages to trace simultaneously his personal sources as a human being and his fundamental resource as a writer, the modern Hebrew language. This quality of the book is the one most lost in translation, although Hillel Hailkin, who does a good job in the psychological and national elements of each speaker's style, does make an effective stab at duplicating linguistic quality in the archaic style of the fifth conversation, the Spanish phrases giving something of the flavor of Ladino rhythms.

I had no other questions about pluralism or the language. But I wasn't quite sure how to address the literary uses of war or Jewish identity in *Five Seasons, Mr. Mani,* and *Open Heart*. These matters seemed so much more complicated, whether I was interested in the relationship between each of the three novels and Yehoshua's cultural diagnosis or the interrelationships among the novels. So when we began to talk about war and identity, it made sense to me to take up the three novels more slowly, one at a time, and not in chronological order, beginning with the two more personal novels and ending with *Mr. Mani* and *Voyage to the End of the Millennium,* which was about one-third complete at the time.

War and its consequences certainly hover around *The Lover* and *A Late Divorce;* one of the most memorable passages in either novel is Gabriel's account in *The Lover* of his wanderings in the desert during the 1973 war. But in no way does war serve as an arena for conventional heroism. In *Five Seasons* Yehoshua goes much further, and war appears only in the imagery of Molkho and his wife's personal combat with her illness, not as a public event. In *Open Heart* war as a theme has vanished entirely. The themes that replace war are personal history and private passion and liberation.

One telling example of the way *Five Seasons* works along these lines is how it treats the Holocaust. Molkho's wife dies in the autumn, and that winter, in part 2, Molkho visits Berlin, the city of her birth, which she was driven from as a child by the Nazis and which she had refused to visit during her life. I told Yehoshua that I felt that he had taken special pains to make the meaning of Molkho's experience of Berlin intensely personal, with only the lightest trace of history or ideology.

"Well," he said, "he loved his wife to such an extent that he wanted also to heal her wounds, the source of her cancer, that came in Germany. So he returns to the city of her birth and tries metaphorically to return her to the place from which she was brutally thrown away."

In *Open Heart,* as in *Mr. Mani,* one of the themes that replaces war is suicide, its possibility, its causes. In *Mr. Mani* his focus is both individual and collective and he goes so far as to trace the theme back six generations and, ultimately, to the very beginning of the Jewish people. In *Open Heart* his focus is one very particular instance. "When you talked about the influence of war on Israeli literature," I said, "you talked about how hard it is to create a character who commits suicide. So here, in *Open Heart*, you seem to set out to do that very thing, and you actually succeed because I at least felt that suicide is a real possibility for Benjy, and that's one of the reasons I think the end is so moving."

"About the end of *Open Heart*," he began, "I must tell you one thing. My plan—and I've talked about this a lot—my plan was that Benjy would commit suicide in the end, that he would not be able to support the contradiction between the facts, on the one hand, that he identifies with Lazar and that Dori is now free for him and, on the other hand, that this relationship is an impossible relationship. And the contradiction between the possibility of having Dori and the impossibility of having Dori would destroy him. This was the original plan, and then when I came to part 4 I saw that he would not commit suicide, that he is too much a 'good boy' in relation to his parents, and that he does not have a strong enough destructive element in him to kill himself. And he resisted me; his mother especially was interfering and trying to prevent him from committing suicide. And this is what happened, and I think that his mother was very smart by connecting him back to his daughter."

'Your comments about Benjy's resistance to your plan and his mother's independence remind me of a great line in one of Grace Paley's stories: 'Everyone, real or invented, deserves the open destiny of life.' Benjy, too!"

It occurred to me that perhaps the greatest novel of suicide is *Anna Karenina*, for Tolstoy takes a character, supremely unsuicidal, and uses all of the art at his disposal to slowly, painfully move her into that tunnel from which suicide is the only way out. Like *Anna Karenina*, *Open Heart* is a novel in which love and suicide are deeply interfused. I remembered that I had asked him about *Anna Karenina* and Tolstoy while he was still working on *Open Heart* but he had not responded. So I added, "Perhaps Benjy, like Molkho, should have been reading *Anna Karenina*."

"Perhaps. I demonstrate in *Open Heart* how difficult it really is to make your hero commit suicide in a very reliable way. And I think that the fact is that I was continually thinking about the difficulties, and when I spoke to you about suicide in general, I myself was encountering such difficulties that I could not overcome them, because if I were to be faithful to my hero he was not really prepared to commit suicide, even though I prepared him very well. And this is exactly what I was saying to you. He approached suicide, but he could not commit suicide. Of course, if it were during wartime, I could have gotten rid of him very easily."

On Jewish and Israeli identity, the fourth feature of Yehoshua's cultural analysis, the mode of *Five Seasons* and *Open Heart* is subtle indirection. In both novels we are never in the mind of characters of ambiguous or ambivalent Jewish identity, like Gabriel in *The Lover* or Kaminka in *A Late Divorce*. In *Five Seasons,* though the story is told in the third person, the point of view is rigorously Molkho's, and never is there any question of the borders of identity. Rather, as the novel moves from Israel into France, Austria, and Germany, we stand well within the human borders of "Molkho, Israeli," and, as he struggles with his private identity as an adult male and a lover, he has the sort of stability and particularity of the characters of nineteenth-century Russian literature. I told Yehoshua how different Molkho felt to me. "Molkho," I said, "wears his Israeli identity comfortably, like an old shoe."

He approved of my analogy. "You put it very well—he wears his Israeli identity 'like an old shoe,' yes, like an ancient shoe," he added, laughing. "He has the most Israeli identity, the most comfortable, the simplest. He does not have to think about it; it comes from inside him. But you shouldn't forget entirely that in *Five Seasons* it's also a question of East and West, Sephardi and Ashkenazi, the Arab countries and Europe."

Open Heart, whose geographical reach is even wider, extending all the way from England to India, is similar in this matter of identity. "There isn't a lot that is 'Jewish,' in *Open Heart,"* I said. "If there is a question of identity, it's more of a matter of the conflicts among the different aspects of normal human identity—child, lover, spouse, parent—and what it means to have an identity at all. For instance, is Benjy possessed by Lazar or is he possessed by the idea that he is the reincarnation of Lazar? This makes me think not only of India and all the transmigration of souls stuff in the Jewish mystical tradition but also of *The Dybbuk* and the way Molkho must exorcise the spirit of his dead beloved wife from his body."

"I would say that the question of Israeli identity has to be taken very smoothly in this novel. In a certain way, like *Five Seasons, Open Heart* deals with the matter of East and West. But I would say that Jewish identity is not presented as a specific label in the book, but rather in the way it comes in any book: a French book, for example, in which you can see the French identity through whatever is done."

"In other words,' I said, "what you might call a 'normal' human sense of identity, rather than the typically 'Jewish' question of the 'tuning of identity' we've talked about before."

"Yes."

" 'Jewish' as a religion is also virtually absent," I continued, because I was also interested in the spiritual dimension of *Open Heart*. "I wonder whether the young characters of the novel, Benjy, Einat, and, of course, Michaela, find India so alluring because it offers spirituality and 'mystery,' and since secular Israelis have conceded all of religious life to the orthodox, the young Israelis fill the spiritual side of their religious needs in other religions, Hinduism, Buddhism, and so on." I reminded him that my daughter and Israeli son-in-law were spending a year in India as we spoke. "For them, as far as I can tell, the fascination seems more cultural than religious or mystical."

"I would not exaggerate the importance of Hinduism and Buddhism," he said. "It's the experience of going to India, the voyage itself, the country, not the spirituality—of course, some are caught there and never escape from being trapped by the mysticism of the East. But for the majority the most important thing is the experience of the journey, the journey itself, the freedom of the journey, not what is represented there but the fact that they are going somewhere where their parents have never been, that totally does not resemble Israel and they can be free there to clear their heads. This is the most important element in these journeys. Especially since most of the young Israelis go right after the army; ever since the intifada army service has been so hard and so dirty because our young men and women are forced to be half soldiers and half policemen."

For Benjy, the force of India is much more than the journey. As a young doctor, intensely committed to rational problem solving, he finds the spiritual, or mysterious, quality of India—also described eloquently in the second, the dreamlike voice of the novel—both alluring and disconcerting. One way Yehoshua dramatizes this disruption is through Benjy's immersion, after his return from India, in Hawking's *A Brief History of Time*. So, when we spoke in February 1996, I asked him to talk about what I called "Benjy's spiritual version of Hawking," in which everything, including all human ideas, is present in the first minute particle at the start of the universe.

"I have to say something now that will surprise you," he began. "Ika and I went to Jerusalem just yesterday to conference about *Open Heart* with physicists, professors of astrophysics, and others."

"How did this come about?" I was thinking that it could happen only in Israel.

"One day an astrophysicist, the head of the physics department at the Hebrew University in Jerusalem, Professor Rabinovitch, called me and said, 'I read your book *Open Heart,* and I think . . .' Immediately, I was scared that he was about to criticize me, to tell me that I have made mistakes here and there about Hawking, but he said, 'I feel that we have to have some communication, that physicists and professors of astrophysics have to speak to writers. Perhaps we can organize something.' I wanted to skip it. I didn't know what to do, but finally we organized it. There weren't so many writers, there was only David Grossman—the others couldn't come—but there were some good journalists and there was one professor from the psychology department of the university, a psychoanalyst, a friend of Ika, who deals with the metaphor of astrophysics in psychoanalytical matters—it was a very fine group. We spent two days, yesterday afternoon and this morning, listening to lectures on astrophysics and discussing Hawking and the novel." By now, a tone of amusement had inhabited his voice. "And it all came from the fact that this professor, the head of the physics department, had read *Open Heart.*"

"Did he want to tell you something or to ask you something?"

"Well, I have to tell you that, just a couple of hours ago, at lunch, he asked me, 'Why did you bring Hawking and his book into your book?' And I said to him, 'Benjy in this book is presented, first of all, as a doctor, a very career-oriented, idealistic kind of doctor, who very strongly believed in medicine and very strongly identified with medicine, and then he is taken to India, and in India he is confronted suddenly with a totally different conception of experience, not so much antiscientific—don't forget that he gets a very good and accurate result in Calcutta—but the fact is that he is exposed to such a mystical sense of things that is all tangled up with his relationship with love. It came as a tremendous shock to him.' "

"And that's the point of the first scene, immediately after his return to Israel."

"Yes," he said.

Medicine and mystery collide directly and explicitly in that scene in which Benjy asks a colleague to fill him in on the "benign" stomach surgery, which is the opening scene of the novel. He learns that the woman died and that the death is " 'a complete mystery.' " This response is too much for Benjy, given his experience in India. So, "in scorn and despair," he responds, " 'What mystery? To call something a mystery, you don't have to be a doctor.' "

I asked Yehoshua to continue with his explanation of Hawking. "Benjy," he explained, "speaks about Hawking in his own way, in of course an amateur way, in order to make a kind of combination between pure science and something that is mysterious: the big bang, the black holes, all this is something that is connected to cosmological ideas about the world. And this is why Benjy brought Hawking in, as an intermediary between the two poles that are afflicting him."

"The connection between *Open Heart* and *A Passage to India* is another way you expand the implications of the novel. When you speak about the wild variety of India and the appeal of a place that is so very different from Israel, I also feel a connection with the way Forster juxtaposes the variety English characters—the insensitive colonial community, an English liberal (in the person of Fielding), a Christian mystic (Mrs. Moore)—with Moslem and Hindu cultures, especially in the force of the landscape itself. India and England, East and West, are central in *Open Heart,* too."

"You should know that the image of India in *Open Heart* comes totally from *A Passage to India*. And not only the book, but the film, which I have seen twice. This is the reason why I knew India immediately because the film was so wonderful that I could connect myself really easily to it. And there is something about Mrs. Moore and the other things you mention. And there's the fact about England, that India is always connected to England."

"Like Israel?"

"Like Israel."

"I especially liked that Indian performance in England, which is one of my favorite moments in the novel."

"I saw that performance in Paris, but I transferred it to England. The performance that is described in the novel is totally accurate. It was directed by Ariane Mnouchkin; she is English, French, and Jewish, a marvelous director, the head of the Théâtre du Soleil, and she created this kind of show."

"I find it fascinating that though you experienced this performance firsthand, your image of India comes from books and movies and, of course, conversations with people who've been there—it makes me think of Bellow's Africa in *Henderson the Rain King*."

"I love to write about places I haven't visited. Sometimes it's not so obvious as in *Open Heart*. For example, in the Yom Kippur War, I was in the Golan Heights, and Gabriel's long monologue in *The Lover* takes place in Sinai."

"Has there been any criticism of your treatment of India," I wondered.

"I haven't been to India and nobody has criticized me for it. Perhaps there was some criticism but I haven't heard about it. The medical material, on the other hand . . ."

"I'm glad you brought that up," I broke in, "because one of the things I really like about *Open Heart* is that it is dense with real work, the concrete detailed work of medicine, and that's so unusual in fiction these days." For Benjy, surgery is like an art; he is slow, scrupulous, and takes especial pains with the sutures as if his aim were to leave no trace of the blood-and-guts drama, now hidden from view. Beyond the esthetic need to make the details of surgery one of the poles of Benjy's existence, the medical material is so alive I began to suspect Yehoshua relished the medical details in themselves, though there was usually a tinge of dread, mixed with exhilaration, in the various medical procedures. So I said, "I know you thought about being a lawyer, but had you ever considered medical school? Did you enjoy the medical research?"

"I never wanted to be a doctor. I wanted to be a lawyer. I was afraid of blood. I didn't want to touch the human body. And now in preparation for *Open Heart*, I participated in a very, very tough operation. To my surprise, it was a great, a really great experience. People were saying, 'You will faint in the operating room.' And I didn't faint. I looked down, deep into the human body without any problems. Why? Because I wanted to do it. But when my son gets a little cut, it is difficult for me even to look at it. So I have to tell you that when there is a specific need to know something, you can overcome any obstacle."

"How did the surgeons treat you?"

"All of the surgeons competed to have me watch them." He smiled, both amused and basking again in the attention the surgeons had lavished on him. "I think there is a kind of loneliness in surgery because no one from the outside ever gets to witness the important work they do. I came back a week after I had participated in that difficult open heart operation. The surgeon asked me if I wanted to see the patient, so I went to his room, and he was sitting up with all his family around him. I went up and introduced myself. 'I'm A. B. Yehoshua, and I participated in your surgery.' He got very excited. 'You see!' he said to his wife. 'You see! I was right! I was right! I told you that just as I was falling asleep I saw A. B. Yehoshua, and you told me I was dreaming!' "

When I stopped laughing, I said, "Before I interrupted you just now, you were about to say that there was controversy about some of the medical stuff, even though you researched it."

"Well, I did my work, and, of course, there were some mistakes. There was a big controversy." He raised both arms in a gesture that captured the absurdity of it all. "Two doctors attacked me about some of the details. Some remarks were right and some were totally wrong, and there were other doctors who answered them. Many people considered the whole controversy a joke; they asked the doctors, 'Why are you demanding such high accuracy? This is a novel, not a medical manual.' " He laughed. "But I figured the book inspired so much credibility that they wanted each detail in the book to be totally accurate. Anyway, I did correct all the little mistakes that were there for the English version and all other versions, and I think that I am now free from any criticism."

The way Molkho and Benjy feel comfortable with their identities as Israelis made me think of them as a new kind of hero, neither an ideological intellectual, nor a kibbutznik, nor a warrior, but a "normal" hero, undramatically heroic and self-critical, who finds special arenas for courage within the limited possibilities of everyday life, in work, in family, and in private identity, especially as a lover. When I asked him whether he too thinks of Molkho as a new hero, a "normal" hero, his response was mixed.

"You are right to speak of Molkho as a new kind of hero, as an alternative to the ideological intellectual and the kibbutznik," he said. "But, of course, I would not be an advocate for Molkho. I am *for* ideology. I am *for* taking a point of view. I wasn't thinking that he was 'normal.' I think I was trying to push him out of politics because he doesn't know anything, he doesn't want to commit himself; he's still at a stage in which he thinks that politics cannot bring anything to his salvation. So you have to take him more as an example of the little man who avoids politics. Benjy, of course, is more conscious of what is happening. He has wider scope. Nevertheless, he is still quite limited. You know," he chuckled, "you can avoid politics even in Israel."

The relative straightforwardness of Molkho and Benjy as characters and the apparently traditional, "classical" form of *Five Seasons* and *Open*

Heart may give the impression that Yehoshua has fashioned formally conventional novels. But that is not the case. In a more subtle way, Yehoshua's third and fifth novels are as formally adventurous as the others. When I asked him to talk about this side of *Five Seasons,* in our very first conversation back in 1988, he immediately began to speak of S. Y. Agnon, generally acknowledged as Israel's greatest novelist, bubbling with enthusiasm. "I don't know if you know Agnon's *A Simple Story.* It is a marvelous novel —it was translated by Hillel Halkin in a marvelous translation. Agnon is the basis for all of our writing. It is amazing that even in writing that has been done just recently, you can see the influence of Agnon. How important he is! A shadow that covers the whole family! You know," he said, smiling, "instead of teaching A. B. Yehoshua, you should teach Agnon." The implication was clear: do not even dream of discussing *Five Seasons* until you have read *A Simple Story.*

There is something particularly satisfying about Yehoshua's return to Agnon as a source and resource, particularly because of Agnon's belief that an alliance between the human will and the communal tradition is the only way to stave off disintegration into human and social anarchy. This is not to deny the Agnonian strain even in the earliest Kafkaesque stories, with their emphasis on the fragility of the codes of civilized life. But with *Five Seasons,* Agnon moved to the center of Yehoshua's creativity.

A Simple Story has the familiar shape of a traditional love comedy, replete with young lovers—Hirshl Hurwitz and his beautiful, intelligent, and independent cousin, Blume Nacht—a conventional and passionless social order, and an adult, Hirshl's mother in this case, who blocks the young lovers' happiness. When Hirshl's mother, Tsirl, sees that he has fallen in love with his impoverished cousin, she sees to it that he marries Mina, the daughter of a wealthy small-town farmer instead.

We took up our discussion of Agnon and *Five Seasons* during a long phone conversation in January 1992. I asked Yehoshua about the affinity between Agnon and *Five Seasons.* "I don't think there is a direct connection between *Five Seasons* and *A Simple Story,*" he replied, "except that Molkho is the same type of person as Hirshl." Hirshl, the hero of *A Simple Story,* and his hero, Molkho, share one crucial trait: mediocrity. "Molkho is so mediocre, really mediocre. He annoys some readers because of this mediocrity. You see, there are from time to time mediocre characters who can make works into great epics because they are not too demanding—this is also true in Agnon's *Temol Shilshom* (Only yesterday). Because they could move with the stream of history, they could be very effective in describing a whole society in a kind of epic. The mediocrity also helps the reader to see exactly the work of the character's unconscious. If he were too talkative, if he were too active, the work of his unconscious would be masked, so his activity is slow, and you can follow more clearly the work of his unconscious."

Yehoshua found Agnon's manipulation of his readers particularly exciting and productive. "It is like some other novels," Yehoshua explained, "in which the hero is very simple and not sophisticated, and through that kind of hero you can bring in immensely sophisticated things. Just because the hero is not sophisticated, you can play about his unconsciousness and bring the reader to feel all the emptiness, all the gaps in the work. You make the reader so creative—the hero does not speak too much, so the reader has to do the work instead of him. And the work that the reader does is very important, very creative."

This talk of gaps and creative readers made me think of the great narratives of the Hebrew Bible, and Yehoshua agreed. "In the stories of the Bible, this is, of course, the system. So little is said, that you have to be much more creative." This demand that the readers be creative applies to *A Simple Story* and *Five Seasons* with equal force and is escalated in *Mr. Mani* in which, as Yehoshua put it, "the reader has to invent and create the other partner," that is, the silent partner, of the conversation. In our most recent conversation, in May 1996, I reminded him of his comment that the "hero" of *The Lover* and *A Late Divorce* is the gap or space between the characters. I added, "In *Open Heart*, as in *Five Seasons*, the gap or space that the reader must fill in is between the reader and the characters, rather than between the characters, as in *The Lover*, *A Late Divorce*, and *Mr. Mani*," and he nodded in agreement.

In the afterword to his translation of *A Simple Story*, Hillel Halkin describes how Agnon cultivates this gap. From the opening pages, Agnon deftly sets us all up for a timeworn romantic story in which Hirshl and Blume, the blocked young lovers, finally, finally get together—and either escape from, get crushed by, or come to terms with the dense social community of Szybusz. The manipulation is consummate; my eighty-eight-year-old Russian-born mother and my fifteen-year-old daughter and my students and everyone else I know who has read the novel have reacted in precisely the same way: rooting for the romantic lovers and against the conventional society.

Then Agnon pulls the rug out from under us, when he allows the old social order (of arranged marriages and tradition) to triumph over the new romantic order (of individualism and romantic love). Although we certainly feel the constraints, the burden, and the costs of the traditional culture—Blume, our heroine, has no place at all in that closed world!—we also feel the force and security and value of the intricate bonds that hold a traditional community together and protect it from the alienation and chaos that threaten to tear it apart. At the climax of the novel, Agnon wonderfully rubs our independent, individualistic, romantic noses in his radically conservative vision in a lovely moment when Hirshl falls in love with his wife, Mina, several years after the arranged marriage. "Mina's blanket moved. Hirshl's lips met hers." The same Mina who had served as Tsirl's agent for squashing and deflecting her son's groping toward liberation now is the agent for Hirshl's final, if limited, liberation from his mother.

Although Yehoshua's secular and liberal political values are far removed from Agnon's religious and political conservatism, the literary response demanded by the ends of *Five Seasons* and *Open Heart* fall into *A Simple Story*'s pattern of sudden, liberating, and overflowing emotion followed by a lot of reflection, both about the central character and ourselves. These reflections, however, move in radically different directions—in Agnon we turn away from Hirshl; in *Five Seasons* we turn, or return, to a deeper look at Molkho's soul.

This difference derives from the characters of the two heroes. Agnon's Hirshl is more limited than Yehoshua's Molkho. Only at the instant that he falls in love with his wife does the distance between reader and character vanish, and it is restored almost immediately when Hirshl, with slender self-awareness, dismisses Blume entirely. "Not only did she never love me, he told himself, she never loved anyone at all."

Hirshl has been liberated from the domination of his mother, but he understands nothing; he does not reflect upon his liberation and experiences no conscious realization about what has happened to him. The transformation is thus only emotional and not insightful. Because his perspective is so much more limited than ours at the end, our reflections tend to move away from him onto ourselves, especially the negative appraisal of the traditional culture most secular readers bring to the novel. And this is exactly Yehoshua's point about the effect on readers of a mediocre, unconscious hero.

In *Five Seasons*, too, there is a "mediocre," mostly not self-conscious hero. But the climactic turn in *Five Seasons*, which comes in the very last sentence of the novel, is an epiphany for both character and reader; it is a moment of wonderful insight for Molkho into himself and for us into him. For the first time in our reading of the novel, we are right with him, and his insight as well as his capacity for insight force us to readjust our judgment of Molkho himself, particularly the numerous traits and actions that have annoyed, frustrated, or amused us as we read. It is as if we had been looking at him with one eye closed and suddenly opened our other eye to reveal him in three dimensions. As Yehoshua risked *A Late Divorce* in one epigraph and the intermittent sanity of a mad woman, here he goes even further: he risks the whole novel in the final seven words.

"The last words of the novel," I said, "reveal that *Five Seasons,* like *A Simple Story,* turns on a man's love of his wife. In Agnon's novel, Hirshl's love of his wife is a sign and reward of his liberation; in *Five Seasons,* Molkho's love of his wife became a barrier to his liberation the moment she died."

"If he wishes to free himself," he explained, "he must fall in love as deeply as he had loved his wife, even though his relationship with his wife was full of struggle."

As Hirshl is liberated from his mother, so Molkho is liberated from his wife. In both novels, a father's concern about a sick or missing son plays an important role in the process of liberation. I asked Yehoshua about Hirshl's sick son, Meshulam, who ends up being raised by Mina's parents. "You're asking me why Hirshl, in order to recover and come to terms with his wife, has to get rid of his son and get him out of the house?"

"Yes."

"Hirshl projects his unresolved and unsatisfying relationship with his mother onto his son, Meshulam. Because I believe that Hirshl's relationship with his mother is the source of his problems, I think that by sending away the self that he has projected onto his sick son, he can liberate himself from his problem and be ready to establish a new relationship with his wife, and that relationship is love."

When I asked Yehoshua to talk about Molkho's love of his wife, he began to talk about Molkho's "unconscious dialogue with his wife, in which he swallows her into himself. He has to take her through himself in this year because he identified too much with his wife, with her culture, with these Ashkenazi things, and he returns and liberates himself in a certain way from the cultural elements of his wife, what she imposed upon him—her intellectual tyranny, to a certain extent, or aggressiveness." Yehoshua paused here. "No, I will not use the word tyranny—it is a story of a kind of a slow, modest, normal kind of a liberation, and, of course— and you are totally right—he *loved* his wife."

This is the love that is strong enough to get him to go back to the Berlin of her birth to try to heal her. "So it is love, it is certainly love," he continued. "And he goes through different metaphors of women, to liberate, stage by stage, the parts of his wife from him, in order now to be a free man, an authentic man again, and to be now in love with others. And when people say to me, 'You see, he will repeat; the second year will be like the first one; he can't get married,' I say to them, 'If you speak like this I immediately will write a volume, the title will be *Molkho Gets Married*— you know, like John Updike's *Rabbit Redux*—to prove to you that after this year, he has achieved his inner liberation."

"And the last line makes it all clear to us," I said.

"Yes, that he's free and that he's able to love again."

The double take on Molkho—as a mediocre man and a man passionately in love—makes him remarkably real for us. I told him that Molkho reminded me of the characters created by Tolstoy and, especially, Chekhov. It is no accident that Molkho keeps reading *Anna Karenina* throughout the novel. "I think of Molkho as a nonintellectual Levin who thinks he should be a Vronsky," I said.

"Oh!" he said. "Chekhov and Tolstoy are everywhere. I would not dare to say that Molkho is like Chekhov. Molkho is too passive even for Chekhov. Of course, Chekhov is a genius, but I think that in recent years I haven't liked his ambivalence so much—he's much too ambivalent— and the fact that he repeats again and again that a man cannot love. Not in all of his stories, because there are some marvelous stories, like 'Three Years' and 'Duel,' in which people can cross the border and create a relationship, in which people can change."

"Or 'The Lady with the Lapdog,' " I said. "But this preoccupation with people at the border between isolation and connection has been in your work almost from the beginning, and several of your stories have an abstract version of this Chekhovian pessimism, this mixture of yearning and futility."

"Well," he answered, "there are many, many stories in which Chekhov repeats: 'A man cannot change himself. He can desire something, he can dream about something, but he cannot go along and accomplish something.' I've become a little tired of this repetition. But, of course,

Chekhov . . . Chekhov is great." It again struck me how tuned in he was to that sentiment of Grace Paley: "Everyone, real or invented, deserves the open destiny of life."

I thought of his threat to write *Molkho Gets Married* four years later, in February 1996, when I brought up Agnon and the craft of fiction again as we discussed *Open Heart*. Here the hero is Benjy, who certainly is more self-aware than Molkho or Hirshl, but he is as blind as they to the wildest yearnings of his soul. Benjy does get married, to Michaela, but the purpose of the marriage is to help his impossible love for Dori. As usual, the subject of Agnon delighted him.

"You are more right than you know to speak about *A Simple Story* and Agnon and the relationship between me and Agnon. I feel very close to Agnon and I learn from Agnon concerning matters of craft, as you say, not concerning subject very much. And you cannot imagine how right you are speaking about *A Simple Story,* and not only about *Open Heart,"* he added cryptically. "You will be amazed in three years to know how your intuition was correct." I figured he was talking about his novel in progress, which would become *Voyage to the End of the Millennium.*

Open Heart is a novel of two climaxes, the first when Dori comes to Benjy after Lazar's death has apparently freed her for him, the second, at the very end, after Benjy's mother had brought his daughter, Shiva, to him from India. Both of these are managed with the kind of consummate craft Yehoshua is so partial to. The first has Agnon written all over it. "What happens when Dori finally reveals herself to Benjy and to us is so typical of you," I said. "The way we are forced to rethink the whole novel from her point of view, realizing that we have been trapped by Benjy's consciousness into believing that she, Dori, is entirely incapable of living alone, much the same way as she has been trapped by Lazar's conscious-ness (and, she realizes to her dismay, Benjy's too)."

"Go on," he said, sounding amused.

"So that, until then, while we may have questioned Benjy's behavior, we don't question his analysis of what Dori needs or wants, so we have been forced or manipulated by you (you devil!)"—both of us are laughing by now—"into complicity in Benjy's idea of her, whatever our sympathies may be."

I told him that for the first time I was feeling a little foolish about discussing his work with him, because, I said, "This is the first time that I have no one else to talk to." I had just finished reading the English translation in manuscript, and none of my Israeli friends who had read it in Hebrew were around, just then. "I know you love that kind of move," I said. "In *Five Seasons,* for instance, which in many ways most resembles this, that sudden readjustment of perspective doesn't happen until the last sentence of the novel! Here at least it's some fifty pages from the end." It is characteristic of Yehoshua that just before the revelation happens, Benjy —with every reader in sync with him—is able to entirely occupy Dori's consciousness, know her with climactic intimacy, imagine every one of her movements, step by step, his heart beating along with hers until the moment that she enters the apartment, only to have this moment turn out to be the beginning of the end. Also characteristic is the irony of the fact that when Lazar is alive Benjy is most appealing to Dori as an alternative to Lazar's imprisonment, and just when Benjy thinks he has the field to himself, he does not, because now she has her own natural, simple, and terrible need: "I want to be alone."

Unlike *Five Seasons,* when the sudden change in perspective illuminates the hero, in *Open Heart* what is illuminated is the heart of Dori, the love object; as in both *A Simple Story* and *Five Seasons,* though we readers are given innumerable clues to the truth about Hirshl or Molkho or Dori, it is only in retrospect that we catch on.

When Yehoshua and I continued our discussion of the novel in another phone conversation a month later, I was still thinking about Agnon. By then I had had the chance to discuss the book with several people. "Hirshl and Molkho and Benjy must all free themselves from a passion that cannot be fulfilled," I said. "Hirshl because he is not strong enough to pursue Blume, Molkho because his wife is dead, Benjy because Dori wants to be alone. But in *Open Heart,* this freedom takes on a strongly feminist cast, because Dori frees herself from the limited roles created in the male imaginations of both of her lovers."

"I'm happy that you find *Open Heart* more feminist," Yehoshua said, "and this is also connected to the novel I am working on now."

"I think Michaela contributes to this feminist strand too, as another sign of Benjy's limited understanding. And this is very important, I think, in the end of the novel. You know, when I speak to people about the ending I get different reactions. My Israeli friends find it terribly sad: that he has finally fallen in love with his wife, breaking into his dream, breaking into his obsession—even breaking into the other voice—but they say it's too late because they are sure she will not return to him. Perhaps these are the same readers who read the end of *Five Seasons* pessimistically, and I know what you think of them. Your own editor, Betsy (Elizabeth Lerner,

Yehoshua's editor at Doubleday), sees it as much more hopeful—romantic that she is. I see it as sadly hopeful but uncertain. I like the fact that though his mother is right to bring Shiva back from India, she is wrong when she says it's up to him, rather than up to Michaela, whether the marriage will continue."

"I think the most important thing about the end," he said, "is that the suicide does not happen, because I could not make it happen."

"And the mood of sadness comes from that."

"I think so. As for Michaela, I don't know about Michaela. Michaela may return or she may not return, Michaela is not so important for me. I know that many people like her. I don't like her too much; to my mind, she is too disturbed. But the most important thing is that now that his daughter is with him, he cannot destroy himself. She is his connection to life, something he has to take responsibility for. And Michaela may or may not return, the relationship may be renewed or not: these are minor things that will happen after I have finished with the novel."

But I wasn't done with Michaela. "I don't know if it's because I've been reading too much of you and Agnon," I said, "so that between the two of you you've trained me to read with a peculiar kind of alertness, but when I was reading the scene when Benjy goes off with Michaela at his friend's wedding, toward the end of part 2, just after he decides it would be good to marry to make himself more acceptable to Dori, I jotted down in the margin of the book, "Will he finally fall in love with Michaela (as Hirshl falls in love with Mina), and will that be the climax of the novel?"

"About Agnon and Michaela, perhaps, you *are* right. Now that I think about it, there is some resemblance. But at the end of the novel, I did not bring his relationship with Michaela to such a climax as Agnon does in Hirshl's relationship with Mina, because he had chosen Michaela on purpose only to help him in his relationship with Dori. Dori has to feed him with all the libido that his mother did not give him. Benjy's parents are good parents, but they are English Israelis, they are dry, pushy about his career, and one of the important things about India is that for the English, India is the sensual side they keep under control."

"As both Italy and India are in Forster's novels."

"Yes."

"And the focus of Benjy's sensuality is on Dori's belly," I said, "with its association of birth or rebirth, that continues your immersion in the physical human body that's so important in *Five Seasons* and *Mr. Mani*. Even the form of lovemaking Benjy chooses with Dori is an image of his desire to be reborn."

"This is why, even though Benjy is brought to India to fall in love with the daughter, he falls in love with the mother instead."

The image for this exchange is the blood transfusion Benjy arranges in India, from mother to daughter. At the same time as Dori's healthy blood infuses Einat's body, the love infection flows in the opposite direction, from the intended lover to her mother. I said, "All the surgical attention to the inside of the body, especially the abdomen, made me think of the idea that all of a child's questions are really one question: 'Where did I come from?' This theme is set in the operation that opens the novel, routine abdominal surgery, after which Benjy, to his surprise, tells the family, 'Don't worry, she's been born again.' "

"Yes, his attraction to Dori's belly is an indication that he wants to be reborn or correct his birth by a kind of rebirth."

"That would make Benjy's obsession with Dori not purely destructive," I acknowledged. "As I've said before, I believe that personal obsessions and collective obsessions can be both 'sane' and destructive. Do you believe it is necessary for Benjy to go all the way into his obsession with Dori in order to liberate himself from his love of his mother to a healthier love, an adult love?"

"I don't feel that Benjy is obsessed," he insisted, in a rare show of impatience, "but more that he is in a kind of need, like babies in utero who take from the blood the food they need to build their bodies, and from time to time these babies absorb some odd elements in order to fill inner needs of which they are not even conscious. This is what is going on with Benjy."

"I see," I said. "And what makes Benjy's mother's decision to bring Shiva from India so shrewd is her awareness, conscious or unconscious, of her son's condition and the danger he is in: Shiva transforms Benjy from son to father. I have to tell you that in the role of Shiva I see another trace of *A Simple Story*, with a twist, of course. In the Agnon novel, for the romance to flourish, for Hirshl to fall in love with his wife, Mina, and to resolve his difficult relationship with his Mama, he had to *subtract* the sickly son; here, again the parent's health involves the child, but here you have to *add* the healthy daughter. In both cases the children are the vehicle for healing and, in fact, loving, as Benjy transforms himself psychologically (and, I would add, morally) from being a child wanting to be reborn to being the father of a child."

"I don't know how far you can take this," he said, taking off his glasses and rubbing his chin pensively. "The end of *Open Heart* gives only a hint about what is happening. His mother brings the child back to him as a handle for him to hold on to life, to stick to life. The problem of Benjy is different from the problem of Hirshl. Hirshl had too much of his mother, and Benjy didn't have enough of his mother. So there is a difference." He paused. "But listen, next month, when I am in Boston, if you will promise me, but really promise me not to say anything, I will tell you a secret about my future literary plan."

"I think I told you," I continued, after I had promised him not to breathe a word, "that I see *Open Heart,* like *Five Seasons,* as a novel for a time of peace, a boring time, in which a writer can focus on private matters sans guilt, so that politics and ideology are, in a manner of speaking, absences that are present, especially in the context of *Mr. Mani.* It is as if you were saying: Our people are making the right choice, so I am free to write about anything I choose, public or private."

"You are asking about the connection between *Five Seasons* and *Open Heart,* and you are right to say that both of them deal with private things. But I wouldn't say that they are peacetime novels, because *Five Seasons* was started after the Lebanon War and it was during the years of—not yet the intifada—but it was, let's say, the height of the occupation. Also, *Open Heart* was not exactly in peacetime but before peacetime. But I would say that these are private kinds of novels, not totally private, but certainly less political, less ideological, even though there are many ideological interpretations of *Five Seasons.* I would not draw this sharp separation between these two types of novels, for example, connecting some to peace and others to war. I would say that there are novels that function through specific individuals and there are novels that function through more typical kinds of characters that represent a wider society, a wider group. For example, the novel I am writing now, and this is a peacetime novel, is a novel about the first millennium, one thousand years ago, and it is very ideological, but not, of course, in the Israeli context."

"When I called *Five Seasons* and *Open Heart* peacetime novels," I explained, "I wasn't thinking so much about when you actually were writing the novels. What I was trying to imagine was the state of the society in which such novels would be most naturally received. My idea was just that *Open Heart* and *Five Seasons* are both novels written for a time of peace, for readers in what I might call a peacetime consciousness, when our concerns as humans are primarily involved with personal fulfillment and personal tragedy, not constantly interrupted by the continual call to collective emotion and solidarity that happens in times like the spring and winter of 1996 with the terrible suicide bombings. In a way, it goes back to that statement you made about creativity and solidarity in Ehud Ben Ezer's *Unease in Zion*—it must have been about twenty years ago. Even during a time when peace is nothing more than a hope or a goal, at least while readers are immersed in the intimate experience of reading these novels (whatever ideological allegories clever critics discover or create), they are occupying a kind of clearing in which their own private feelings as private individuals are validated and given enormous value."

"Perhaps you're right," he said. Although Yehoshua seemed to be resisting my idea, I believe that profound political implications emerge from the remarkable aliveness of the characters of these novels. He insists that *Five Seasons* and *Open Heart* provide respites from politics, but one effect of the double take on Molkho, Benjy, and Dori is to make both the characters and our response to the characters a paradigm for the sorts of things that should engage a normal people living a normal life in a normal land. In all their everyday imperfection and virtue, these three characters, and every other character in *Open Heart,* in their opacity and their unique-ness, provide a dramatic answer to all the fundamental questions about identity Israelis have been forced to ask themselves in the face of the intifada and the ongoing peace process that followed: "Who are we? What sort of people are we? What kind of nation do we want to be?"

The alternatives are the familiar ones: secular or theocratic; demo-cratic or authoritarian; peaceful or warlike; tolerant or fanatic; Eastern or Western; Sephardic or Ashkenazi; collective or individualistic; normal or abnormal. The Hebrew title of *Between Right and Right,* his fierce collec-tion of essays, is *Bizchut Hanormaliut* (In defense of normality). That we can be blind to the heart of so apparently normal, transparent, "medio-cre," and limited human beings, like Molkho or Dori, amounts to a celebration of the human richness in the private domains of love and work, as opposed to the public worlds of politics and war.

It is as if Yehoshua were saying to us, with the spirit of Chekhov more present than ever, this, this is what life is about: the idiosyncratic human responses to private loss, the unpredictable private acts of moral courage, responsibility, and transformation. Politically, *Five Seasons* and *Open Heart* represent an alternative, a kind of clearing, in the middle of the frenzied jungle of Israeli public life. If we accept Yehoshua's attempt "to penetrate in the most slow and detailed way" Molkho's movement until a year after his wife's death, we should be equally patient in the painstakingly slow movement toward peace.

We can imagine *Five Seasons* and *Open Heart* as novels for a better time. It is as if Yehoshua has leapfrogged over the contemporary ideological rigidity to a time of so healthy and vital a peace among Israel, the Palestinians, and the Arab world that novels like *Five Seasons* and *Open Heart* would be simply what they appear to be, personal novels of death, grief, and renewal, of isolation and connection, of love, obsession, and rebirth—in a reading liberated from a historical context that insists on subtle political interpretation of every private action and realization.

5

Approaching the End of the Millennium

Yehoshua is right, of course, when he acknowledges the complementary relationship between *Five Seasons* and *Mr. Mani* and the similarity between *Five Seasons* and *Open Heart*. Whether we were discussing structure or character or theme, it was clear that the characteristic tactic of both *Five Seasons* and *Open Heart* is indirection—in sharp contrast to the direct, outrageous, and confrontational approach Yehoshua takes in *Mr. Mani*. And the subtlety of *Mr. Mani* is of an entirely different order than the Agnonian craftiness of *Five Seasons* or *Open Heart*. The thematic difference between *Mr. Mani* and the other two novels became pretty clear to me when I thought about how *Mr. Mani* handles the theme of war. Although war figures only in imagery and memory in *Five Seasons* and vanishes entirely from *Open Heart*, it is one of the main contexts of *Mr. Mani*. The first three conversations are set during a war, the fifth at a time of revolution. More pointedly, starting from the very beginning of the novel in the prologue to the first conversation, many of the characters' biographies are marked or measured by wars. But as in *Five Seasons*, the central theme is not war but history. In *Five Seasons*, the history is private; in *Mr. Mani* the history is both private and public. In neither novel does Yehoshua exploit war as it is used in conventional war novels, as, what he earlier called, "a mine of dramatic situations."

So it is no surprise that it is not in war but in the exploration of the identity theme that *Mr. Mani* reaches its most profound depths. Yehoshua is subtle and direct, heartbreaking and exuberant when he takes on the identity theme in all of its historical, psychological, moral, and even mythological implications. He explores Jewish identity and Israeli identity in all their nuances and all their tragicomic wildness—and all the vectors of this exploration converge in Yehoshua's attempt to understand the present. Among the strange chorus of Mr. Manis is one who believes all the inhabitants of Israel, including the Christians and the Moslems, are Jews who have forgotten they are Jews, another who preaches to Arab peasants, "Get ye an identity and be quick," and a third who announces that he has canceled his own Jewish identity. What we feel profoundly as we move back through five or six generations of Manis is how human identity is a dense amalgam of private character, personal history, and collective history.

One of the things that pleases Yehoshua most about *Mr. Mani* is the way he managed to find a fictional embodiment for many of his political ideas, so that for the first time in his literary career he has fully fused his own multiple identities: as public man and active citizen and as private man and artist. "I have always wanted to see the links between the psychology of a person, his personality, and his political views," he told me during his visit to the United States in 1993. "So I combined the ideological elements of the crossroads of our history with the psychological interaction between the generations. And I wanted very much to relate these two things to each other."

I asked him for an example. "As you know, when I wrote the third conversation and published it, I did not know whether I would be able to finish the book. But I don't think I told you that I dedicated that chapter to Lova Eliav, to my friend, Lova Eliav, whose seventieth birthday we celebrated in December of 1991 in a wonderful ceremony." Arie Lova Eliav, formerly a senior military officer, ambassador, diplomat, administrator of settlement and emergency projects in Israel and Iran, member of Knesset, secretary-general of the Labor Party, winner of the Israel Prize for "exemplary lifetime service to society and the State," has for many years been the leading dove within the Israeli establishment. In his April 7, 1974, *New York Times Book Review* article on Eliav's prophetic manifesto, *Land of the Heart* (published in Israel in 1972 and in the United States in 1974), Nadav Safran characterizes him as "a statesman who believes it is possible and necessary to engineer the conditions that favor peace, without illusions, but without cynicism and self-deception either."

"It really was a marvelous celebration," Yehoshua continued. "Many people came simply to tell him that he was right, that he had been right all along. This man, who was a total political failure because his party did not succeed, was a symbol to all of us in the peace camp of the clear thinking at the end of the 1960s and the beginning of the 1970s after the Six-Day War." Eliav is not only a friend; he also represents a paradigm for the sort of human being Israel requires most, a pragmatic visionary.

In 1993, before Ezer Weizman was chosen, Eliav was one of the candidates for the presidency of Israel, and he was attacked ferociously in the Israeli press. I asked Yehoshua to comment on this. "Of course, we regret that Lova was not elected president." He spoke slowly, his tone weighted with his strong affection for his friend. "But Ezer Weizman is a very combative dove, and he will also be good for peace. Lova was a little hurt by the fact that he was attacked in the newspapers about being a *tzaddik,* a saint, which made him appear ridiculous. And I know that he was very much hurt by his experiences during his candidacy for the presidency."

"But Lova remains for you an image of a man of foresight?"

"Yes. Of course. And I have always asked myself why there are people, at a certain time in history, who can see all the elements of a conflict and see the solutions, while the majority are blind and take years to understand. Why was it, in the middle of the 1960s, that there were those in the United States who were saying, 'Vietnam will be a disaster; we should not continue.' Without knowing all the elements of the problem, without even knowing where Vietnam is on the map, they still could understand through the codes of America and Vietnam that this was not a war America had to make and that it would be a failure. How could they dare to say that America would fail in this battle?"

It was the same thing with the Six-Day War. "How did it happen that there were Jews in Israel who said right after the Six-Day War, 'There is a Palestinian people. You will not be able to dominate it. The Arabs will refuse to make peace if you refuse to give back the territories. The settlements will be a disaster.' Why can certain people think so clearly? What is the source of their enlightenment?"

By the *Mr. Mani* synthesis of ideology, psychology, and history, Yehoshua dramatizes his answer to this riddle. The inclusion of Jewish history in this novel is his way of participating in a fundamental change in Israeli literature. This is his first novel that is preoccupied with the past. I asked him whether he was alone in this shift. "Not at all," he said. "If you examine Hebrew literature during the past forty years, you would find that only recently have we become concerned with the past. And this is a change, and I think *Mr. Mani* is a part of a whole change in the relationship between Hebrew literature and the past."

I asked him to describe the way it used to be. "Until now, we were always preoccupied with the present." He spoke affectionately of "the sense of the past that European writers have continually. Even when he is writing about his contemporaries, a European writer can always go back to the nineteenth century or to the eighteenth century."

"You are talking about the physical past, right?"

"Yes. When I think about the place itself, we don't have the past like the Europeans, like a Parisian, for example, who can go out into the street and touch a church that was built in the eighteenth century or the seventeenth century. Europeans can visit a library that holds old manuscripts and a whole physical environment. But we don't have the past in the present physically."

As he said this in 1993, the physical reality that was leaning in on us was the crowded New York City coffee shop, but the city that was most present as we talked was Jerusalem, and not the Jerusalem of the present, but the series of snapshots of the historical Jerusalem, represented in *Mr. Mani*. "In a way," he said, "when I returned to the past—and I don't know whether I will ever do it again—I returned to the physical past— this was the way I explored Jerusalem in the novel, so if *Mr. Mani* had gone just from Athens to Crete to Auschwitz without Jerusalem as the center, I would not have written it. Even though the conversations take place in various places, the real subject is Jerusalem. When it comes to identity, it is important to identify with places, because when I think about Israeli identity, I think about territory, language, and the legal and social structures that connect the people to each other. In a way, this idea is my contribution: you cannot have an identity without also having a history of the place; identity is in the geography, the territory, and it is in this sense that Jerusalem is so important."

"This physical idea is so very different," I said, "from my father's relationship with Sambor, the town in Poland where he was born."

"Yes, when Jews deal with their past in Europe now—imagine, for example, a Jew who goes back to Russia: he isn't concerned with his village as a geographical place; he is concerned with the community that was, let's say, in Lvov or in Lida or your father's Sambor.

"When he goes back, he deals with families and with the structure of human relationships, but he does not see Vilna, for example, first of all as a place, in a geography, near a river, near all those things that make Vilna's smells and colors whatever they are."

"That must be one of the reasons," I agreed, "that so many Jewish Americans—my father was a good example of this, too—find it quite easy to think of Israel as if it were the old country, as if they came from there, as if Israel is their homeland, even though they or their families came from Europe."

"Yes, yes," he said softly.

I asked him to describe the general effect on Israeli literature of this absence of an available material past. "An Italian writer or a British writer or a French writer," he said, "can so easily reconstruct the past of his people. He can rely on himself, and he can find a way to describe the past and to invent his stories in a setting of the nineteenth century or the eighteenth century without any problem. This was not true in Hebrew literature."

"Why?"

"Hebrew literature was a literature of the present and even of the boiling present, the immediate present. If you ask how many novels were written after the 1950s even about the War of Independence itself—you would see that even the War of Independence was already in the past. I blame the Israelis for reading so many newspapers. You have to picture the Israelis every Friday going home after work with a pile of newspapers; they read three evening newspapers and a local newspaper. It is a cult of newspapers. It's because they want to understand, they desperately want to understand. They think that if *Yediot Aharonot* doesn't give then the answer, perhaps *Ma'ariv* will have the formula: what is the solution to their confusions and their troubles? This attachment to the immediate present is also dangerous and has dominated Hebrew literature."

"And these thoughts directly affected your conception of *Mr. Mani.*"

"At that moment in the cemetery, I knew that I had to return to the past. But not a simple return to the past. From the beginning, the conception of the novel was to start in the present and go to the past only to serve the present. I am not going to the past in order to escape from the present. I have a problem now in the present—this is my situation—and all the elements that the present gives me are not sufficient to explain to me the source of the trouble or its solution. And this is why I dug down to another layer in the past. And that layer was not sufficient, and I had to go backwards, and backwards, and back and back again. But the point of departure is always the present."

As he spoke, I had three ideas at the same time, which I shared with him. I noted that on the personal level of *Mr. Mani*, the problem in the present is Gavriel Mani's nightly flirtation with suicide, and he agreed.

"As you speak," I added, "the image of archaeology comes into my mind, in which the physical and the temporal are one and the same." But stronger than this image was my recollection again of Faulkner's description of his composition of *The Sound and the Fury*. In Faulkner's case, the issue is not a desire to understand the present but a wish to understand the force and meaning of Caddy Compson in her brothers' lives. But the formal problem is similar. *The Sound and the Fury* began, Faulkner said, "with the picture of the little girl's muddy drawers, climbing that tree to look in the parlor window with her brothers that didn't have the courage to climb waiting to see what she saw. And I tried first to tell it with one brother, and that wasn't enough. That was Section One. I tried with another brother, and that wasn't enough. That was Section Two. I tried the third brother, because Caddy was still to me too beautiful and too moving to reduce her to telling what was going on, that it would be more passionate to see her through somebody else's eyes, I thought. And that failed and I tried myself—the fourth section—to tell what happened, and I still failed."

"This going back and back again in the reverse direction," I asked, "is the reason why you are so insistent about not defining *Mr. Mani* as a historical novel?"

"Yes. An historical novel is always a novel that starts to accumulate time. There is a basis, a starting point in the past from which you proceed, slowly, to a later time. But in *Mr. Mani,* the question is in the present. And I go to the past not because I like the past but because I need the past, because I cannot solve my problem through the components of the present. And this is the dominant structure of the novel, moving from present to past, in what you call the reverse direction."

I asked him to talk about the narrative discontinuity that results from his focusing on a series of crossroads. "I wanted the novel to be a combination of dramatic elements and epic elements. I cannot write an epic history of Israel or of Jerusalem during 180 years. It would be pretentious; it would be something that could not be fulfilled. I don't have enough material to reconstruct the life of Israel during such a long period of time. What I can do is pick moments in a dramatic way, in which people speak about a certain confusion or a certain conflict they have encountered, and try from this conflict to understand a particular historical period. That's why the form had to be conversations, in which two people speak to each other. But only one of them had to have a story to tell. In that story the person speaks about a man. And we would, little by little, discover a family through the conversation of strangers who have encountered members of this family during a certain period in their lives, and, little by little, we would understand the dynamics between different generations."

"What with suicide, incestuous sexuality, and murder, the dynamics of these relationships between the generations are not too simple," I noted.

He burst out laughing. "The question, for one thing, goes beyond the biological. As you know—and this was another thing I only discovered after I had finished the book—it is possible that Efrayim Mani, the son of Joseph Mani, is not his real son, but that Joseph Mani"—he was talking about the third conversation—"just took a pregnant woman who had come to Beirut and helped her to deliver the son, and when she died, he kept the child. And so the child is not *his!* In the second conversation, someone pointed out to me, he is blond with blue eyes. Of course, he could have gotten this from his mother, but perhaps Joseph Mani himself is not the father. So the question is not biological. It is more than biological, because a father can adopt his children."

"And you weren't thinking of this at all while you were writing the novel?"

"No. And after *Mr. Mani,* I wrote a play, *The Babies of the Night,* about the adoption by Israelis of Brazilian babies—it was accepted by the two main theaters in Israel, and it opened in Haifa in 1992. Out of the blue, out of any context, I didn't know for what purpose, I wrote this play about three couples that come to Rio de Janeiro to adopt babies." The play is a complicated one, with many characters and a complex multilevel set. "You know, it was one of the texts that I worked hardest on in my life. It kept changing and changing and changing. I never in my life will write another play! It is so difficult! But my point about *Mr. Mani* is that the question is not biological, it is not even genetic, it is far more. It is the unconscious elements that come from fathers and sons conceived in the widest terms."

I brought up his old affinity—and affection—for Faulkner and asked why he decided to tell the story through conversations rather than the interior monologues that are the method, except for two chapters, of *The Lover* and *A Late Divorce*. "You know very well my admiration for Faulkner," he replied, again that tone of amused complicity in his voice. "Nevertheless, the monologue in itself, the monologue as an aesthetic method —I feel that it is a little artificial. And I felt that I could not continue with this technique. This is why I returned to the dialogue. Dialogue is a one to one. Monologue? What is a monologue? Who gives a monologue? The monologue is a kind of aesthetic invention. In life a person does not give monologues."

"So you distinguish the monologue from stream of consciousness," I said.

"Of course. Stream of consciousness is another thing. Stream of consciousness is not Faulkner. From time to time there is some stream of consciousness. But as a method, stream of consciousness is quite different. But an interior monologue, in which each person tells a piece of the story, is an artificial device. So I returned to the dialogue. But the dialogue in this book could not be realized as a real dialogue, because this is a novel in which someone tells a story to someone else. And the other, like a psychoanalyst, only tries to help him with little questions that he introduces from time to time. So in order not to expose the artificial aspect of this dialogue, I took out one side."

"As usual, you weren't very easy on the reader, were you?"

"No. I said to the reader: You will have to help me, and you will participate in this novel by re-creating the other side of the conversation. At each point, there is not only one question or one answer, but there are several options, and the reader has to choose among them. And by not getting caught up in the reading itself, but from time to time having to stop and say, 'What was the answer of the silent partner, what was his or her comment,' you do a kind of re-creation of the text."

I told him again that I thought that he loves to take this sort of artistic risk in his fiction. "Well," he said, smiling, "I was worried about this technique and wasn't sure whether I would get the active participation in the reading of the book. And I was quite amazed that so many readers accepted the challenge to such an extent that in my next book I will omit the other side of the conversation also—I will just give empty pages and the readers will create the dialogues by themselves." I laughed, and he added, "And this was the technique until I came to the last conversation."

"Why are there five conversations and not more or fewer?"

"When I wrote the novel, I knew it had to be conversations, but I did not know why I chose five and not six and not four. But after I finished the novel, I asked myself, 'Why five?' And then I understood: I am in Israel five generations. When I write my curriculum vitae, I always write: 'Born 1936 in Jerusalem, fifth generation.' What is this 'fifth generation'? It is not a sign of ownership. What difference does it make if I am fifth generation or third generation or second generation? It's nothing. People say to me, 'You are from the *Mayflower.*' I say, 'No, it's not the *Mayflower.*

The *Mayflower* is when the Bolsheviks come from Russia to Israel at the beginning of the twentieth century; that is the *Mayflower.*' But the old community of the Sephardim were not aristocrats at all. People said they were aristocrats, but they never were considered aristocrats. But the fifth generation was always important for me. I have always wanted to repeat and mention it."

"Do you now know why it is so important to you?"

"It is a sign for me that I am, in a certain way, in a position that is different from others. It is important in my discussions with the Arabs that I am fifth generation. It is equally important in my political discussions with Jews. In my dovish political discourse it was important for me to say, 'I am fifth generation, so I also know those others who were here in the nineteenth century. For me, Zionism was not started only in the beginning of this century with the Balfour Declaration.' This is the reason there are five conversations. But I did not realize this until after I had finished the book."

The time and place he selected for each conversation enable him to participate imaginatively in five turning points of modern Jewish history; each of the turning points has to do with identity and its implications. "Each conversation had to be at a special time," he said, "and here enters the ideologue, the writer who also has an ideology. I tried to find crossroads in Jewish history. At each crossroads I wanted to ask, 'What was another option in Jewish history that was not realized?' " The Hebrew phrase associated with these options is *kivun negdi,* the opposite direction or countermove. Each crossroads is "a kind of laboratory in which I simply placed the other option, the one not taken." I asked him to talk about his reasons for picking each of the crossroads.

The first crossroads is 1982, the time he began writing the novel, the time of the Lebanon War. Hagar Shiloh, a twenty-year-old university student, speaks to her mother, Yael, at Mash-abei Sadeh, a kibbutz in the Negev desert. Hagar's father, a war hero, was killed during the Six-Day War in 1967; her boyfriend, Efrayim Mani, is in the army in Lebanon. I could not help noticing how often Yehoshua comes back to the Lebanon War as a watershed for him and his nation, so I asked him why it troubled him so. His answer was succinct. "It was the first time that I saw Israel making war by its own free will, without any provocation, a war for the sake of war, with the crazy idea of going to Beirut and imposing a peace treaty upon the Lebanese. How could people think such a crazy thing?"

It is hard for Americans to understand the profound impact of the

Lebanon War on the liberal intellectuals of Israel. When I asked him to explain this more fully, he referred to the last years of Menachem Begin and his funeral in March 1992. "You saw the funeral of Begin—it was very emotional. And the way this person locked himself in his home for nine years without going out was like a Shakespearean drama—such a deed has some of the stature of a Shakespearean tragedy. When he died, there was such a strong outpouring of emotion toward him—partly because he had punished himself. And the Lebanon War is the only possible explanation for this self-imposed imprisonment. Imagine, a person who was a prime minister staying at home and not even going to one political convention, a person for whom politics was the oxygen of his life. Not speaking, not explaining, doing nothing—just once a year going out to the cemetery on his wife's memorial day. And that was all! And this was because of the Lebanon War."

"Don't some people attribute his withdrawal to his private grief after his wife's death?" I asked. "And I read an article in which Avishai Margalit says it was his pride."

"Well," he said, brushing these other theories aside with a dismissive wave of his right arm and a grave tone of voice, "the explanation which was given in Israel by his friends recently was the Lebanon War. So you can understand that, if Begin, who led this war, fell into such despair, what it was for those of us who were totally against it! The first day of the war was an odd kind of revelation for us: what is Israel doing? For all of us, who have fought so many wars, war is very important. And to go like this to war!" He shook his head sadly. "We are not the Romans, we are not the French or the Germans! After six million dead, you don't risk going to war on your own initiative. We were born and we were brought up with the conception that war is always an evil, that war is imposed upon you, that you never choose a war. And the fact Begin had started this war, *milhemet b'rera,* a war of our own choice, was something totally new to the values of the Israelis. So this was the starting point of the novel. I don't say that the war in Lebanon was the most important event of the state of Israel, but it was a kind of event that came from a different set of values; it changed the values that Israel had held for a long time."

The second crossroads is 1944. The conversation partners are Egon Bruner, a young German soldier, and Andrea Sauchon, widow of Egon's grandfather, Admiral Werner Sauchon, a German war hero who died in 1935. I was interested in why Yehoshua did not set the second conversation in 1948, the year of the creation of the modern State of Israel. I said,

"Did you skip 1948 because 1948 was a year in which the Jewish people, for once, made the right collective choice?"

"Other people have also asked me why there was no conversation in 1948, and, to some extent, you're right," he said. "But there is also a practical reason. The gap between each conversation had to be at least twenty, or thirty, or forty years, to really erase all the memory in order to show how the unconscious works. So that Efrayim Mani, for example, would not know anything about his father's deeds or what was happening in Jerusalem when his father was young. So I didn't want the period to be too short."

"I see. This operating principle of at least a twenty-year gap between the conversations made it impossible to include both the Holocaust and the creation of the state."

"And I wanted the Holocaust," he continued. "The Holocaust was very important to include. Besides, 1948 already touches my own environment, my Sephardic environment, and perhaps I would have had to speak about my family, I would have had to take material directly from my family memory, and I did not want to do that. I wanted to re-create an imaginary family, without referring at all to something that is personal. Of course, I admit that the personal things came in, as in all my books, in diverse ways —but not officially, not directly."

"What about 1944, then?" I asked.

"As I said, the Holocaust is very important for me. And I wanted very much to get it from a totally different angle. You know I do not come from a family that was in the Holocaust—my wife, Ika, of course, does—but I wanted to oppose with all my heart the conception that you cannot run away from your Jewish fate, that Hitler decides who is a Jew and who is not a Jew because he has the power to kill the Jews. He has the power to put me in the concentration camp, so he decides if I am a Jew or if I am not a Jew." I told him how often I had heard American Jews say this.

"I cannot bear this idea," he exclaimed, "and I wanted to oppose it, not because it is my will, but because it is reality, it is objective reality: the Jew is always free to choose his Jewishness. Even in the Holocaust. If a Jew says I am not a Jew, and Hitler brings him into a concentration camp and kills him as a Jew, still he is not a Jew. And the fact that Hitler killed him did not make him a Jew. I respect *his* will and not Hitler's."

He seemed to be getting at something radical about Jewish identity. "I am interested in the freedom of a Jew to choose his identity. Jewish identity is only in the mind," he said. "And we see it now with the Russian Jews who are coming now after seventy years without any Judaism, without any content of Judaism, and still they are Jews, only by their identification."

I asked him why he set this conversation in Crete. "I wanted to explore all the elements of Jewish identity in the place in which, I would say, civilization was born. And Crete, according to the legend, is the place in which Europa was born, and Crete, in general, is one of the most important places in human history." The Hebrew word for "Europe" is "Europa."

This did not quite mesh with the version of the myth I am familiar with, in which Europa is born in Canaan, kidnapped there by Zeus in the form of a bull, and carried to Crete, where she is raped by Zeus the eagle. "One of the things I thought you had in mind," I said, "was to counter the Nazi anti-Asian myth that would cut Europe off from Asian barbarians."

"Yes. You're right," he said. "Europa was born in Asia. But the continents were competing: Who will have her? Who will have her name? Finally, Zeus, by kidnapping her and taking her to Crete, gave her name to Europe and not to Asia. And perhaps by returning back to Crete, the Nazis, who were trying very hard to dominate Europe, wanted to take Europe at her sources, as if to say, 'We are capturing Europe in her homeland, where she was born, we are taking Europe from her roots.' They conquered Europe—except for England; all of Europe—and the European side of Russia—was in Germany's hands."

"And what does Egon find at this source, at the womb of Europe?" I asked. "What else, but a Jewish family!"

"Yes."

"And you like the idea of the air invasion in part because of the eagle."

"In part. And the air operation itself fascinated me, first of all, because it is so dangerous to come by air. And this way the Germans demonstrated their spirit at its best, even though they lost a lot of people. Afterwards, it was forbidden to do another operation like this because it was too costly. They lost a lot of their best units. I was fascinated because it was not an operation that was done only from military calculations, as a pragmatic operation. Crete was not so important militarily, and it could have been taken slowly by ship. So the invasion of Crete is the type of operation that is done when a country is at the peak of its victorious movement."

"I see. The invasion was German Romanticism in action."

"Yes. There was something large in it. Their best thinking was present in the operation. And I wanted to catch this moment of success in order to approach it realistically and mythologically to show what was so dangerous in it." These words brought to mind one of the few lapses in Hillel Hailkin's generally successful translation. Near the very end of his dialogue, Egon Bruner tells his grandmother how infuriated he is by the survival of Efrayim Mani's wife and son, "by the thought that we'll soon have to leave this place for the swamps and the fogs again, and that *they* will continue to look out at this brilliant bay through these ancient enchanting olive trees—that thought so aggravates me . . ." Hailkin skips the telling Hebrew words after the "enchanting olive trees": "and they will continue to pollute the blue and pure womb of ours."

"Did you also want to draw any connection between the Minoan civilization and the ancient land of Israel?"

"As you know, when the people of Israel came from Egypt, at the same time, about one thousand four hundred years before Jesus Christ, the Philistines, whom we call the *p'lishtim,* the Cretans, came to Israel from the island of Crete." He paused for emphasis.

"At the *same* moment," he repeated, "two people came to Israel: the Jews, or *am yisrael,* came through the desert, and the Philistines came through the sea, and they were bitter enemies. And the Philistines gave their name to the Palestinians. So you can take that as the start of the Israeli-Palestinian conflict. Of course, I don't mean 'Palestinian' in the modern political sense; I am talking about the conflict on this land between two people, the Jewish people and the other people."

Nor is this all there is to Crete. "Crete is also many, many things," Yehoshua continued enthusiastically. "There were lots of things I discovered—and this was quite amazing—when I came to Crete. It was the nearest point to Israel reached by the Nazi machine during the Second World War. So it was very dangerous to us. And, of course, the ancient civilization of Knossos and King Minos—the civilization without religion. These are just a few hints about the many, many things that are inherited in Crete that are in this chapter."

The third crossroads, the first one written, takes place in Jerusalem in 1918. The conversation is between Lieutenant Ivor Stephen Horowitz, military advocate in the British army, and Colonel Michael Woodhouse, a military judge and war hero, who lost "his right arm and part of his vision" at Verdun in 1916. "It was the crucial time of the Balfour Declaration," Yehoshua said. The Balfour Declaration of November 2, 1917, begins with the words "His Majesty's government view with favour the establishment in Palestine of a national home for the Jewish people."

"The fact is," he continued, "that at this time, if the nascent Palestinian identity would also have guaranteed a nation its people, and the country would be have been divided into two countries by the 1920s, perhaps the Holocaust would have found a Jewish state already prepared. This was the original program of Zionism, of Herzl: to avoid the Holocaust, or to avoid its consequences by having a place of rescue for the Jewish people. But this opportunity was missed by the Zionists, by the Arabs, and by the British. All three of them were blind. The fact is that the British did not prepare a solution to this dispute by, at that time, creating two states and dividing the country, as they would do in Pakistan and India twenty years later."

"So you disagree with Gandhi," I said.

"Yes. In my opinion, against the opinion of Gandhi, who was somewhat utopian, by dividing the country the British avoided a lot of bloodshed that would have continued for centuries in an India that included Pakistan. The split and even the transfer of population avoided a lot of trouble. But that was not done here in 1918. The Palestinians were too weak, without their identity, and they didn't understand. The Zionists didn't understand. The British didn't understand. All three of them. And this is the theme of the third conversation."

"But what about the personal side, the nonideological side, of Joseph Mani's story?"

"Of course, we also know that Joseph Mani's desire to be anti-British was also because he had felt betrayed by his father, who was very much British. The fact is that he wants to cut." Yehoshua is referring to Joseph Mani's cutting of the map of Palestine in two. According to Lieutenant Horowitz, Joseph Mani's political identity was born when, a mere child of twelve, he, all by himself, cut the umbilical cord of a newborn baby. "He wants to repeat the cutting by his father with the knife, the cutting of the babies from their mothers, or to repeat the cutting of his father on the railway, the way he committed suicide—all these elements are psychological, but they can be transformed in a fantastic way to ideological conceptions." This cutting motif extends through the last conversation of the novel all the way back to the cutting that happened and did not happen on Mount Moriah at the climax of the Binding of Isaac.

Yehoshua is particularly fond of Lieutenant Horowitz, the speaker of the third conversation, who by the end of the conversation has begun to switch his identity from that of a Jewish Englishman to that of a fledgling English Jew. "He is courageous, he is very courageous," Yehoshua said. "He is the only speaker in all the conversations who risks his position. He could, after the conversation, have been sent directly to prison, with the colonel, his silent partner, telling him, 'You, the prosecutor, instead of accusing the defendant, you come and try to prevent the trial!' " There is also a second, a personal side to Yehoshua's affection for Horowitz. "You know, I wanted to be a lawyer, and my juridic libido was invested in the third conversation." To me, as a reader, the legal consciousness depicted here is neither more nor less convincing than the medical consciousness depicted in *Open Heart*. It's probably a sign of Yehoshua's mastery as a novelist that, if he hadn't disabused me of the notion, I probably would have assumed that his "medical libido" was at work in *Open Heart*—and that at some level at some time he must have at least entertained the notion of becoming a doctor himself.

Although Horowitz is the only English conversation partner, England has a very strong presence throughout the history of the Manis, beginning with the British consuls of Jerusalem in the fifth and the fourth conversations who are patrons of the Mani clan, continuing with the British army on Crete that is in the background of the second conversation, and ending with the most recent Efrayim Mani—the Efi of the first conversation— who abandons Hagar Shiloh and their child to pursue his doctorate in London. I asked Yehoshua how *Mr. Mani* was received in England. The novel had been published there by Peter Halban in April 1993, just a few weeks before this conversation in New York City.

"I have not seen all the reviews, but, in general, it seems that it has received good press."

"Would you say a little more about the powerful presence of Britain in the novel and in Jewish and Israeli history?"

"The presence of Britain in the novel is very strong. It's also strong in my life, to a certain extent. My father worked for the British government until the foundation of the State of Israel. Britain is very much present in *Mr. Mani* because Britain was the country that delivered the Balfour Declaration, and without the Balfour Declaration nothing could have been done. And this is very important. But at the same time, as I said before, Britain left the Palestinian problem unresolved, and this is still with us right now. So the importance of Britain in the history of Israel, not only in the last 90 years, but more, in the last 130 years, is very significant."

I was also interested in English anti-Semitism. Early in the third conversation, one of the ways Horowitz reveals his sense of his own identity is through his appraisal of the anti-Semitism of Major Clark, the chief advocate, who is his superior officer. "And his anti-Semitism," Horowitz tells Colonel Woodhouse, "is the most natural thing in the world; I mean it's all a parcel with his views on women and horses, which are very solid indeed and have survived their encounter with the facts with hardly a scratch. But he wouldn't harm a fly and in fact there is no greater gentlemen." I asked Yehoshua, "Do you think there is anything special about English anti-Semitism? Does their romantic attachment to the Arabs play a part?"

"I don't see any specific kind of anti-Semitism coming from the English," he said, "different from French anti-Semitism or other anti-Semitism. For me, anti-Semitism is the same reaction. From the beginning of the history of the Jews in Persia in the biblical Book of Esther, there has been the same pattern of anti-Semitism; it can be stronger, it can be weaker, but it is more or less the same pattern: The Jews are strangers, and they are not willing to really identify with the country in which they are living." His words and his intonation paralleled the accusation by Haman, the villain of the Book of Esther. "They have always a second drawer in their life in which Israel and the Jewish people are found. So I don't want to enter into the varieties of British anti-Semitism. But I *would* say the British definition of anti-Semitism is the most accurate one." He laughed. " 'An anti-Semite is a person who hates Jews more than they deserve.' This is the British definition and the most correct definition, one that I myself agree with, because the Jews hate themselves to a certain extent. If you hate them more than they deserve, you become an anti-Semite."

The fourth crossroads is 1899, the time of the Third Zionist Congress, and the Holocaust casts the same shadow over this conversation as it casts over the third. In this conversation, Efrayim Shapiro speaks to his father, Shlomo, at their small country estate in Poland on the outskirts of Auschwitz immediately after getting off the train from Israel. "These," Yehoshua explained, "were the days of the end of the nineteenth century when the Jewish people had just become conscious of their own secular identity. And the fact is that if they had come to Israel at that time, they would have helped Herzl, who was so isolated and so alone and so opposed by the majority of the Jewish people."

"And the Shapiros didn't come," I said, "because Efrayim, for a mélange of reasons and desires far too dangerous for him to acknowledge to himself, thwarts the wild and powerful love between Moses Mani and his sister, and that's why they don't come to Israel, even though, as it turned out, the father would have loved the idea."

"But if they *had*," he continued, with sadness in his voice and eyes, "if they *had* come, the Jews could perhaps have held the whole country at the beginning of the twentieth century. But they missed the opportunity."

"And that explains my favorite sentence in the book," I said. I was referring to the chilling throwaway line Yehoshua gives to Dr. Moses Mani near the very end of the chapter. " 'Who knows,' " he says to Efrayim, " 'perhaps in a few years you will be able to take a train straight from Jerusalem to that Oświęcim of yours without having to brave the sea!' "

"Yes," Yehoshua replied. "The way in which Auschwitz and Jerusalem are linked, you see it very well."

The fifth historical crossroads is 1848, the era of the European revolutions of 1848. "This was the time we call 'the springtime of the peoples,' the moment in which the Jewish people had to decide: are we only a religion or are we a people? They had to recognize themselves as a people if they wanted to join the other nations or they could have gone down in history as the emancipated 'Sons of Moses,' speaking of themselves only as a religion. Napoleon had asked them in 1806, 'Are you a religion or are you a people?' In 1848 they decided they are a people. And in this way they entered modern history as a people, with all the confusions, all the problems, and all the conflicts. Perhaps they could not have done otherwise." This "otherwise" option would erase the Jewish national identity and replace it entirely with the national identity of the country in which each Jew lives. Yehoshua's implication was that the option of entering modern history as a religion and not as a people would have had unpredictable and radical consequences ninety years later. That is, the Nazis would have seized power in a European world in which there was no such thing as a Jewish people.

The fifth conversation differs in several ways from the others. For the first time a Mani, Avraham Mani, is the speaker and he is as important a character as the Joseph Mani whom his story is about. Also, Avraham Mani has two silent partners, not one, and for the last part of his story his conversation partner, Rabbi Hananiah Haddaya, cannot answer him because the old rabbi has suffered a severe stroke that has paralyzed him and shattered his capacity for speech. I asked Yehoshua to talk about this silent listener. "And this rabbi, this paralyzed rabbi, I remember how the idea came to me—to invent this rabbi who cannot answer. For me, he's a kind of god, if you like. I don't want to say it quite explicitly since I am a secular person, but God, for me, is a term, it is not a presence in itself, it is not an objective thing, but a term which people use to define themselves. The rabbi for me was a kind of god."

"Here, again, you speak of God, though your interpretation of the Binding of Isaac starts from the assumption that there is no God. You don't believe in God, but you also seem to argue with God a lot. Would you like to talk about this?"

"I do not believe in God but I am very much preoccupied with the human conception of God. God is a human conception, and the fact is that people speak about God repeatedly and at length. Because I am so interested in human beings, I have to be interested in the way they think and speak about God. This is my concern. This is why God comes so often to my work, as one human conception."

On the human level, Rabbi Haddaya's condition had special force for me because my father had a similar condition. I asked, "Have you had any personal experience with someone who suffered a stroke?"

"Yes. The invention of a rabbi that understands but doesn't speak came from an actual event in our family. Ika's mother had a stroke, and for one year we had to establish a kind of relationship with her such that we would speak to her and know she understands although she could not answer. And this situation, which can lead you to a terrible despair, came to be a very human and touching relationship. I remember our children and ourselves talking to her with no answer, and yet there was a relationship. We didn't know what she understood, but we knew she understood something. She smiled. She reacted. And we could identify with her unspoken answers. But not one word."

"How long did it last?"

"One year. But, Bernie, you know what it is like, better than I."

"Yes, with us, it lasted for seven years," I told him.

"With your father."

"Yes."

"Not speaking?"

"Not speaking, probably not understanding. The speech centers of his brain were completely shattered, and there was a lot of despair." My father suffered a massive stroke in Kfar Saba while he and my mother were on their only visit to Israel in 1977.

"It was their first visit?" Yehoshua asked.

"Yes. My father was a passionate Zionist."

"You know, Bernie, I completely believe that it was not only physical but also mental, this stroke, because I know, for example, about an uncle of mine who always dreamed of coming to Israel. But just before coming, he was so afraid of coming that he died." This statement followed from Yehoshua's idea, developed in *Between Right and Right*, that there is a profound fear of emigrating to Israel deep within the souls of the Jews of the Diaspora; the root of this fear is the unconscious conviction that only in Israel are Jews judged, only in Israel are Jews called to strict account for their moral failures, because only in Israel do Jews have communal power in the world.

"My father," I said, "had the stroke the day before he was to leave. Just before he collapsed he and my mother had been talking about buying an apartment in Kfar Saba, so profoundly had he been affected by the visit. So he *did*, at least, have his visit to Israel."

"Yes, he did have his visit. But I think emotionally, he was so shocked in a way. When was this?"

"It was in 1977. And, you know, that was when I met Linda. And she returned to the States a year later."

Yehoshua smiled sadly, and shook his head. "I won't say any more about your taking a new immigrant away from Israel. You know how I feel about it."

"Thanks," I said. "I was wondering what was your point in having this last conversation partner not only silent but incapable of speech.

"The idea came to me to put the rabbi in the same situation as Ika's mother," he said, "especially because we always talk to God and God doesn't answer and we always have to guess at his answers. And in a way his silence, the silence of God, dominates all the other conversations in the novel and is the source for the silence of all the other people: the father in the fourth conversation, the colonel in the third conversation, the Nazi grandmother in the second, and the mother in the first conversation."

The silence reminded me of the biblical Abraham's virtual silence, as well as God's talkativeness, during much of the Binding of Isaac story. I wondered about one Hebrew phrase from the end of the conversation. "I was struck with the phrase *l'haded et asurov*," I said, "which Hailkin translates as 'release him from his earthly bonds.' As I understand it, literally it means to sharpen or tighten his bonds. And that to me evokes the Binding of Isaac."

"My intention," he replied, "was to make *asurov*, his bonds, his ties, more sharp, more painful. I combined two sentences in one of the *piyu-tim,* one of the ancient songs, that is always sung on the second day of Rosh Hashanah when the Binding of Isaac is read in the synagogue. So, in an ancient *piyut,* there were two phrases which I combined on my own to create this new expression, *l'haded et asurov,* to strengthen his bonds, to sharpen his bonds." The *piyut* he was alluding to, *et sha'arei ratzon le'hippate'ah* (To open the gates of favor), one of the most remarkable in the whole High Holiday liturgy, is only included in Sephardic services. Composed by the twelfth-century religious poet Judah Samuel Abbas of Aleppo (d. 1167), it begins the service on the second day of Rosh Hasha-nah at which the *shofar,* the ram's horn, is sounded, immediately after the torah service when the Binding of Isaac, Genesis 22, is read. With the refrain, ". . . the Binder, the Bound One, and the Altar," the poem is a wild meditation in fourteen stanzas on the biblical story and includes a trembling Isaac, trembling angels, and divine intervention. The stanza in question is the eleventh, in which Isaac speaks to his father:

> "My speech is trembling from the slaughtering knife—
> Please sharpen it, my father,
> And at the moment when I am bound, be strong,
> And at the moment when I am entirely burned up,
> From my flesh take with you what remains of my ashes
> And say to Sarah, 'This is the savor of Isaac' "
> . . . the Binder, the Bound One, and the Altar.

As Yehoshua spoke about each of the crossroads, it became clearer and clearer that, in theme, the Holocaust plays a complementary role to Jerusalem in the novel. As the novel broods on the space of Jerusalem, so it broods on two moments in time, the mythological time of the Binding of Isaac and the historical time of the Holocaust. I asked Yehoshua to go into this in more detail. "For me," he said, "the Holocaust makes it necessary to examine the Jews and Jewish history from the beginning. After such a failure—and I see the Holocaust mainly as our failure—I have to understand how, from the beginning, we dragged ourselves, we pushed ourselves into such a corner, in which we were murdered in such a terrible way."

He was speaking very carefully. "I think that after such a catastrophe, you cannot just say, 'Okay, there was a catastrophe, there was an episode, there was a failure, but I am going on.' You have to reexamine all your history from the beginning. I always say it in a blunt way. In a room like this, I would gather all the sages and the leaders of the people of Israel, from Moses to the prophets to Rabbi Yohanan ben Zakkai, with Rambam, and Rabbi Nahman of Bratslav. . . . And I would show them *Shoah* or other films of the Holocaust." Yohannan ben Zakkai, the leading rabbi of the first century, managed to persuade the Romans to spare ten rabbinic leaders just before the destruction of Jerusalem in 70. Rambam, Rabbi Moses ben Maimon, Maimonides (1135–1204), is the greatest Jewish philosopher and rabbi of the Middle Ages. Nahman of Bratzlav (1772– 1811), who likely thought himself the messiah, was the great-grandson of the Baal Shem Tov, who founded Hassidism, and one of the most complex and brilliant figures in Jewish spiritual history; he visited Israel briefly in 1798–99.

"After they finish watching the film," Yehoshua continued, "I would say to them, 'Okay. This is where we are going to end up. Now you are to return to your own time. Tell me, now that you know what will happen in the end, will you change something in Judaism as you built it, as you conceived it, as you foresaw it? Or will you keep the same conception? Now, Moses, we are going back three thousand three hundred years. Tell me, now that you know what will happen. Will you change something, in your conception, in the Torah you are giving, in your behavior? Rambam, what would you do in order to avoid it? Or would you not do anything? Would you say, "This is how it is; this is our fate; I don't know how to change it?" ' "

Yehoshua continued to choose his words with particular care. "I think that the serious leaders among them would say that we have to do something to avoid the Holocaust. Moses, for example, could decide: 'I will cross the Jordan River and I will enter the country in order that there will be a grave there. Jews will have a bigger problem leaving, because my grave will be there and they will, therefore, be more attached to the Land of Israel.' Yohanan ben Zakkai perhaps would say: 'Instead of a *minyan* of ten people, I will have to say now that the *minyan* will have at least three thousand people, in order that the people will not have the possibility of dispersal.' Or Rambam, who lived in Egypt, would say perhaps, 'I am leaving Egypt and coming to Israel to settle there.' Perhaps Nahman of Bratslav would say: 'I will not return to Poland; I will stay in Israel.' In fact, of course, after several weeks in Israel, Nahman felt so very frightened that he went back to Poland."

"So every one of the crossroads of the novel reflects your analysis of the Holocaust," I said.

"Yes. The reexamination of Judaism after the Holocaust is extremely important for me," he said, "and that was the way I constructed the novel. The novel points out some crossroads in our history and asks whether there was another option. And if there were, what conditions made it possible and why wasn't it chosen? The family of Manis represent these questions, each one in his own way."

As I juxtaposed in my mind the family of wildly idiosyncratic Manis against Yehoshua's image of a gathering of all the historical leaders of Judaism, I laughed and told him that this gathering of the leaders, of Moses and so on, sounds like a Jewish equivalent of a decorous House of Lords or Senate. And all the characters of the novel—conversation partners and Manis alike—were a wild and chaotic Jewish Commons, a Jewish House of Representatives. "This is what I wanted to create," he said, a *havurah* through the generations, all of them sitting together." Literally, a *havurah* is a group, but the Hebrew word carries the strong bonds of a *haver,* a friend, a comrade, a lover. In the second conversation, old Joseph Mani mixed the stories of those who dug and those who were dug up at Knossos as if all of them were *b'nai havurah ahat,* the members (literally, the children) of one *havurah.* The word *haver* has assumed a special poignance in the wake of the Rabin assassination. His motto during the last years of his life was *shalom haver,* peace, friend, and on Rabin's first memorial day, one year after the assassination, everywhere you looked in Israel there were bumper stickers with the phrase, *haver, ata haser,* friend, you are missing.

"I must tell you," he continued, mock desperation in his voice, "that there are many connections that I myself didn't realize that exist among all five conversations, not only among the Manis themselves but also among the speakers. The partners who are having the conversations are related to each other and to the Manis."

"Some of these connections have a disturbing 'what if' ring to them," I said. "Here are two of my favorites. If Efrayim and Linka Shapiro of the fourth conversation had moved to Israel at the turn of the century, then, not only would the Shapiros have been spared the Holocaust, but perhaps the Mrs. Shapiro of the first conversation who gives Hagar Shiloh the key to Gavriel Mani's apartment—and perhaps helps save Gavriel's life—could have been the daughter-in-law of Efrayim Shapiro, whose decision, in the novel itself, not to move to Israel, precipitates the suicide of Moses Mani, Gavriel's great-grandfather. It's also likely, given their ages and where they live, that Hagar went to high school or the army with Ivor Horowitz's grandson, the first in the Horowitz clan to emigrate to Israel. It's enough to make my head spin."

"The most important thing to me," he said, "is to imagine Hagar Shiloh sitting right next to Rabbi Hananiah Haddaya, and it was very important to me to show the relationship even between this kibbutznik kid, Ashkenazi, sitting in the kibbutz in the desert in 1982, and this old Sephardic rabbi, sitting in Athens in the nineteenth century. They are related and I wanted to present this relationship."

However representative the Manis may be, their individuality is equally important to Yehoshua. "You cannot say about them that they agree ideologically," he said. "On the contrary, some of their ideas are in conflict with each other. Still, I wanted to demonstrate the possibilities by having one person, by himself, stand at a crossroads, see that history is going in one direction, and decide that there is another direction. And this applies to the time of the Balfour Declaration in 1918, when there could have been the partition or the division of the land into two states. Or to the time of the Third Zionist Congress at the end of the nineteenth century, when people were so reluctant to collaborate with Herzl. Or to 1848, when the Jewish people could have said, no, we are not a people, we are only a religion; we do not want to enter modern history as a people."

Yehoshua is prepared for the typical American reaction whenever he speaks of the Holocaust as a Jewish failure, the way so many American Jews are quick to understand him to mean that he sees the Holocaust as the moral and spiritual responsibility of the Jews, the way they are so eager to bristle at the notion that he is blaming the victims.

He is certainly aware of the possibility of being misunderstood. "I tell them, 'Don't misunderstand me.' I am not talking about the Jews of Germany or the twentieth century, who resisted the Germans or were victims—if I were in their place, I would have behaved the same way. This is not the question. The question is Judaism itself, Judaism as a conception, the idea that we can live in exile, that we must live among the other people, in the flesh of other people, at the same time as we keep saying to the other people, 'I am not here. Next year in Jerusalem!' "

"It's clear to me that you are not blaming the victims," I said.

"Of course not! I do not blame the Jews of Germany or the Jews of eastern Europe. I am talking about Juda*ism*"—he put particular stress on the "ism"—"the failure of Juda*ism*. This is the failure of Moses. This is the failure of the total conception that says that we can stay a people while not in our land, that we can maintain our identity while not in our land. There always were warnings, all through history, that this will end in catastrophe. And it ended in catastrophe. Just open Deuteronomy to see what happens to the Jews when they are out of their country."

I asked him to talk more about the Diaspora. "I say that there is a permanent contradiction in the lives of Jews outside Israel, and the contradiction always cries out for conflict. I am amazed that the Jews were not destroyed in the Middle Ages. How did they reach the twentieth century, when they could have been destroyed at many, many points all through history? The question is not the Jews. The question is Judaism. How Judaism has re-created its conception in which . . ." He was at a loss of words for a moment. "Here is a metaphor. We are a people that does not walk on the sidewalk, only in the street. And we always say, 'For us, this is the way we behave in history; we don't have to go on the sidewalk and wait for the red light. We go faster. We go through the street itself in between the cars.' And afterwards there is a catastrophic accident. What can we say?" He paused.

"We can't say this was just an accident. The situation was calling for such a disaster. It wasn't by chance that this disaster came to us."

I asked him about the argument that says that by having Jews in both the Diaspora and Israel, we keep from putting all our eggs in one basket. If we all lived in Israel and there were a war there, the whole people could be wiped out. "Listen, if anyone says that to you, ask them this: Suppose someone from Holland came to you and said, 'You, as an expert on preserving a people, give us advice, good advice, about how to preserve the Dutch people better in history.' Would you say to them, 'Take the Dutch people and spread them all over the world, and this is the way to survive'?"

"But you know, Bulli," I said. "You'd by surprised by how often I hear American Jews say that the best strategy for avoiding a new Holocaust is to keep half the Jews in the Diaspora and the other half in Israel." I had the temerity to bring up Roth's *Operation Shylock* again and one idea Roth plays with in it: Diasporism—the flip of Zionism—that because of anti-Semitism all the Jews of European ancestry should leave Israel and return to their European homelands!

"I don't know if I have to repeat myself again about the Diaspora and all those matters," Yehoshua said, exasperated. "For me, it is not a question of strategy, of security. To divide the Jews into two parts, and to put here some Jews and there some Jews!" His tone is mocking and derisive. "I don't think that such a crazy idea would come into the mind of another people, the Dutch, the Norwegians, the Thais, the people in Peru or in Uruguay—nobody would think that the best strategy is to put some people in one country, others in another country, to spread the people all over to keep it from trouble. The strategy is a total failure and the great failure is the Holocaust, in which we adopted this strategy and finally we got six million dead. I think it is immoral to live in the Diaspora. This is my theory, and I've explained it many, many times: I think that if a person is a Jew, he has to take total responsibility for his life, and all the component realities of his life have to be Jewish. He cannot live only with his Judaism on a bookshelf, in which there are just ideas, while he lives in another reality, which is American, English, or whatever." I had the sardonic thought that if these conversations ever get published, this book too would just be added to the bookshelf.

"In other words," I said, "the security argument is nothing but a rationalization for not leaving the Diaspora, making *aliyah,* and settling in Israel?"

"Of course! For me, it is not a question of security; it is a moral question, it is a question of identity, and in this I am behaving totally like all the other millions and millions of people in the world, and this is the way that the Jews also have to behave—we have to adopt this normal sense of identity."

I asked him whether his perspective on the Holocaust was affected by his identity as a fifth-generation Sephardic Jew of Jerusalem. "For us," he said, "the Holocaust was a failure. First of all, you have to know that before the Holocaust the Jewish people was 95 percent Ashkenazi." The Ashkenazim are the Jews of European descent. "The fact is that in Israel now it is half Sephardic and half Ashkenazi, and the Russians have been coming in huge numbers. But still the Sephardim, whom you call the Oriental Jews, are a small percentage of the Jewish people. After the Holocaust there was a certain change, but still the vast majority is Ashkenazi—it is 80 or 85 percent of the Jewish people."

"How did you react after World War II?"

"I was like the other Israeli guys in whom all was repressed. The Holocaust was repressed. I remember that the fact that there were six million dead became known to us only after the war was over. No one was talking about the Holocaust during the war years themselves. And now so many books are being written about the repression of the subject of the Holocaust in the Jewish community in Israel during the 1950s."

"What do you think of this repression? It reminds me so much of the way the first generation of emancipated African Americans repressed the middle passage—the transport of Africans from their homes to the New World and slavery—a repression that has been broken only very recently in African-American literature." The poet Robert Hayden opened the door to the subject in the early seventies, but novelists subjected themselves to its horror only during the past ten years, in Toni Morrison's *Beloved,* for example, and Charles Johnson's *Middle Passage.*

"In my opinion, it was a healthy repression. And I say this knowing all the problems and questions which this sentence can raise." It was 1993 and we were sitting in that coffee shop in Manhattan when he said this. "Let me put it this way." He leaned in toward me across the table. "In 1948 and 1949 we were not tourists on vacation. We could not, for example, enjoy New York with all of its facilities and afterwards at five o'clock go into the Holocaust Museum and grieve, knowing that others would carry out all the tasks that make a city function morning and night. In Israel we had to do all the work ourselves, and, in the years immediately following the Holocaust, if we had been always preoccupied with the Holocaust, we would have paralyzed, knowing about the Holocaust, speaking about the Holocaust, remembering the Holocaust—it would have been a total trauma which would have paralyzed the national spirit."

"But what could you do?" I asked.

"After the creation of the state, when the refugees from the Holocaust arrived, we said, 'Stop! We don't want to hear about you. Right now we have a lot of work to do, so come in and enter immediately into the work of the country. Because if you come in with your horrible story, we will all sit like this,' "—he let his body sag—" 'immobilized and horrified and we won't be able to do anything.' This was one of the reasons for this repression, and *everyone* did it."

"How long did this last?"

"There was not a day for the memorial of the Holocaust until 1955 or 1956. And it was started by a religious director in the Ministry of Religion. There was not even an official day for the memorial of the Holocaust in Israel until this one individual did it on his own initiative. Because it wasn't important." Although a law establishing "the Holocaust and Ghetto Uprising Remembrance Day" was passed in 1951, nothing much happened until the mid-fifties. Finally, in 1959, the Knesset, prodded by Rabbi Mordecai Nurok of the National Religious Party, passed a comprehensive Holocaust and Heroism Remembrance Day Law. And not until two years later, shortly before the Eichmann trial, was the observance of this day formalized and "Holocaust, Rebellion, and Heroism Memorial Day" was fully integrated into the Israeli calendar.

"When did things really change?"

"Begin started going around with all of his Holocaust talk and he spoke of it daily in every political speech, following the explosion of interest in the subject of the Holocaust after the Eichmann trial in 1961, when we had become strong enough to encounter the experience."

I asked him again how his perspective as a Sephardi affected his thinking. "As a Sephardi, because I didn't even have any family in Europe, the repression was not emotional but intellectual. This is why I always feel that when I speak about the Holocaust—and, as you know, it's extremely important to me—I am a little free of the kind of emotion that disturbs a clear debate about it."

"What feelings *do* you have?"

"I have the anger of a Sephardic Jew of the fifth generation, whose parents and whose great-grandfather came by themselves—not because an anti-Semite was making them come, but on their own initiative. It's the same on my mother's side, a Moroccan Jew who left Morocco in the twenties. And I feel that if these Jews of my family could do it, what were the others doing? And this is the source of my anger, my permanent anger with the Jewish people, that they come to Israel only because somebody is hitting them, only because they do not belong. And this is also my natural way of belonging to the country—I fit in to Israel like a French peasant to France. My belonging is unconditional. I did not come to build something new; there are no conditions from Jewish history that, in order to justify my coming to Israel, I have to be good or I have to build a new society."

"It sounds as if you can maintain a kind of detachment."

"Exactly. In a way, this Sephardic element gave me a kind of a clarity, a cool clarity, and this is why so many Jews cannot stand my arguments. But, as you heard already"—we both started laughing—"I am well-prepared for any argument when I speak about the Holocaust as *our* failure, and not only as what the non-Jews have done to us. Of course, the responsibility of the non-Jews is clear. But I think that it's extremely important that we understand how we pushed ourselves into this corner."

We hadn't yet talked about the setting of the first conversation, and I asked him whether the desert is supposed to provide one kind of answer to the millennia of wandering that ended in the gas chambers. "Let me answer you this way," Yehoshua said. "My feeling is that the novel itself is optimistic, because, finally, at least in the last chapter which is the first chapter, I bring this Mani, this disturbed element of the Manis, these people who were always living with a tendency to commit suicide—I bring them to the desert, to Mash-abei Sadeh, where they can continue in the most healthy, in the most normal way, which is how I see Zionism."

The desert is a very important image to him. "My feeling is that the remedy for the Jewish state is to turn to the desert. From time to time, we have to return to the desert. The desert is the place where we have a lot of space of our own; in the desert, we don't take anyone else's land. We have space there for all the Jewish people, and half of the territory of Israel is desert. If we do not encounter the desert, if we do not challenge the desert, if we do not find a way to live in the desert, we will always be in conflict about boundaries: here *is* the West Bank, here is *not* the West Bank; this house in Silwan is in Israel, this house in Silwan is across the border?—and we have all the familiar problems of mingling with the other people." Silwan is an Arab village southeast of the Old City, between the Mount of Olives and Mount Zion, just beyond the pre-1967 border of Israel. It is the home of the young sheik who is a friend of Joseph Mani and the companion of Avraham Mani in the fifth conversation.

"In the desert we are alone," he continued. "It is one of the most problematic of all the problems for the Jewish people: we never can understand ourselves except by being with others, by being with the gentiles. Why can't we be alone by ourselves, as the Danish can be by themselves, as the French can be by themselves? Why do we always need the non-Jews in order to understand ourselves? We cannot understand ourselves when we are alone. Is this a defect of ours? I see it as a defect. I see it all the time, and I am not at all amazed to see anti-Semitism as a permanent malady and continuing malady all over our history—as we have seen in the last years. Because Jews cannot be by themselves. This incapacity is a permanent problem of our people."

"But the end of the first conversation suggests that it need not be permanent."

"Yes," he said. "The book is optimistic because of the continuation of the family in the desert, with a little, little grandchild of the Manis who will return to the desert and perhaps build his life there. The suicide threat of the Manis always threatens all of us. I believe that we can overcome it."

I was struck again, especially, in the climaxes and resolutions of the novels, by how much credit Yehoshua gives to his readers. I was reminded of the ending of *A Late Divorce*, which depends on the astuteness of a madwoman and an epigraph, and the last words of *Five Seasons*. "You do like taking risks with your endings," I said, "the way, for instance, the very last line makes us rethink everything we had thought as we read *Five Seasons*."

"Yes," he said, "that Molkho is free, and that he's able to love again."

"But as I think back on *Mr. Mani,*" I said, "I realize that I wish you would have indulged me in one full and rich description of the desert as a landscape to balance Jerusalem which is so fully realized as a physical terrain. Here's the desert, an image of a whole other way of thinking about everything. And there it is, hinted at in the prologue and the conversation itself, but emphasized only in the epilogue to the chapter. I wonder why you didn't dramatize it more or why you were so understated about it." It occurred to me that I was asking him to be a lesser writer than he is. But I was also thinking of the wonderful way he had handled the desert in the surreal wanderings in the Negev desert of another Gavriel, in the most memorable monologue of *The Lover.*

"I don't think I was so quiet about the desert. First of all, when I describe the mother, Yael Shiloh, I show how she has really been integrated, for a long time, into the kibbutz, loving the desert, seeing the desert as her home. She is not just a pioneer who comes in with all the ideological stuff; all the kibbutznik ideology and all the connection to the desert have become completely natural behavior to her, and this is the motivation to go to Mash'Abei Sadeh. Second of all, Hagar says, 'Yes, I love the place.' She does not love the kibbutz so much, or the people there. And she stays there, finally she stays in the desert with her child, because of her child. She cannot raise him in the city because she lacks the means to do it, so she has to come back to the kibbutz. Also, during the course of her conversation, from time to time, she says, that with all her attraction to Jerusalem, still she is happy to leave Jerusalem to go back to the desert, not in ideological terms, but just returning home."

"So, it's the normality of it for both Yael and Hagar that is so important to you."

"Yes, the desert is becoming a home to them—as the desert already has become home for people who have been living there for fifty years. There are already seven or eight kibbutzim, so that for a half a century, people have been connected to this place. This is an achievement in itself. It proves that this can be done." He paused.

"I wonder about the desert in America. It is important for me to examine it—in Nevada and places like that. Are there people who are doing various kinds of work while they are living there? What is life like in these places?"

"I think there is real attraction to it in the same way, but here it is so mixed up with American individualism," I said. I told him that my most powerful experience of the desert was not in the United States, but during a brief camel and Jeep tour in the Judean Desert right after my daughter's wedding there—how overwhelmed I was by the experience: the isolation, the clarity, the feeling that every human superficiality could be burned away.

"Yes, going to the desert . . ." His voice trailed off. "And we have to remember that Ben-Gurion always considered the desert as the test of the sanity of the Israelis, and he said it, and I remember very well one sentence of his. It is on a big rock at the entrance of one of the biggest and most important military bases in the middle of the desert, at which my Nahum was stationed: 'In the building of the Negev, the Jewish people will be tested.' "

"And you are suggesting this is the image that will even heal the Manis."

"Listen," he said, smiling, "you don't have to push it too hard."

"I know," I said, "but that's exactly my point, that *you* don't push it too hard, you're understated about it—even though it's so important."

"So Gavriel Mani, a person of Jerusalem, comes to Mash-Abei Sadeh. With all of his history, as odd as it is, to come to a kibbutz, there in the Negev, is a little bit bizarre; it's certainly not his style, but it is not the style of many, many others. And don't ignore the personal dimension to it, that, first of all, the fact that he returns through Hebron is related to the fact that his grandfather was there in the same place in 1918, meeting for the first time the British army when he attached himself to Captain Daggett in order to serve as an interpreter there."

"But the focus in the first conversation is: 'Mr. Jerusalem Meets the Desert.' "

"In a way, in a way. The fact is that there is a kind of dialogue here, and this remains the framework of a dialogue between Mr. Gavriel Mani, who's the grandfather of Hagar's child—Efrayim, the father, doesn't want to take this child—and he manages to have some sort of relation with his grandchild, his daughter-in-law, and her mother, and there is a kind of a promise that the two elements can come together."

"Because until then, until he leaves Jerusalem, he is so closed in."
"Yes."

"There is also the scene when Hagar looks out from the window of the hospital onto the desert—this time it is not the Negev desert, but it is also the desert, the part of the Judean Desert that's on the West Bank."

"Yes," he said. "It's the Judean Desert. And that connects with the political conception about the question of dividing the land with the

Arabs. I said to myself, even if we think that we are partitioning the land along the cease-fire borders of 1949, it can be regarded by the Arabs as injustice, because, even if they get back all of the West Bank and the Gaza strip, they are getting a quarter of the original Palestine, and we get the other three quarters. So I asked myself, 'What is this three quarters, what does it consist of?' Finally, if you examine it, you find out that half of it, or even more, is the desert. I don't say that it doesn't belong to the Arabs, but to them it was . . ."

"Nothing . . ."

"Yes, nothing. It had no attraction at all to them. Very few were living there. Nobody was living there. And so from the point of view of justice, the country was divided half and half, because if you take out the Negev, they get one half of the land and we get one half, and this is a real half for both sides. And we get a desert and they—well, if you include Jordan— they also have a lot of desert and this is a not a problem. They do not envy us for having the Negev because they really have a lot of desert of their own. In Jordan alone, the deserts are huge; the size of Jordan is almost four times the size of all of Palestine. So because of the desert, I can, in a way, feel comfortable in my discussions with the Arabs. But the desert, of course, is our challenge: to make the desert thrive. If you speak about the Jewish people, if you speak about the future, if you speak about bringing some new methods to the world itself, it can be accomplished through working in the Negev and trying to make something valuable for everyone from the desert. And we have some experience. So for me it is the way of the Negev that provides the best direction."

I told him again of the impact of the desert on me, and I wondered about his experiences of the desert. "That's a good question," he said. "I myself was in a kibbutz not far from Mash-Abei Sadeh, Kibbutz Hatzerim. I was stationed there during my military service and afterwards for a couple of months; I had friends there. So my feeling has always been that this is the challenge. I was very pleased that during his military service, Nahum was mainly in the Negev. I remember saying to him, 'To have three years of experience of the desert cleans you in a certain way, cleans your soul.' "

While the desert of the first conversation suggests hope, setting the fifth conversation in Athens has, for me anyway, more ominous implications. As I read that chapter, Athens seemed right to me. I felt that this sense of rightness had something to do with the way classical Athens had destroyed itself as a nation in just one century, but I couldn't put my finger on the real reason. Somehow these thoughts reminded me of the fleeting paranoia I have felt at odd moments. I remember, for instance, attending Harvard Hillel services at Memorial Church in the middle of Harvard Yard during the early hours of the Yom Kippur War in 1973 and imagining, of all things, that a pogrom was about to be launched at us by Harvard students. Even though it happened so long ago, this is a typical and still fresh example of a moment when I found myself half believing that what the world really wants is that the Jews go the way of the ancient Athenians. After the Jews are gone, all the nations of the world could shake their collective heads and say, "What a wonderful civilization it was while it flourished! Too bad it didn't last longer!"

I was astonished when it turned out that this fantasy wasn't too far from what was on Yehoshua's mind. He believes that the choice not taken in 1848, the option to be a religion and not a people, resembles the fate of classical Greek culture. "For most people," he observed, "Greek culture is not listed under the heading of Greek nationality. It is only civilization, only religion, only philosophy. Plato and Aristotle: you don't think of them as Greek national figures—and this also could have happened in Judaism: it could have been a religion, a philosophy, a civilization, but not an historical people. I don't know whether it was possible or not possible for the Jews to choose religion over nationality, but this choice is, as I said before, the meaning of the crucifixion or sacrifice of Isaac." According to Yehoshua's theory, Abraham pretends he is going to sacrifice Isaac to transform a private religious idea into the religious belief system of a new people. "Once again," he continued, "I am talking about the combination of nationality and religion; you cannot separate them. And this is the trouble and this is the problem and this is the disease inside the Jewish people. You can only try to modify it; but you cannot change it totally because it is in the marrow of our people."

I wondered how this religion-nationality division applies to American liberal Jewry. Yehoshua agreed with me that America, right now, is the best Diaspora land for Jews ever. I told him that I can see the danger (or the possibility) of American liberal Judaism (if it does not fade away) becoming an entirely new phenomenon in the history of Judaism, that is, a resolution of the religion-nationality duality entirely on the religion side, because I now know many liberal American Jews who really think of themselves as Jewish Americans, with barely a trace of peoplehood or nationality in their imaginations or their identities. "On the other hand," I said, "I keep meeting liberal Jewish-American college students for whom a six-week group visit to Israel when they were seventeen or eighteen has profoundly transformed their sense of who they are. Clearly, their Zionism has very little continuity with my father's Zionism or mine, but it is still a very powerful experience of identity for them, and a purely positive one. What do you make of all this?"

"I agree with you that America is capable of producing a new kind of Jew, in which Judaism will be just a religion and that Reform Judaism can make a split between Judaism as religion and Judaism as nationality, and push Judaism towards a pure religion." In Israel even the anti-Zionist ultra-Orthodox Jews think of themselves as a people awaiting a purely theocratic state, ruled by the Messiah. "I don't know how far it can be pushed and still retain Jewish meanings, that is, whether you can subtract Israel and the national elements from the religion. It is very difficult, but I don't exclude the possibility that in the future there would be some kind of synthetic Judaism, a kind of a mixture between Protestantism and Judaism, or whatever. Among the many, many varieties of religious life in America, there can be a kind of new religion, the Sons of Jesus, the Sons of Moses, whatever it is. But they are no longer Jews."

"This is the problem," I said.

"Yes, this is the problem. For me, they are excluded from the Jewish people. I don't say anything against them. They can do what they want, and I wish them all the best. But remember, you cannot speak anymore about five million, six million Jews in America; you hardly can speak today even about two and a half million—the others aren't Jews anymore. They are Americans of Jewish origin, with a new kind of religion that is a kind of a symbiosis between them and American Christianity."

I described a lecture by Amos Oz at my congregation, Beth El, in Sudbury, Massachusetts, in 1987. Many people in the audience had taken enormous offense at some of Oz's words. What sin had he committed? He simply had expressed his concern for the next generation of American Jewish youth. I heard people say afterward, "Who the hell does he think he is, criticizing us!" I told Yehoshua my wife's theory about the prickliness of American liberal Jews when it comes to Israel. "Linda thinks that American Jews desperately want to preserve their individuality, what they perceive to be their individuality, with respect to Israel, and that's why Amos's words, which seemed benign to both Linda and me, offended them so much. She sees a mutual arrogance, of American Jews towards Israel and of Israelis towards the United States."

"The problem is not arrogance!" Yehoshua was adamant. "The problem is that I'm afraid America will absorb Israel. I am thinking of myself, of how I have to defend myself against the Diaspora. Because the Diaspora *is* the dominating power in Jewish history. And my question is *not* what will happen in the Diaspora. What happens in the Diaspora—we know what happens in the Diaspora: disaster is what happens in the Diaspora: all the destruction, all the assimilation, all that has happened already. The question is: how will I protect myself from the diasporic forces that have always dominated the Jewish people."

A sharp example of these forces at work comes from the occupied territories. By 1993, when he spoke of these forces, he had already been saying for twenty-six years that Israel should get rid of the territories for its own good. To him, the Israeli addiction to the territories is emphatically not Israeli nationalism gone haywire. On the contrary, this self-destructive addiction reflects the power of those irrational diasporic forces that invariably choose religion over nationality. In this case, the Jewish settlers and their supporters allow the religious and cultural "value" and "meaning" of the territories to override the reality of national self-interest. I myself believe that the yearning for Samaria and Judea reflects a latent desire to reproduce the conditions of Crown Heights one mile west of Jerusalem. I said, "Your analysis of the Diaspora and its power is part of your fundamental perspective as a Zionist-Jewish-Israeli, isn't it?"

"You know I'm far more critical of Jews than of Israelis—because the question about the Jews is not the question of what they are doing and what they are not doing, but the fact that, if they are not in Israel, they are in a situation in which they are not obliged *as Jews* to act or not to act. When you are in a total reality, when you are responsible for everything around you, you, collectively, can do good and you can do evil. But Linda, for example, was not responsible as a Jew for the prison where she used to work; she is responsible as an American." My wife had worked as an art therapist at a women's prison for two years. "This is the only way to think about it—and the whole context is American. If you decided to vote for Bush or for Clinton, it was not a Jewish decision but an American decision that applies to all Americans. As a Jew in America, you only can sit at Beth El and discuss with the rabbi abstract matters that cannot refer to anything real. The only decision you can make is about the synagogue, whether or not to put a garden in somewhere."

"You're saying that even when our congregation adopted an illegal refugee family, we were acting as Americans in consort with American churches that were doing the same thing, while in Israel, because it is a Jewish state, you have total responsibility."

"Of course. Here we collectively can do good and evil, because we have the power to kill and we have the power to liberate. We live in a total reality."

"What would you say to the many American liberal Jews who find the roots of their Judaism in the prophetic tradition, the call for universal justice, that asks all Jews to participate in *tikkun olam,* the repair of the universe? Is this a possible bridge between liberal Israelis and American liberal Jews?"

"You cannot do *tikkun olam* if you are not doing the *tikkun olam* yourself," he said. "You cannot only preach about *tikkun olam*—what is the sense? All you have to do is look at the Jews now—there are so many Fascist Jews and there are Jews who are so hawkish. They don't do *tikkun olam;* they only look out for themselves. But even in the case of the best Jews, those that speak about *tikkun olam,* in America they can only *speak* about it, but the question is what they will *do,* not as individuals but as a group. In America they cannot do *tikkun olam* only as a Jewish *tikkun olam,* because when they fight for the blacks in the South, they do not fight as Jews, in my opinion—they fight as Americans, and they have to join with Christian Americans. The solution has to involve other Americans. If they say, for example, 'We have to increase the unemployment allowance,' this would increase the taxes of other Americans. If they wish to change the conditions in Harlem or Los Angeles, this also has to affect other Americans, because the responsibility is, as I said before, in the American context, not in the Jewish context. This is my main criticism about all these 'Jewish' ideas. And this is the reason why the Israelis, whatever they do, are responsible as Jews—of course, I am ashamed here and I'm critical there, but I see all the good things and all the bad things inside a real society."

The key distinction for him is between the compulsion required by laws enacted in a Jewish state and the voluntarism of all deeds in a Diaspora Jewish community. "You are helping me begin to make sense of a cousin of ours," I said. I told him about one of my cousins who works as a social worker with new Ethiopian immigrants in Beer Sheva, and, at the same time, votes for Tehiya, a right-wing party that supports the transfer of all Arabs from Israel to Arab countries. "In America," I said, "such a combination is virtually impossible to imagine. It would be like Teddy Kennedy calling for the nuking of Baghdad."

"But, of course . . ." Yehoshua was smiling broadly.

"And you say, 'Of course' . . ."

"Yes, I can see it very clearly, and I can picture your cousin even working with the Arabs as a social worker. There are some very nice guys among the Tehiya, who treat the Arabs in a most friendly and casual way. But at the same time they have their terrible and crazy ideas about the final solution of the Israeli-Palestinian question." Our eyes met, and it was clear that he had chosen his last words carefully.

Read from the point of view of an Israeli in the 1980s and early 1990s, the thrust of *Mr. Mani* is to try to shove or at least nudge his people toward some sort of modification or transformation of the religion-nationality paradox that is the collective illness of the Jewish people in both Israel and the Diaspora. *Mr. Mani* would replace the pernicious and diasporic combination of nationalism and religion—which would, for instance, hold on to the West Bank at all costs—with a more flexible amalgam of nationalism and religion that is open to living in peace with another tangle of nationality and religion, the Palestinians. The Joseph Mani of the fifth conversation, the 1848 conversation, is absolutely convinced—it is his idée fixe—that these Palestinians whom he calls Ishmaelites, these Arabs who inhabit Israel, are Jews who have forgotten that they were Jews.

When I asked him to appraise this idée fixe of the first Joseph Mani, the first words out of Yehoshua's mouth were emphatic: "Joseph Mani is not crazy!"

"But are there any historical examples of anyone thinking that way in 1848?" I asked. "Or are you imagining that option from the point of view of the present situation?"

"Well," he answered, "I don't know about a real figure, but I can easily imagine that there could be a real figure who would say these things. I know that early in this century, there was an element in Zionism or even in pre-Zionism that thought that the Arabs were the *bnai yisrael,* the children of Israel, that stayed in the country after the destruction of the Second Temple in 70 c.e. Little by little the Jews left the country, and those who remained were, perhaps, converted to Islam. Ben-Gurion and Ben-Tzvi, the first prime minister and the second president of Israel, were both preoccupied with the origins of the Palestinian Arabs here, and there was this theory that they are the ancient, the forgotten *bnai yisrael,* and this idea was very much backed by some of the Zionists. I admit that 1848 was probably a little bit too early for someone to have had this idea. But ideas are running around all the time. And you can always find a crazy person who says things like that."

These speculations brought Yehoshua's thoughts back once again to the intifada and its meaning for his people and himself. "You know," he said, "the fifth conversation was written during the bitter days of the intifada in 1991 and 1992; this was my way to cope with the intifada. You should examine the description of Joseph Mani entering their houses, and putting his hands on the children, and speaking about the suffering that he will bring upon them." A withering sadness fills his voice as he continues. "They are becoming our Jews, in an ironic way, they are becoming our Jews. And the combination of identities, the pain of identity, and the pain of sliding from one identity to another, and all these crazy elements" —he laughs—"all of it comes from my identification with their suffering, especially in the first years of the intifada, when so many children were killed."

In the fifth conversation Yehoshua brings together virtually all of his artistic, personal, and ideological preoccupations: his relationship with his father and his Zionism; the intifada and the Binding of Isaac; Jewish identity, Israeli identity, and Palestinian identity; the real and mythic Jerusalem; the relationship between Israel and the Diaspora; dramatic dialogue and authorial authority—all these issues and themes and techniques are seamlessly woven together and lead to a remarkable climax that reverberates backward and forward though all of Jewish history, without losing a sharp focus on the present crisis.

He, too, likes the fifth conversation most. "It is for me," he said, "as Faulkner used to speak about the first monologue of Benjy in *The Sound and the Fury*. You know, this kind of writing I will never again achieve in my life. This is what I think about the fifth conversation, especially the last pages of it."

This assessment of his whole career, made in April 1993, led me to ask what he was working on then. "I have already finished half of my new novel," he said, referring to *Open Heart*. "It is a long novel, more classical in form, more in the line of *Five Seasons*. It will be about five hundred pages long in Hebrew, much longer than *Mr. Mani* or *Five Seasons*, which were both about 340 pages long."

"What's it like?" I asked. "Is it ideological, like *Mr. Mani,* or does it turn towards more personal matters?"

"It is not at all concerned with the Sephardic, political, and identity themes. I'm through with all of those subjects, at least for now, and I'm involved with a totally new kind of thing—it will be a long and very classic story of love."

"Have you shown it to anyone?"

"When I finish a whole chapter, when I am at a crossroads"—he smiled—"and I have to examine whether it's good or bad, I give it to Ika, and she tells me." He looked at her, deep in conversation with my wife, and smiled.

I was curious about the tone of the new novel. I said, *"Five Seasons,* even though it begins with a death, is a very funny book. I love the scene at the opera, for instance—it's hilarious, besides being revealing." In Berlin in part two of the novel, Molkho, who is possessed so profoundly by the spirit of his dead wife, is bewildered and annoyed to discover that the part of Orpheus in Gluck's *Orpheus and Eurydice* is sung by a woman. "It is a side of you," I reminded him, "that surprised me when we first met."

"Yes," he said. *"Five Seasons* is a funny book. It's very funny. But the novel I am writing now is not funny. It will be a long and very classical story of love."

"Like *Anna Karenina?"*

"I don't want to say any more about it."

Listening to him talk about the novel that would be *Open Heart* with the familiar mixture of modesty and pride made me ask how he could be so sure that the last conversation of *Mr. Mani* will remain the pinnacle of his work. "You know literature better than I," he began as I laughed, "and you know very well that writers do their best writing in their forties, perhaps in their fifties. After his fifties, nobody has written his great novel. All writers decline, and this is the start of my decline, unfortunately—but I am fifty-seven and this is the age. I hope the decline will not be too rapid and the angle will not be too sharp."

"I hope so too," I said.

• • •

Three years and one novel later, when the English version of *Open Heart,* that large novel of impossible love and possible suicide, was about to be published in the United States, I again found myself discussing a work in progress with him, this time, his sixth novel, *Masah el tom ha'elef (Voyage to the End of the Millennium).* These final conversations took place in Boston during his nine-day book tour for *Open Heart* that ended on May 2, 1996. The many dramatic events that have punctuated these three years define a radical change in the history of the Jewish people and the Jewish state: the dawning of peace.

Because his cultural diagnoses invariably infected his fiction in all sorts of ways—and because he is a member of Lova Eliav's visionary company —I thought it wise, before I asked him about his work in progress, to revisit some of the themes we had wrestled with over the years, especially, war, identity, and pluralism.

Thinking back to his 1990 analysis of the forces shaping Israeli litera- ture I was struck again by the complexity of the interplay among his literary works, his ideas about literature, and his ideas about his society; to use a mathematical analogy, at any moment, in any work, any of these three elements may be the independent variable, with the others the de- pendent ones. The paths between these three matters are no two-way streets; they have all the intricacy and mystery of a mirror maze with at least three entrances that also turn out to be exits, or a skein of tangled wool with three ends, not two or four. Even when ideology is one of the central concerns in the genesis of a novel, as in *Mr. Mani,* new meanings emerge from the text itself, such as the fact that "mani" can mean *ma ani,* what am I?

"Facing the Forests" is perhaps the most dramatic example of the contrary movement, from literature to history, if we think of it as a story that began in the realm of personal psychology and morality and later acquired an ideological mantle. "It was only the passage of time," I said, "and the cunning of history that made 'Facing the Forests' a prophetic story."

"Yes, it wasn't written to be prophetic."

"You told me that you are looking forward to the time when the ideological dimension of the story diminishes."

"When I wrote 'Facing the Forests,' the Palestinian problem was so repressed it was only in the background—the way Indians used to be only in the background in American literature. And, in literary terms, that's where it should be."

A particularly telling example of the flow between literature and life involves the theme of war. I found it fascinating that his observation in 1990 that war was becoming exhausted as a *literary* theme for writers anticipates his conviction in 1996 that war is becoming antiquated as an *identity* theme for all Israelis. On the literary front, war gave writers a relatively easy theme and scene machine and delayed the evolution of a subtle, flexible, and vernacular literary language; on the human front, it delayed direct national confrontation with many profound conflicts among Israelis because of the solidarity virtually all Israelis feel when Israel is under attack or when the siren sounds throughout the land on Memorial

Day. "To this day," he insisted on May 1, while visiting Boston during his 1996 book tour, "an act of terror in Netanya or Tel Aviv generates a feeling of solidarity among a yuppie secularist, a religious separatist in Mea She'arim or Bnai Brak, and an Oriental Jew in a remote and neglected desolate development town."

I reminded him of the words that were my very first encounter with his ideas. "You are insistently summoned to solidarity," he had said, back in the seventies, "summoned from within yourself rather than by any external compulsion, because you live from one newscast to the next, and it becomes a solidarity that is technical, automatic from the standpoint of its emotional reaction, because by now you are completely built to react that way and to live in tension. Your emotional reactions to any piece of news about an Israeli casualty, a plane shot down, are predetermined." Whatever else was true about this solidarity, it papered over the sharp differences among Israelis. "I remember that you joked about Begin having mercy on writers and giving them the Lebanon War in 1982, so they would have something to write about, but that was more than a joke." And it was not only about literature.

"Yes, this wartime mentality was one of the three pillars upon which Israeli identity was constructed; the other two pillars, which grew from the power of war or the threat of war, are the high value placed upon immigration from the Diaspora and the settlement of Israel. With the dawning of peace all three of these are weakening and beginning to disintegrate." Much of his current social and political thinking appears in a controversial essay, "Israeli Identity in Time of Peace: Its Perils and Prospects," a version of which appeared in the November 1995 issue of *Tikkun*. "This article," he said, "made a lot of noise when it was published in Israel." One of the central points in this essay is that for an Israel at peace with its neighbors, neither *aliyah* nor building settlements along every border of the country is any longer a matter of life and death.

I remember how he always used to needle me for taking my wife, who had lived in Israel for ten years, back to America, so I asked him to elaborate on his new ideas about immigration, especially in the light of how he had celebrated, in classic Zionist terms, the great emigration from the former Soviet Union in the 1980s and 1990s.

"I will tell you something that will shock you. For the first time a slight majority of Israelis have said that we don't need any more immigrants. Eighty thousand people arrive every year, and in the last six or seven years the immigration from Russia has amounted to a 25 percent increase in our population. Imagine America, in a period of just six or seven years, absorbing sixty million people who don't speak English and teaching them the language, giving them homes, and *decreasing* unemployment! It was amazing! And now for the first time a majority of Israelis no longer believes in the sacred idea of immigration, which was so important in the demographic battle with the Arabs. Peace changes all. Four million Danes do not lose sleep because there are seventy million Germans across the border."

"But the population of the Arab countries still remains so much larger," I said.

"So what?" he replied. "When I was young, Egypt had twenty million people; now they have sixty million. And they have only grown weaker."

"But when you talk about immigration and Israeli identity, it's not only the fact of immigration that's so important, it's the idea."

"There are important moral elements tied up with immigration," he agreed, "openness to immigrant culture and helping the newcomers, for example, and I'm afraid these values will erode."

"You also referred to settlement, to the whole idea of the *halutz*, the pioneer."

"Remember that settlement was not settlement for economic reasons; it was gaining land in the conflict with the Arabs over the land. The aim was to seize a bit of land so that the Arabs could not. In peacetime, people can think over whether or not it is a good idea to build a new settlement. Perhaps some of the unsuccessful towns in northern Israel could be dismantled, to enable the people to move to where they can find work and also to free the area for nature reserves and so on. We are a crowded country, and in peacetime we do not have to settle every border. The French are not preoccupied with the fact that large tracts of land along the Swiss border are empty."

"But settlement, too, is a powerful idea."

"Yes, the myth of settlement, the culture of settlement is an important element in Israeli identity, because they carry the important ideas of working the land and equality."

I was beginning to understand why he sees the dawning of peace as a perilous time for Israeli identity, as these three "pillars" dissolve and deep old conflicts bubble to the surface. "You see peace as a real danger," I said, surprised by my words as I uttered them.

"The threat is that a great gap will open in Jewish identity, which until now has been filled by war, settlement, and immigration: a dark hole will open, and dark holes do not stay empty, so something will fill it, and four great rifts in Israeli society can lead to terrible consequences. In Bosnia there was peace, then there was five years of war, and now we all hope that peace will be restored. For us, there has been no peace for 120 years, and the Jews who came to Israel came from permanent conflicts in their environments. So it's really a peace after two thousand years; and I don't mean that as a beautiful saying, but as the real thing."

The four rifts he singles out are between rich and poor, between the religious and the secular, between East and West, and between Israel and the Diaspora. "The war," he explained, "has shifted the Left from its historic role as a Social Democratic party. We have devoted all of our energy to the peace process and the rights of the Palestinians, so that now there are extreme gaps between rich and poor. The man serving tea at a *Histadrut* meeting used to earn just a little bit less than the general secretary. Now the ratio of wealth between the lowest class and the highest class is 1 to 12, which is much worse than in Europe. In Sweden the gap is 1 to 6, in France 1 to 8."

"The religious division is even worse," I said.

"Yes. What you have to understand is that for the past six or seven years, Israel has been a totally secular country. It is much more secular than America, which, on paper, is a secular country. Even marriage, the last bastion of the religious hold on Israeli life, will soon be free of religious domination. Already 30 percent of youngsters are having civil ceremonies abroad, which are recognized in Israel. But, Bernie, you know this better than I . . ." He was referring to my daughter, Gabi, who was married in a civil ceremony in Cyprus in the fall of 1991, and afterward had a Reform ceremony in the Judean Desert. Of the two ceremonies, only the civil ceremony has legal standing in Israel.

"Soon there will be a ship three kilometers off shore." He laughed as he continued, "And you will be able to get a marriage certificate by fax. You know firsthand that the people who have civil marriages do so on political grounds because they do not want to be married by the rabbinate, and so secularism is becoming an absolute. At the same time, the *haredim,* the dark orthodox, close themselves more and more in ghettos, becoming more and more extreme and more and more autonomous."

"Why do you think they are becoming so extreme?"

"Dov Sadan told me that the Jews were far more moderate when they lived surrounded by other Jews in the *shtetls* in Europe than they are now, in Israel. They are becoming more and more extreme and more and more radical as a consequence of their continuous confrontation with secular Jews." Sadan, formerly professor and head of the Yiddish Department at Hebrew University, is one of the preeminent scholars of the whole body of modern Jewish literature and its roots.

"You're not including the religious Zionists in this inaccessible group, are you?"

"No. I am not talking about the National Religious party. They have always been at the center of Israeli life, trying to influence the whole life of Israel through their *halachah* [the body of traditional Jewish legal codes]. They wanted to answer the Israeli reality with *halachic* questions. But their dream of a Greater Israel has been broken into pieces."

"And the other religious parties . . ."

"The other religious parties, Shas, the Agudat Yisrael, and the others, want to use Israel as a *shabbas goy* [a Sabbath Gentile]; secular Israel would do all the forbidden things, while they perfect their spiritual lives." He laughed again. "Here's something else that will shock you. These parties have not yet formulated a position on the most important issue facing Israelis, war and peace. They don't care about it. Issues of peace and war are for them what the Vietnam War was for the Lubavitcher rabbi in Brooklyn. The war is a concern for the *goyim* and means nothing at all to them. This is shocking, but I understand it very well."

I also asked him to elaborate on the division between East and West, between the "Oriental" Jews from Asia and Africa and the Jews form Europe and the Americas.

"Let me answer this way. As soon as peace leads to open borders Israel will become a much more Oriental country. Immediately a quarter of a million Palestinian tourists from Kalkilya, Ramallah, and Jerusalem will fill up the beaches, with food brought from home, and sing songs about their beautiful country. They have always complained that we have taken the sea from them. And soon Saudi sheiks will come to gamble in casinos, which some clever Israelis will build on the beaches. This will put the Oriental Jews in a new situation because of the great rift between them and the European Jews. They have always complained that they have not been allowed to fully express their culture. Before the Holocaust 97 percent of the Jews were Ashkenazi, but in Israel, soon after the creation of the State half the population was Sephardic. Now the Russian immigration has shifted it back a little, but you must never forget that the Jews who came from the Arab countries suffered a triple shock." I must have looked a little puzzled.

"Yes, a triple shock. Like all Jews everywhere, they went from being a minority to being a majority. They also went from a traditional culture —not so much religious as traditional—to a secular culture. And they went from a postfeudal society to a technological Western society. And the shock made them ashamed. When German Jews came to Israel they said, 'The Nazis may have taken our homes and our passports and our lives,' but—and this is to their great credit—they also said, 'The Nazis cannot take our German culture from us, and we are devoted to Thomas Mann and Goethe and Schiller, to Bach and Beethoven and the rest.' But the Jews from the Arab countries were ashamed to express their culture."

"And you're saying that this will change in peacetime."

"In peacetime they will express their culture more openly because of the greater presence of the Palestinians and because of the Israeli Arabs. And the Jews of Western inclination, who see New York, Los Angeles, and London as their spiritual centers, those Jews will feel a kind of disgust for what they think of as primitive."

"And I suppose that this will also exacerbate the conflicts between Israel and the Diaspora."

"Yes, it will, and the detachment has begun already, and we can feel the alienation. In the U.S. in the last thirty years Jewish identity has been revitalized through three existential components, the memory of the Holocaust, the rescue of Soviet Jews, and the economic and political support of Israel. The rediscovery of the Holocaust, which was entirely ignored by Americans in the fifties, much longer than the repression in Israel, is an amazing phenomenon."

"Entirely ignored?"

"Yes, kids would come to Israel during the 1950s who never even heard of the Holocaust until they came to Israel. But in America there is now a kind of a cult of the Holocaust. But now that the great museums and centers have been built and as the survivors disappear, little by little, from the sea of life, the Holocaust will shift from a living, burning experience to something more academic, historical, and institutional. Also, the fight for liberation of the Russian Jews has disappeared entirely with the opening of the gates of the former Soviet Union. As for Israel, in peacetime, the need for money and political support will diminish entirely."

"You are exaggerating."

"Not at all. In any case, only 1 percent of Israel's budget comes from the Jewish organizations of the Diaspora. And why should a Jew from Baltimore write a $3,000 check for an Israel in which one million citizens take vacations abroad every year and thousands gamble in the casinos of

Turkey? We can no longer pretend we need the money, especially in peacetime. As for political support, there's no problem. When Peres says to Clinton, 'Come,' he comes. And the Congress sometimes supports us too much, as in that decision to move the embassy to Jerusalem, and we sometimes have to slow it down. And during peacetime we will not need so much special support from the U.S. We will have relations with our neighbors, and we are already recognized by 170 countries. And our little ritual about *aliyah* that both Israelis and Americans are so attached to will stop being important. You know: we say, 'You have to come.' You say, 'We don't want to come. We will come only under certain conditions.' We say, 'Come.' You say, 'I won't come.' " By now I am laughing.

"You are pleased that someone comes to you and says, 'Come, come, come.' And we feel morally superior when we ask. This whole game will cease. What I want now is a new dialogue with Americans, not just this old insistence on *aliyah* that I myself was insisting on just a few years ago, but a new dialogue that takes into account all the changes that come with an Israel at peace."

With all the rifts and the changes in the core of both Israeli and Diaspora identities, it is clear that the dangers are real and pressing. I asked, "What do you see as the worst possibilities?"

"You can see it already. The extreme materialism in Israel. After all the years of conflict, of intense ideological debate, it is only natural to see Israelis plunge deeply into hedonism."

"And you think something can be done about it?"

"We have to think ahead. In recent times, the process of identity change has become so rapid that it seems impossible to do anything about it. Who could have imagined that a huge, strong, strict empire like the Soviet Union would dismantle itself so rapidly? No one was prepared, so there has been a degradation of so many aspects of human life that it is possible the Communists will be returned to power in the elections. This was also the case in the unification of Germany. People talked about a long, long process taking over twenty years and not ending until the twenty-first century, and it was done in just two years.

"So it will be rapid, and if we are not prepared to fill it with positive elements, the black hole in Israeli identity will be filled up with some of the worst garbage from the world-CNN culture."

"You seem to be saying," I said, "that the pluralism in Israel which found its way into the forms of *The Lover* and *A Late Divorce* is now, in a time of peace, a profound cultural threat that has to be confronted."

"Pluralism." He pauses, frowns, and gathers his thoughts. "I am afraid that from time to time there may be too much pluralism. And now my concern is not so much in promoting pluralism, but in finding the new elements that will unite us in the face of the disintegration of the Israeli identity. The key word for me now is integration and not pluralism: integration between religious and nonreligious, integration between East and West, Oriental and non-Oriental, integration between poor and rich, integration between Israel and the Diaspora. Integration: not everyone going into his own little corner once peace is established."

In retrospect, once more, the forms of his novels have proven "prophetic," as novels of multiple voices (*The Lover, A Late Divorce,* and *Mr. Mani*) give way to novels of a single voice (*Five Seasons, Open Heart,* and *Voyage to the End of the Millennium*) and the recognition of pluralism gives way to the call for integration. It also crossed my mind that the *havurah* he imagined for the characters of *Mr. Mani*—all the conversation partners and all six generations of Manis—also anticipated this call for integration.

Six years ago, in 1990, as we discussed "Early in the Summer of 1970," he had told me with dismay that he had, in the twenty years of fierce ideological debate between 1970 and 1990, lost his ability to imagine the old Bible teacher from the inside and would use a character like the teacher only "as an instrument in the political debate"—I had assumed, wrongly, that the teacher was a religious man.

"No, no," Yehoshua said. "He was one of those secular, socialist, Labor Party hawks, who was incredibly patient in dealing with the Arabs, because he was certain about the destiny of the Jewish people." A familiar type, to Israelis, anyway, the old teacher was shaped by a faith in the historical destiny of the Jewish people that assumed quasi-religious dimensions. We had discussed at some length the possibility of entering the old teacher's imagination. However, even by 1990 the possibility of sympathetically entering the mind of a religious Zionist hawk was so remote it did not even occur to either of us as something worth mentioning.

In 1996, just six years later, Yehoshua's thinking on religious matters has leapt forward, if only to keep pace with an Israeli government that began in 1993 to face the enormous challenge of making peace with the Palestinians, which, he noted, "has been the heart of the conflagration here for the last 120 years." His thinking about the religious conflicts has evolved, as he grapples with the current crises facing Israelis. Perhaps the first indication of his new thinking was the fact that in *Mr. Mani* a man of decidedly religious sensibility, Avraham Mani, assumed a central role in a

Yehoshua novel for the first time. In April 1996, on the eve of his departure from Israel for his U.S. book tour for *Open Heart,* he referred again
to the storm that had greeted his article "Israeli Identity in Time of
Peace." "I have been preaching in support of a dialogue with the religious, and the Reform Jews and the secular Jews attack me because they
think I am surrendering to the religious."

During his visit to the United States a month later, I asked him to
elaborate. "My feeling," he said, "is that it is very important now for
Israelis to attach themselves to religious elements that can be turned into
cultural elements. The most important issue now is to transform religion
into culture and for secular Israelis to find ways to relate to this."

"How do you propose to do this?"

"As I said, we must create a new dialogue between the secular Jews,
who are both the majority and the winners, and the religious Zionists,
who were our bitterest enemies. It is a question of identity. The question
of *Jewish* identity will become far more important in peacetime; war, immigration, and settlement will no longer be on the table. We must, as secular
Jews, connect ourselves with Jewish identity."

"It wasn't very long ago that you focused on place, language, and
social structure as the ingredients of identity," I said. "This is a real change
for you to emphasize so strongly the *Jewish* element in Israeli identity."

"Yes. And that identity is only in *texts.*"

"Texts as opposed to what?"

"Listen, if a French boy goes to see Michael Jackson in Paris, or
Madonna, or whomever you send over to him, he shouts, he sings at the
concert, speaking in English. Still, after the show is over, he walks out and
sees the Louvre, the Notre Dame, or the Châteaux de la Loire—and he
can relate himself to his history easily, just by walking in the street and
looking around—really easily. All you have to do is observe a Frenchman
talking about a chair in a shop, a Louis Quatorze or Louis Seize chair, and
you see him polishing his identity."

"And an Israeli kid?"

"An Israeli kid goes to see Michael Jackson in the same way. And
when the show is over, where can he go? To Rachel's Tomb? To the Cave
of Machpelah [the traditional burial place of Abraham and Sarah, Isaac
and Rebecca, and Jacob and Leah in Hebron]? He will visit some graves
from three thousand years ago and through them understand his past? It
is very depressing." He shook his head, and a rueful smile crossed his lips.
"You cannot get much from the grave of a Jew—which was probably the

grave of a sheik that was transformed into the grave of a Jew. Our Châteaux de la Loire, our Louvre, our Florence, our Michelangelo are texts. Our Louis Seize chair is a text. It's unfortunate, but what can I say? It's better to have a statue by Michelangelo than a religious text that you have to dig in and pore over to find some vitamins for your history and your identity, but that's all we have."

"Wait a second. Are you saying there is nothing material at all?"

"Well, the Jews lived a thousand years in Poland, and what are the signs that they were there? Graveyards and texts. And so it is in texts that even the nonreligious must go to find their essence and their history."

"So that's why a dialogue with the religious Zionists is so important."

"Yes. The religious, who work with the texts all the time—not as scholars, but in human dialogue with the texts—they can be very helpful to us, and this is why the dialogue with them is very important."

"I see," I said, "but this seems to be the worst of all possible times to try to get secular Israelis even to think about the religious elements in Judaism."

"They have been our bitterest enemies. The most terrible demonstrations against the peace process were done by the religious. I told you about my conversation with my son after he told me that Rabin had been killed, that I knew that only a religious Jew could have done it."

"While I had assumed that only a religious *American* Jew could have done it."

"And, now, if there is an uprising against the Oslo II agreement they will lead it. But we, the secular Jews, the majority, the winners, must build a bridge to the religious Zionists."

"Do you see any hints that this is a real possibility?"

"Right now it is very difficult, of course. The secular Israelis hate the religious in such a terrible way because the religious have become a kind of a monster, a three-legged monster, especially after the assassination of Rabin. One leg of this monster is the ultra-Orthodox, with all their nastiness and ignorance, the way they keep themselves out of the army and sit in their *yeshivot* and study. Another leg is the superfascists among the West Bank settlers. A third leg is Shas, the Sephardic religious party, and their cult of graveyards and their financial corruption. So the image of the religious is simply terrible."

"It sounds pretty hopeless to me."

"Not in peacetime. In peacetime we have to cut this religious monster into pieces, casting what is bad to one side and what is good to the other, and then we must try to have a dialogue with the good side. I speak mainly about the religious Zionists. After the defeat of the idea of Greater Israel"—this is the great dream of the religious Zionists of an Israel in which all of the West Bank is incorporated into the body of the nation— "they will either become ultra-Orthodox and become more and more extreme in their religious conceptions or they will return to the center of Israeli society. This is what I hope for very much, and we must exert great effort to make this happen. This is what I preach now, and for this I have been cursed by a lot of my friends, who say that I am giving up now that we have won a total victory." Once again, the cunning of history casts a sardonic eye over human statements: the election of Benyamin Netanyahu, the increased parliamentary representation of religious parties in the Israeli elections less than a month after these words were spoken, as well as the skirmish over closing Bar Ilan Street in Jerusalem in July, all suggest that the religious Israelis, Zionists and non-Zionists, are not ready to concede defeat.

"Do you have any particular steps in mind?" I asked.

"I would, for example, agree to have all stores closed on the Shabbat —of course, not the cafés . . ."

I laughed.

"Seriously, I mean the commercial stores. I would say to the religious side, 'I agree to be more strict about Shabbat if you would permit public transportation on Shabbat'—because public transportation affects only the poor, so why not end the restriction on public transportation in exchange for more strictness about opening stores on Shabbat."

"You're saying that the secular Jews should do this for their own good."

"Absolutely. In the future, the two great parties, Likud and Labor, will not need the religious in their coalitions. Likud and Labor will be more like Republicans and Democrats. These are silent, calm elections by Israeli standards now because Bibi Netanyahu keeps speaking about peace, peace, peace—his general theme used to be terror—and Peres speaks about security." These words were spoken a few weeks before the elections. "We must make concessions to keep a Jewish atmosphere in Israel, and secular Israelis must give up some of their advantage in order not to push the religious Zionists into a ghetto."

"You keep emphasizing that the first steps must be taken by the Western secular Israelis. Is this also true for the second rift you were talking about, the one between Oriental and Western Jews?"

"Western Jews must make it a mission to try to find a way into the Mediterranean world. The Arabs have been stressing this over and over. You should know that Arab intellectuals oppose the cultural peace process, not the political peace process, but the cultural one. Zionism was invented just ten years after the word "anti-Semitism" was invented, which means that Zionism originates as a negative idea. If Herzl hadn't seen the Dreyfus trial, would he have created Zionism? The Arab intellectuals say to us, 'Your minds and hearts are in the West. We accept you here as a fact. We don't want to fight with you anymore. But can you really be our neighbors? Do you belong in this part of the world?' This is the challenge. In addition, the Arab world now is in very bad shape. No one can now respect the Arab world, with the bloody dictatorship in Iraq, the instability in Lebanon, the poverty in Egypt, and the fundamentalism in Algeria and the Sudan. But these are our neighbors and the Arabs were a great nation in the past. The question the Arabs face is how to awaken the great Arab nation again and bring them back as a participant in the course of history. And perhaps we can help them in this process. And recognizing ourselves as Middle Eastern, that our roots and sources are not Eastern or Western, but Middle Eastern, can help in the matter of identity."

In the relations between Israel and the Diaspora, too, he sees the need for dramatic changes. "We also need a new dialogue with the Diaspora, beyond the focus on 'Who is a Jew?' My answer to 'Who is a Jew?' is simple: a Jew is someone who identifies himself as Jewish."

"That reminds me of one of the themes of the second conversation in *Mr. Mani*," I said, "that Jewish identity is a matter of the mind not maternity. But surely that's not yet the legal definition."

"This is not the official definition, true, but it is the practice. And Israel cannot continue with this legal definition. There are now thousands of people in the world who would declare themselves Jews in order to escape from their situation. We never even dreamed about this possibility: that non-Jews would wish to become Jews and change their identities to better their lot. There are thousands of people in India who are ready to get a Reform rabbi to convert them, and then they could immediately come to Israel and be accepted."

"It sounds as if you are proposing to change the Law of Return and the definition of 'Who is a Jew.' Is that true?"

"We cannot change the definition of 'Who is a Jew,' but we can decide who will be an Israeli, who will be a citizen of Israel, and in the near future this will no longer be automatic." He waved aside my objection before I had a chance to say anything. "We have to have an intermediate period during which people will be examined to see whether they are qualified to be citizens of Israel—I am not thinking of a refugee, a real refugee. On the basis of the Law of Return, people who declare themselves Jewish can come to Israel, but a certain period of time has to pass before they can be recognized as citizens of Israel. The country has to protect itself. I have already seen some extreme Zionists, who are *totally* faithful to the moral conception of the Law of Return, who now believe that citizenship cannot be automatic."

"What kind of demands would you make on the new citizens?"

"It is very hard for me to say this—you know what I have said in the past about the Law of Return and the importance of keeping Israel a Jewish State. But citizenship should have more meaning and significance. Citizens would have to know Hebrew, the laws of Israel, the history, and so on."

"I know that learning Hebrew is a particularly sensitive issue for you."

"Yes, all citizens must renew their relationship with the Hebrew language, and this criterion for citizenship is also one of the criteria for there to be a real dialogue between Israel and the Diaspora. Hebrew must be studied seriously in the Diaspora—I mean seriously. The language that Jews will use to speak to each other cannot be a broken, primitive English."

"Or broken, primitive Hebrew," I added. "But do you really think it is possible to get American Jews to seriously take up the study of Hebrew?"

"I think that instead of taking $300 million from the U.S., we should give back the money to set up programs to get Americans in the U.S. to begin taking the study of Hebrew seriously. We have new methods. We have language laboratories and many means to make it easy—it won't be some old-fashioned Sunday school, but really modern methods."

"Is there anything the Israelis can do?"

"We writers have to reform the Hebrew language, which is still a language with twenty-two consonants and no vowels. I said this to you years ago. We writers have promised ourselves that as soon as a Palestinian state is established, we will establish vowels in the Hebrew language in order to ease the way to learn the language."

"Why is Hebrew so important?"

"With Hebrew you can relate in an intimate way, not only to your sources as Jews but also to the reality of Israel. A TV discussion in Israel could be relayed to the U.S. by satellite or cable and you will really be able to participate in the life of the country, not only through big headlines in the *New York Times*. In peacetime, Israel will not be in the *New York Times*, not one word, as you don't find a word about Holland or Denmark. Our happiest day will be when no one will know the name of our prime minister! Do you know the name of the prime minister of Denmark?"

I laughed.

"Neither do I. You know, I visited a tiny village in Greece a few years ago—it was when Shamir was still prime minister—and someone asked me, 'What about Shamir?'. And I said, 'What do you know about Shamir?!' This is the problem: people know too much about us. But in peacetime, the only way to communicate with us on a profound level is through Hebrew."

"Do you have any other ideas, in addition to learning the language?"

"Of course I do," he said laughing. "We should undertake joint projects. In Rio de Janeiro there was recently a large conference on the environment, and there were representatives from all the countries of the world, and there were representatives from the Vatican and Islam, but nobody represented the Jewish civilization in the matter of world issues, like the environment, drugs, unemployment, or birth control."

"What are you proposing?"

"Now that we are no longer in terrible trouble as a people, now that survival is no longer an issue, we must go in two vectors, one profoundly inward and one outward to the world. In peacetime we have to turn again to the world, and, between our total experience of Israel as a country and your total experience of Jews in the world, we can give a Jewish point of view, through our sources and experiences, and help solve some of the problems."

"How important is this for you?"

"It's very important that Israel should start to give something to the world. When Martin Buber came to the great German philosopher Hermann Cohen in the 1920s and asked him to join the Zionist movement, Cohen replied, 'What? After two thousand years of suffering and developing a special vocation, the Jews will create a small Albania in the Middle East!' Buber said, 'No, it will not be another Albania; it will be a different country, a better country, and we can integrate some of our hopes and some of our mission by having a country of our own.' Of course, Buber was right. Twenty years after Hermann Cohen said this, thousands of German Jews were wandering from one port to another asking for one little Albania that would take them in. And no one in Auschwitz was speaking of the spiritual quality of suffering. But to their credit, the Zionist leaders, including Ben-Gurion, as practical and realistic as he was, repeated that Israel has to have some sort of mission, to be a light to the nations. The unique way in which religion and nationality are integrated in the Jewish nation—which you and I have talked about a lot —can, I hope, keep us from the danger of becoming completely preoccu-pied with ourselves, now that peace gives us a real opportunity to be a 'normal' country."

"What do you have in mind?"

"Now is the time to do something real, not only talk, to create, for example, a learning corps, like President Kennedy's Peace Corps, to try to close the gap between the First World and the Third World. Most of the West has given up on the Third World, but Israel is right on the border of the Third World; the Third World is just four kilometers from the Knesset in Jerusalem, in the refugee camps. We have been specialists in learning— and there is a great surplus of teachers—so we can give something back in two-or three-year missions teaching biology, mathematics, or comput-ers . . . imagine an encounter in the Congo between a young teacher from St. Louis or Paris and another young teacher from Netanya. The point is to *do* something rather than talk about it. An Israeli-Jewish learning corps could resemble the Swiss with the Red Cross or the French promoting their culture all over the world."

There was still one rift to deal with, and that was the great social rift between the rich and the poor. "On this issue I must address my col-leagues on the Left. I am afraid of liberalism. I am afraid that in peacetime all of the energy that has gone into the peace process and the rights of the Palestinians will be directed at civil rights, the rights of homosexuals, beaten women, children, and so on, and not at the gaps between the social classes, which have become so great in the last few years."

This distinction between liberalism and social democracy is one sign of the gulf between the Israeli sense of community and American individu-alism. I asked, "Do you see such a change in the Left as a real possibility?"

"I hope so. We have been going in an American direction here. And the American model of identity is not a good model for us. We are in a totally different category than America. We are not a country created by individuals seeking liberty. We were created by a nation, an historic nation, an ancient nation with a thirty-three hundred year history that returned to its land to renew its national life. In America you find something you do not find anywhere in Europe: there are places you cannot enter. When I visited Chicago last week, people told me, 'You can't go here, you can't go there.' You accept the high level of crime the same way you accept the extreme gap between rich and poor. But we cannot have such gaps. For all our differences, we are finally one people. So the Left in Israel must return to its Social Democrat identity. If the Left is satisfied with liberalism rather than social and economic justice, it will be very bad." I was fascinated to hear the man who had spoken so vividly about the heterogeneity of Israel now calling for a sense of oneness.

"It sounds as if you don't see any large 'pillars' that would replace the three huge ones that have been losing their power and meaning."

"No, no large ones, like war and survival, but many small ones. We must do many small things to bring us together in peacetime. There were those in England who, years after the end of World War II, talked with nostalgia about the good old days of the blitz. God forbid that in twenty years we will say how beautiful were the times of war, because we were so united! God forbid such a thing should come to pass!"

I was interested in following up on his comments about American identity, because it seemed to me that American liberal Judaism might be a bridge for secular Israelis between pure secularism and some sort of religious identity. I described the reaction of American liberal Jews to the aftermath of the Rabin assassination. "You can't imagine how strongly people reacted to the rituals improvised by the kids at the site of the assassination. We saw it all on TV: the memorial candles from old European tradition; the notes, like the notes people shove into the *kotel* [the Western Wall] in Jerusalem, as if they were trying to make the site of the assassination, a secularly spiritual alternative to the *kotel*, located significantly in Tel Aviv, the center of secular Israeli life. Most of the Americans I've spoken to believe that these improvisations indicate a spiritual need that neither secularism nor religious orthodoxy could fill. Of course, it is partly wish fulfillment, but I know many people who take this as evidence of a yearning for spirituality or ritual that uses but improvises on traditional matters, very much along the lines of American Reform Judaism."

"I think the most important element of the kids' actions after Rabin's death was a guilt feeling: why didn't they support him more during his struggle for peace? Why did they allow him to be alone? But the question of the candles and the notes—it was a combination of things from other places, a little bit religious, a little bit Buddhist; this is not exactly my cup of tea, but these are kids. And I have the right to be old and to feel a gap between generations. It would be terrible if there were no generation gap and if I were not already considered as an old fool who has to be kicked away."

"It sounds as if the kids had a much stronger effect on Americans than on you."

"You have to know that I was not so impressed by the reaction of the youth to the murder of Rabin. Only on the political level was I affected, seeing their support for the peace and watching them wake up a little from their passivity. This was most important. But the religious reaction, the sentimental reaction did not impress me so much. In general, you know how upset I am by the sentimentality now in the world and in films and in books. Now, towards the end of the century, there is more inclination to go towards sentimentality in many aspects of art: either violence and postmodernism which cuts all experience to bits or, on the other hand, a kind of soft and mellow sentimentality."

I also thought liberal American Judaism might be a bridge between the religious and the secular partly because many American liberal Jews deal with the religious texts very much along the lines that he suggested. I listed many of the trends in American liberal Judaism that, I said, "don't seem to appeal much to Israelis: the spirituality of 'liberal' or 'progressive' Judaism, including all the study of Buber and commitment to *tikkun olam,* the 'neo-hassidism,' the meditation, the democratic religious communities, the including of traditional meditative melodies in liberal services, and, most important, the explosion of egalitarianism reflected in the religious services, the prayer books, and the women rabbis and cantors. Is there a place for all this in Israel? Dani, my Israeli son-in-law, studies the kabbala and insists that it is not 'religious.' "

"You are speaking about the Jewish spirituality movement in America. I believe that in a time of peace, in a more relaxed time, these books and ideas will have more of an influence on the Israelis. The Israelis have been so preoccupied with their own specific situation that they were not open to Buberism, women rabbis, and things like that. I also believe that Israelis have not found real connections with Reform Judaism and the other things you mention because they felt, on one hand, that this is not authentic Judaism as they live it daily and, on the other hand, they were feeling that it is too Americanized and too . . ."—he searched for the right word —"too smooth for them. But I would say that this will change in peacetime. With peace, the general relation with American Jews has to change, away from the moral position of superiority I have touted so strongly to a partnership."

"In your lecture on 'Democracy and the Novel' [presented at a symposium at the University of Michigan in 1995] you say that for Americans, democracy 'is the very skin of your body,' that we 'are the only nation in the world whose national identity is almost genetically related to democracy.' Could you elaborate a little more on the pressure from American identity?"

"I am a little afraid of this hedonistic secularism of the Israelis. Israel imitates America but it is not America because in America there is a deep nucleus of religious conceptions. And it is not Europe because in back of the atheistic conceptions of Europe there are wonderful churches and wonderful religious music and wonderful memories of religious time. So what will Israelis do? They will copy the American web of nothingness without the religious sentiment of America. And this, of course, has to be changed."

"What do you have in mind?"

"One of my concerns is that we have to move a little away from what I call the American model of identity. We are not America. America and Israel are two different types of identity. We are not a country like America where individuals immigrated to find their personal liberty. We are a more solid collective society. As I said before, we are an ancient people. We have to turn ourselves to the direction of Europe and try to copy their models and not the American models. It is very, very dangerous, and I say this with all due respect for America and especially with my great gratitude to America for all that America has done for Israel. Without America Israel could not have survived. But it very important now that we detach ourselves a little from the American model."

"You seem to be saying that the danger is that some caricature of American individualism is what will fill Israel identity unless new elements are nourished. What are the chances that this pressure from America can be resisted?"

"The American identity has influence all over the world. But the fact is that we don't have enough protection for our identity. As I said before, unlike a French kid or an Italian, we don't have a material record of a continuing life here that can protect our own identity—we don't even have as much as the people of Iceland, a tiny people, on their large island. This makes us more vulnerable, more exposed to American identity than other nationalities, like the Chinese, the Japanese, the French, and others."

He asked me what I thought about his ideas about America. I said, "I agree with your idea that, for Americans, democracy 'is the very skin of your body,' and I think you're probably very sharp when you suggest the Israelis should look to a European model, because so much of Jewish identity is bound up with nationality, religion, and language, like the European. But when you attribute to America 'a deep nucleus' of religious identity to balance the hedonistic secularism (or individualistic democracy gone wild) of America, I would answer that the 'religion' of America is a secular religion that worships the icons of democracy (the Bill of Rights, the Constitution, the flag). The dark side of the individualism is reflected by many things, one of which is the incredible level of violence in America, some of which has something to do with good things (passion, a sense of justice, a sense of honor) gone awry. Whenever I ask my students to define freedom, all give a variation on 'doing or thinking or saying what I want without restrictions'—very rarely (even after I give examples from prisoners of conscience saying they are freer than their jailers) does anyone entertain the possibility that freedom is doing what you ought to do, or that the only free choice that matters is choosing between good and evil."

"I appreciate your comments about America," he said. "And perhaps you are right. And I feel it, that the holy things in America are connected with democracy, not so much with religion. These things are all you have to make up for what, compared to Europeans, you lack in history, the past, and the other tribal elements of a people."

His mention of tribal memories of a people naturally made me think of *Mr. Mani* again and the way in which memory, both individual and collective, is not a passive faculty, but rather what William Carlos Williams calls "a kind of accomplishment," and I thought it was time to ask him about the novel he was working on, *Voyage to the End of the Millennium*. I wondered which among his current ideas found fictional life in the new book. I began, naturally enough, with identity. I asked, "Would you like to say anything about the issue of identity or of memory in the new novel, compared to the others?"

"The question of identity, yes." He sighed. "It has to be taken very smoothly, very normally, in this novel. In *Five Seasons* and *Open Heart* identity also has to be taken very smoothly. In both, it's mostly a question of East and West and this element has begun to dominate my writing and it is also very much in the novel that I am writing now. There is a tension between East and West, a confrontation, an integration."

I reminded him that when I told him that I found *Open Heart* feminist he had connected it with this new novel.

"Well," he said, "this is probably a good time to describe it to you. The novel is about a rich merchant in North Africa who takes his boat with all the merchandise that he didn't sell, along with his Arab partner and his two wives, to go and see his nephew who is his business partner. Abulafia, his nephew whom he loves extremely, had married an Ashkenazi wife in Paris. When she heard that he has a relationship with his uncle who has two wives she very much wanted her husband to sever the partnership."

"When does this take place?"

"In the tenth century, just before the end of the first millennium. This was the time when there was this *herem,* this ban from Rabbi Gershom ben Yehudah, *Me'or ha-Golah*"—the Light of the Diaspora—"that bigamy is forbidden among Jews. So this merchant is on his way to Paris in his boat in order to convince his nephew, who had decided to sever their relationship, not to do so. He argues that bigamy is possible and honest and it should be allowed. I'm not sure what the feminists will say to me in America when this novel comes out. Perhaps they will like it. Why not? Anyhow, I say that this is the plot of the novel, and I am now in the heart of it."

"Again it sounds as if you have to do a lot of research, as in *Mr. Mani* and *Open Heart.* Was it as demanding as the research for *Open Heart?*"

"Yes. I did a lot of research for *Open Heart.* And here I have also done a lot of work because there are so many different areas I have to treat. I have consulted with three professors of medieval history, both general history and Jewish history. They read the first third of the novel, and they made some suggestions, but in general they were very satisfied with the mood, with the general atmosphere. And now I've been telling everyone that I will put their names in the novel in order to get a guarantee against any future attack. That's what I should have done with the doctors who helped me with *Open Heart,* so that when those other two doctors attacked me, they would have referred themselves to the experts and not to me."

"I can hear in your description of the novel at least two of the things that you've been talking about, the issue of religion and culture and the conflict between the East and the West. Here religious ideas seem to be forcing the merchant to choose between the love of his nephew and the love of his wives."

"The main ideological question is the confrontation between East and West, or, at that point in history, between South and North, especially because these two Jewish civilizations, the Sephardic and the Ashkenazi, stood at the very, very beginning of the Renaissance. I am not talking about the Arab-Jewish civilization, which in the tenth century is only beginning its rise to what will become the Golden Age of Spain, the sources of which came from North Africa. And the sages of Ashkenaz were not so highly cultured at the time of the novel. But this Ashkenazi culture is the talmudic culture, of the learned and pious Jews, which started along the Rhine, a community which would be struck and destroyed by the First Crusades one hundred years later, at the end of the eleventh century. But this is not my business, I am just describing three months of this rich Jew's journey to renew his relationship with his partner."

There was much I wanted to ask, but I remembered how little he had shared about his earlier books while he was still working on them. I said, "When we talked earlier, while you were working on *Five Seasons* and *Open Heart,* you seemed much more reluctant to talk about a work in progress. This time you seem to have shown it to many more people."

"It's true. I have talked about it quite freely. Never in my life have I revealed the contents and the plot of a novel as I have revealed the plot of this one. I hope it will not bring me bad luck. I don't show every paragraph—I wait until I have a complete section. The new novel is divided into three parts. When I completed about 110 pages, about one-third of the novel, I showed it, not only to Ika and the medievalists but to a total of fourteen or fifteen people, because I wanted to get their reactions. I now think that this is important, because if you are going down the track of a long novel, it's a long way, and you have to be sure that you are not losing your way, so you must have more reactions."

"What were the reactions like?"

"They were very good. I am working very hard and, as I said, I am being very much assisted by the medievalists. I hope the writing will continue smoothly."

"As I remember, you used to show your novels only to Ika as you completed a section, and you showed them to Amos Oz."

"But Amos always shows me his novels only when they are finished. Only in *Black Box* did he show me a part of a novel, and I told him to stop." We both laughed. "He didn't listen to me, of course."

Between his essay "Israeli Identity in a Time of Peace" and his lecture "Democracy and the Novel," I had a good idea of what is on his mind politically and artistically as he composed *Voyage to the End of the Millen-*

nium. In his lecture, after discussing six ways in which "the novel, more than any other artistic form, has encouraged and been in support of in the democratic revolution," he reverses field and shows how the "fashionable" conventions of contemporary democracy have contributed to the "stranded condition of the novel" in contemporary Western culture. What I found fascinating is how his new call for novelists to rebel against these fashionable democratic conventions reverses the artistic stance that began his literary career. In our earlier conversations we had discussed how, in the 1950s and 1960s, he and the other authors of the Generation of the State had felt suffocated by the great panoramic ambitions of the Palmach Generation of writers, who came of age before the War of Independence. Now he decries the absence of the great integrative novels of moral weight and range that characterize the early twentieth-century masterpieces by Thomas Mann, William Faulkner, Marcel Proust, James Joyce, and Virginia Woolf, and he discerns a real social need for integrative novels that tell a whole culture's story to all of its members.

In his lecture he singles out six related traits inimical to the creation of great novels characteristic of early twentieth-century modernism, six symptoms that infected novelists of the second half of the century and kept them from taking on the whole society in novels of moral insight (like *The Magic Mountain*) and defiance (like *The Sound and the Fury*). Of the six symptoms in his diagnosis the three most important are: 1) the way psychological understanding tends to wash away moral problems; 2) the rise of antiheroes who throw readers back into their own limitations instead of heroes that represent possibilities of moral action or of insight that readers yearn to experience; and 3) the fact that authors have become unwilling to undertake "a comprehensive view of reality" and "grand-scale integrations that are the very essence of great literature" because of the widespread derogation of elitism, the predominance of "experts" from the social sciences, and the rise of "minority" voices, each with its own special authority. This condition is not peculiar to recent Israeli fiction. Yehoshua detects it in the whole body of fiction produced in democratic countries in the second half of the twentieth century.

A good case in point is Bellow's work because his novels seem to pull in different directions in two of the traits, the nature of the hero (or antihero) and a writer's willingness to take authority upon himself. I told him that I was rereading *The Adventures of Augie March.* "It's twenty years since I read it," I said, "and I had forgotten how ambitious it is. It really cuts a swathe across the whole society. It's a great novel!"

"I haven't read *Augie March* in a long time," he said, "and I don't remember it well enough to answer you. But certainly, Bellow takes authority and shows great daring in his other novels, in *Herzog* and *Mr. Sammler's Planet*, but you would not say that Professor Herzog is a hero, you wouldn't want to be like him."

"As opposed to Hans Castorp, or Dilsey, say, or Quentin Compson," I said, bringing the discussion to *The Sound and the Fury* once again.

"Yes, Quentin's struggle with incest is very moving, despite all the suffering and all the horror. And, in fact, you know that I consider *The Sound and the Fury* the most important work written this century, and, as I said before, it is through Dilsey, the black servant, that the reader understands the whole metaphysical world in chapter four of the novel."

"I am interested in your thoughts about some recent American attempts to respond to your diagnosis. It seems to me that Toni Morrison, probably the closest thing we have now to a national writer—and also the writer most profoundly influenced by Faulkner—has at least attempted to meet the bulk of your challenges, especially the one you consider most important, what you describe as 'the increasing frailty of the moral aspect in the contemporary novel.' For one thing, in all of her novels, she demands *both* psychological understanding *and* moral accountability, that, to paraphrase your words, to understand is not necessarily to forgive. It occurs to me that Toni Morrison could also be thought of as a real version of the fictional Dilsey, as someone who uses a minority position—with the moral and social 'problems' that that orientation brings—as a crowbar to pry open and penetrate the inner core of the whole society."

"Especially in her novel *Beloved*," Yehoshua agreed. "Toni Morrison definitely meets my requirements about literature, the novel, and morality, raising the question about the right of parents to kill children in order not to give them a dreadful life, the life of slavery."

"Or *Jazz*," I continued, "in which she is willing to break the narrative code she has set up to allow for the possibility of transformation and liberation, perhaps in a way parallel to your breaking of your narrative code in *Open Heart* when Benjy breaks into the dream voice at the end of the novel." Both Yehoshua and Morrison seemed to be using techniques of postmodernism for decidedly moral ends.

"I just finished *Jazz*, and it's quite interesting along those lines."

"I would like to find out a little more about the literary ramifications of your call for integration," I said. "We've talked about your abandoning of multiple voices in *Open Heart* and *Five Seasons*. Do you see a connection between the relatively integrated points of view in these two books with your call for integration in the politics of identity and 'grand-scale integrations that are the very essence of great literature'?"

"It's fair to say that I abandoned the pluralistic point of view, the multiplicity of voices in the novel in favor of one man, one hero speaking. But you must remember that both Molkho and Benjy are limited persons. So in both *Open Heart* and *Five Seasons* it would not be accurate to say that I have created an omniscient hero or a narrator who can address the whole situation. In *Five Seasons* Molkho is very much bound to his unconscious; he is, in fact, unconscious all the time, and he doesn't even see or understand the most evident things that happen to him."

"Which is quite different from the kind of integration that you were calling for in your lecture on democracy and the novel."

"Yes. This is not really what I was speaking about when I talked about Thomas Mann and Hans Castorp of *The Magic Mountain* or a classical novel like *Crime and Punishment* or even, for example, *Herzog,* in which the writer takes authority . . ."

"And the new novel?"

"In the new novel I really do take total authority, and I wouldn't even say that I have a main speaker. There is no multiplicity of voice but rather a pluralism that comes only through the authority of the writer himself. In the new novel there are very, very few dialogues—it is a novel without dialogues, or with very few dialogues, because even when people speak to each other they speak through me. I interpret what they are saying. So it is the contrary of *Mr. Mani,* which is a novel only of dialogues."

I was impressed and surprised once more by Yehoshua's restless experimentation. Here he is, a master of dialogue, eschewing dialogue, as a few years earlier, he had abandoned the interior monologues of *A Late Divorce* for the one-sided dialogues of *Mr. Mani.* "What you're telling me is that in the new novel there is only an omniscient narrator?"

"Yes, there is just the narrator, an objective narrator, living at the same time of the novel. No, that's not it—the author is an historian. But everything is described very much in the third person."

"And there is not even a second voice in any way analogous to the dream voice of *Open Heart?*"

"Well, let me tell you that I was tempted to include three short chapters which look at this novel from the point of view of a modern writer. But when I showed the first third of the novel to all those readers, there were differences of opinion."

"As in *Open Heart*."

"I had included one short paragraph that spoke about the way we modern people can absorb, can relate ourselves to people who lived one thousand years before us. Some readers accepted it and some were a little reluctant. Finally, I decided to entirely get rid of this extra voice, partly, I must admit, because of the disturbing experience I had had with *Open Heart*, even though you yourself were one of those who liked this voice. Perhaps I will leave only one paragraph at the beginning of the novel, a very short one that will be something of an introduction, but I still haven't come to a final decision."

"I am also interested in the question you raise in your lecture about heroes, calling for heroes who hold out the possibility of large moral and intellectual transformation as opposed to antiheroes, who only hold a mirror up to our limitations. To some extent, I believe, you *have* created heroes. The various Manis, for instance, are all intellectual heroes, in their willingness to oppose the direction of history. But, as far as morality goes, we see courage only in flashes, with the second Joseph and the first Efrayim Mani, with Lieutenant Horowitz, as you've said, even with Hagar Shiloh, and perhaps most profoundly with Avraham Mani's willingness to break taboos at the end. Benjy too is willing to break social and intellectual taboos. And even Molkho shows a dogged persistence in his inching towards liberation. In *Open Heart* I also believe that, though the main weight is on liberating Benjy from the psychological contradiction that threatens to tear him apart, there is also something terribly immoral in the prison his consciousness inflicts on Dori (and which you force us to share). In a way, in his love, he acts entirely as if he were God—sort of like Adam in *The Lover*—and Dori (and Michaela) were simply creatures and nothing more than means to satisfy his ends, so that, in the end, along with the psychological liberation he achieves through his daughter because of his human, mortal love of her, he achieves a moral liberation as well. But still, all of these characters are, as you suggest, morally or spiritually limited when compared to Hans Castorp or Dilsey or Quentin Compson. What about your new novel? I don't know whether you feel ready to address this now—but I can't help believing that in the merchant-hero of your new novel you are responding to at least some of these moral challenges."

"You are perhaps right to suggest that my new novel faces moral questions more openly than my previous books. My criticism about the frailty of the moral aspect of the contemporary novel is also a self-criticism. I don't think I was doing enough in my own work. I thought that the questions of war and peace and the other political questions were the moral questions of my novels. But, of course, that's not right, because political questions are only a thin layer of what I would call moral questions."

Even though he has given me only a small glimpse of *Voyage to the End of the Millennium*—I am not one of the fifteen who have read the first third of the novel—I cannot resist conjuring up many more connections between the new novel and his diagnosis of the crisis facing Israeli identity under peace, much the way *Mr. Mani*, for instance, traces the religion versus nationality paradox all the way back to its mythological source. He had already spoken about how the novel addresses the East-West rift more directly than *Five Seasons, Mr. Mani*, and *Open Heart*.

The new novel seems to be pushing both the East versus West (or as he put it, north versus south) dialogue and the religion and culture dialogue back to medieval sources, to a time when neither East nor West was dominant (before the Crusades, before the Golden Age of Spain). "You have proceeded from Avraham Mani, your first hero whose sensibility is profoundly religious, to placing a religious issue at the center of the plot itself. I figure the debate about the ban against bigamy is both a cultural and a religious issue."

"Yes," he said, "it can cause the same sort of rupture as would now be caused if Reform rabbis performed traditional marriage ceremonies between homosexuals."

"And if a debate about bigamy can be transformed from a religious debate to a cultural difference," I said, "then the conversation switches from dogma (requiring a ban) to custom (requiring respect for difference)." Bigamy seems to me to be an inspired choice, right up Yehoshua's alley, because it can strike at so many levels, the most personal and sexual, *and* the familial, *and* the social, *and* the religious (because of Rav Gershom's ban), all at the same time.

"You know, Bulli," I suggested. "I have begun to imagine the novel, given what you have said about the role of texts in Jewish civilization, as a textual Notre Dame (or, at least, Ste. Chapelle), as a source for the cultural uses of religious life."

His noncommittal silence made me swerve toward something more specific. "Going back to the end of the last millennium seems to be a grand idea," I said, "as is going back to a time when the rabbi and the Judaism of the rabbis were vital and had real political authority, as opposed to the frozen, dried out parody of 'traditional' rabbinic Judaism in Me'ah

She'arim. I can't wait to see what kind of hero you have devised, how large he is, morally and intellectually, and what his end will be."

"You'll just have to wait," he said, a droll smile covering his face.

"Listen," I went on, undeterred, "since you have been willing to talk about this novel more than previous works in progress, here are three more questions—which, of course, you're free to ignore or evade. First of all, have you come up with old, no longer viable identity tags relevant to the end of the first millennium that are somehow equivalent to the dying markers of our generation, in Israel and the U.S., on our journey to the end of the second millennium?

"Second, is one of your intentions to educate the Western secular community about the marvelous sources of the religious and the Oriental elements in Judaism and remind the Oriental community of the creativity and vitality of the old Ashkenaz community?

"Third, you mentioned that the merchant has an Arab partner. Does this mean that the dawn of peace has diminished your anger and guilt enough that you now feel, in the words you used earlier, 'clean enough to take an Arab personality and character and to describe him in a kind of objective way'? These questions are all different ways of asking the same question: are you are trying in the new novel to throw some fresh light on Israeli identity in a time of peace?"

"I don't think I put the question of Israeli identity under peace into my novel. It's too, too early to speak about it." He shook his head in mock dismay. "You are going too far and too fast. But let me just say this. I hope, that by its far temporal remove from the present turmoil, the new novel can make its contribution to peace by informing Jewish and Israeli identity with new references that were irrelevant or hidden during the times of war. In wartime we have been much too dominated by events, and even *Mr. Mani*, which went back 180 years, was dominated totally by the situation of Zionism. With this new novel I am going back beyond Zionism, beyond all the modern issues, to try, if it is possible, to discover the unity of the Jewish people. But, Bernie, enough! If you ask me so many questions about the new novel, I will not be able to write it. And I have to write it because I don't yet know what I will find."

As he spoke of getting back to work on his sixth novel, my mind drifted back once more to our first conversation in the winter of 1988 and a comment he had made in the early seventies that has become something of a refrain for us over the years. "Because our spiritual life today cannot revolve around anything but these [political] questions," he had told

Ehud Ben Ezer, "when you engage in them without end you cannot spare yourself, spiritually, for other things. Nor can you attain the true solitude that is a condition and prerequisite of creation, its source and its strength."

When I asked him how he feels about these sentiments now, he expressed a belief in a more dynamic relationship between creative isolation and the burden of solidarity. "I now see the isolation in a positive sense, and I can return from solitude to society with the energy and insight needed to attempt to define a far more profound basis for morality. I do not just accept the morals of the society, but I examine morality through an individual character who liberates himself and afterwards is more equipped to analyze the morality of the society. Once he knows himself, he can also know the society, the Jewish people, or anything else."

Epilogue
Yehoshua Criticism in English

Beginning in the late 1970s, articles about Yehoshua have been appearing in English-language literary journals, predominantly those that focus on Hebrew literature or on Jewish matters.

Overviews

Nili Wachtel (1979), in an article covering Yehoshua's work up through *The Lover,* identifies "the fundamental sin operating in Yehoshua's world: loving from afar. It permits one to love without 'effort,' without an 'obligation.' " Arguing that all of Yehoshua's work, both symbolic and realistic, revolves around "universal human themes," Wachtel is alert to the particular connections between fictional and social reality and writes of Yehoshua's disappointment that the Zionist dream of "freedom for the nation to rule itself, to grow and develop normally, to shed some unwholesome tendencies acquired in the Diaspora," has not been fulfilled.

Yael Feldman (1987) provides a challenging overview of the relationship between ideology and literature in Israeli literature of the 1980s, in the context of the continuing engagement of the generation of the State with the art and values of the Palmach generation. She divides her analysis into four related topics: "autobiography as identity crisis," "psychoanalysis as metaphor," "Zionism vs. Judaism," and "the center cannot hold." She points out that Yehoshua's psychohistorical essays in *Between Right and Right* "openly lead Zionism to the psychoanalyst's couch" and applies this synthesis of psychoanalysis and history to *The Lover* and *A Late Divorce*.

Lev Hakak's (1993) domain is the sociologist's office rather than the psychoanalyst's couch, and building on Feldman's analysis, he investigates Yehoshua's "realistic-psychological" works and shows how "Early in the Summer of 1970," *The Lover, A Late Divorce,* and *Five Seasons* may be analyzed as depictions of contemporary Israeli society. He breaks his analysis into six distressed areas (the individual and society; the Israeli family; Israelis and Arabs; Ashkenazim and Sephardim; the religious and the secular; and the Diaspora and Zionism) and sees Molkho in "his patience, moderation, and sense of balance" as a glowingly positive role model. Hadak also provides a clear summary of the Hebrew criticism through 1987.

Joseph Cohen (1990) provides a sound overview of Yehoshua's career from the early stories up through *Five Seasons*. He summarizes each major work and points out salient formal and cultural features. He emphasizes Yehoshua's kinship with the great modernist novelists, especially Joyce and Faulkner, observing that "Yehoshua interiorizes reality, undermining temporal and spatial linearity, and, like those two modern giants, he has a gift for lyricism in his prose that lifts us out of the ordinary world and propels us into a subjective one where 'real' life goes on inside people's heads rather than in their external environment."

Gilead Morahg's Work

In a series of articles between 1979 and 1993, Gilead Morahg, the leading English-language critic of Yehoshua's work, focuses sharply and subtly on Yehoshua as symbolic writer. Morahg's work ranges from a general essay on the image of the Arab in Yehoshua and other Jewish Israeli writers (1986) to a close analysis (1988a) of the symbolic structure of "Flood Tide," the final story in Yehoshua's first book. In a 1979 essay, which covers the fiction up through *The Lover,* he argues against the Israeli critical consensus that regarded the early allegorical stories as "manifestations of despairing nihilism." Instead, he argues, Yehoshua's stance is humanistic outrage at human inability or unwillingness to engage in authentic, mutually confirming interactions. He grounds his analysis in Martin Buber's formulation that "actual humanity" rests on the fulfilling of "the wish of every man to be confirmed as what he is, even as what he can become, by man." What causes anguish in Yehoshua's fiction is characters' "arrested capacity for mutual confirmation" and the consequent "loss of their sense of individual value." In the early stories, characters wind up yielding to social authority in degrading attempts to confirm their own value as individuals.

A second essay (1979–80) is a close analysis of *The Lover* along these lines. He points to Yehoshua's innovations in the use of multiple narrators by playing "the isolating discord" of the narrators against the "harmonious unities" of the narratives: their structure, language, and "unarticulated perceptions." This contrast between surface and structure implies a tragic perception that "although the potential for genuine human contact may be there, people are constantly failing to realize it."

In 1982 Morahg shows the limitations of a second critical consensus, one that proposes a linear movement in Yehoshua's career from "allegorical structures and universal themes" to realistic attention to the specifics of Israeli life. Morahg proposes more continuity between the early and later work, suggesting that a progression from "allegorical symbolism" to "realistic symbolism" describes Yehoshua's development more accurately. He identifies "Three Days and a Child" as pivotal in this progression and shows how Yehoshua's complex use of symbolism in *The Lover* illuminates the characters and reveals the ways the characters also represent the Israeli society.

A fourth essay (1988a) picks up two threads from the earlier essays, the degrading effects of yielding to social authority and the symbolic connection between character and culture, and applies them to "Early in the Summer of 1970," *The Lover*, and *A Late Divorce*, using *Between Right and Right* as a lens. Morahg argues that the most important social authority Yehoshua examines symbolically in these works is "a religiously oriented system or actions and beliefs that is distorting the natural connection between the Jews and their land."

In his most recent essay (1993) he develops the connection between this religious dimension and the Diaspora, expanding his discussion of "Early in the Summer of 1970," *The Lover*, and *A Late Divorce* and adding *Five Seasons* to an analysis that sees Molkho "as one of those new Israeli Jews whose identities are finally free of the traumatic conflict between the Diaspora and Zion."

Yehoshua's Sephardic Roots

Several articles analyze the Sephardic roots of *Mr. Mani* as personal exploration and political endeavor, especially in relation to the relationship between the Jewish and Arab communities in Israel. Gila Ramras-Rauch

(1991) examines *Mr. Mani* from the perspectives of Yehoshua's emotion-ally nuanced relationship with his father and Yehoshua's exploration of his own Sephardic identity and his "hitherto unacknowledged Sephardic literary forefathers," such as Yehudah Burla and Yitzhak Shami. These explorations are matters of both style and ideology, especially in the old Sephardic respect for Arab nationalism and intimacy with the Arab com-munities of the Mediterranean. She detects in *Mr. Mani* a " 'regression' to the romantic depiction of the Arab as typically found in the writing of the prestate generation."

Muhammad Siddiq (1992), in a comparative study of *Mr. Mani* and *The Trench* by Abd al-Rahman Munif, also considers *Mr. Mani* "a Sephar-dic response to the Ashkenazi cultural challenge and hegemony" that challenges the "Zionist master narrative" created by the "Ashkenazi liter-ary establishment." Siddiq also reveals an affinity with Yehoshua's analysis of democracy and the novel, noting that the novel's "interest in the expe-rience of ordinary individuals as the object of moral contemplation and aesthetic pleasure makes it, perhaps more than any other genre, intrinsi-cally egalitarian and anti-totalitarian."

Arnold Band (1992) argues that as ideologist Yehoshua proposes "Se-phardic Zionism" as a more constructive alternative to Israel's "Ashke-nazic-Zionist and Exilic heritage." Identifying Yehoshua as a comic novelist of psychoanalytical sophistication, Band defines virtually all the characters in *Mr. Mani* as a gang of self-deceiving individuals who "do not understand themselves and the motives for their behavior in personal relationships" and, in compensation, "fashion group-identifications (Sephardism, Zionism, Pacifism, Universalism, Nazism, Religion), which they delude themselves to believe will solve their problems." He notes a parallel turning toward Sephardic roots in father and son. Like Ramras-Rauch, Band connects the personal, the literary, and the ideological, ob-serving, for example, that Ya'akov Yehoshua turned toward the Sephardic community of his childhood after his father's death in 1955, in much the same way as A. B. Yehoshua would turn toward his own Sephardic identity after Ya'akov Yehoshua's death in 1982. Like both Ramras-Rauch and Siddiq, Band does not connect the Sephardic critique of Ashkenazi Zionist ideology to Yehoshua's interrogation of the entire history of the Jewish people.

The Sephardic-Ashkenazi divide also comes up in Risa Domb's analy-sis of *Five Seasons,* which is a typical illustration of the tendency of critics to subject all of Yehoshua's fiction to ideological interpretation. "Molkho's obsession with classical music," for instance, is "the effect of Ashkenazi brainwashing." She argues that Yehoshua uses Molkho to forecast "that a new and healthier future might be possible only after the death of the domination of Ashkenazi culture, which is analogous to the death of Molkho's Ashkenazi wife." She has interesting things to say about the role of music, hell imagery, *Anna Karenina,* and, especially, the complicated use of place and landscape in the novel; she is particularly attentive to the texture of Molkho's visit to Germany.

The Arab in Israeli Literature

As Ramras-Rauch's comments suggest, because of the pre-Zionist interaction between Sephardic Jews and Arabs in various Mediterranean communities, the representation of the Arab in Israeli literature is connected to the Ashkenazi-Sephardic divide in Israeli society. For Warren Bargad (1977) and Gilead Morahg (1986), the presence of a distinctly Sephardic attitude or style is not an issue in the image of the Arab in Israeli literature. Bargad illustrates and Morahg summarizes the treatment of Arab characters in Israeli fiction in the first seven decades of the Arab-Jewish encounter as, what Morahg calls, "abstractions" and "depersonalized figures who serve as schematic catalysts for the internal dilemmas of their Jewish counterparts, and it is only these Jewish characters whose inner worlds are much more deeply penetrated and extensively portrayed."

Morahg analyzes *The Lover* as one of six novels of the late seventies and early eighties in which "Arab characters are no longer static and stereotypical points of moral reference for a central Jewish protagonist; rather they are sharply differentiated individuals whose development in the course of the narrative is integral to its thematic signification." Ken Frieden (1993) analyzes "Facing the Forests" and "Three Days and a Child" as stories that contain images in which modern Israeli enterprises efface an Arab past.

Gila Ramras-Rauch explores these issues in depth in her book, *The Arab in Israeli Literature* (1989), which argues "that the image of the Arab in Israeli literature is closely tied to the self-definition of the Israeli." She locates the literary role of the Arab in Yehoshua's fiction biographically and ideologically by making connections to Yehoshua's own literary identity and to his diagnosis of the crumbling of the Zionist-Labor center of Israeli culture in the 1970s and 1980s. In a comprehensive literal and symbolic analysis of "Facing the Forests," she concludes, "Tragically, the

Israeli discovers a new basis of Zionism in the burned soil, a Zionism born of fire and war, and perceived with all its tragic ramifications in the reality of the land and its people." She also summarizes novelist Meir Shalev's radical reading, which argues that the story represents a violent struggle against the Zionist founding fathers over the true meaning of the land.

In her analysis of *The Lover* she gives less attention to the anguish of isolation than to the conflict between freedom and dependence. "Love, responsibility, commitment, the past—all spell dependence, while aloneness spells freedom and the right to be."

She situates Yehoshua's depiction of the Arab within a broad historical sketch of Israeli narrative, identifying two modes, one realistic "based on verisimilitude and proximity to reality" with an "external, spatial" orientation, the other "symbolic, meta-realistic, ironic" with an "internal, temporal" orientation.

She also identifies many of the pervasive features of Yehoshua's work: the elements of destruction and disintegration, the art of ironic inversion (of myths, archetypes, reader expectations, social values), the attention to a personal (rather than societal) viewpoint that is characterized by moral indignation and anarchic tendencies, and the strong "mythic element" and the "biblical substructure" in his work. She sees Yehoshua's basic stance as that of a tragic ironist addressing the complexities, ironies, and paradoxes of his society.

Feminist Approaches

Esther Fuchs (1984), in one of a number of feminist analyses of the characters in Yehoshua's fiction, concludes that Yehoshua's female characters, up through *A Late Divorce,* are exempted from the experience of time "and allowed refuge either in myth or in stereotypical female roles." Inexorably blank, they often serve "as an allegorical representation of the land of Israel—an inanimate and impenetrable entity."

Fuchs expands this analysis in her book *Israeli Mythogynies* (1987). Although acknowledging the fuller mimetic presentation of Dafi and Asya, she argues that none of Yehoshua's women (through *A Late Divorce*) escapes three androcentric categories: "the desirable but unattainable young woman, the inaccessible or undesirable wife, and the old woman." Dogmatically ideological, Fuchs minimizes both the complexity and the development of Yehoshua's art, even managing to interpret the lovely lovemaking scene between Dafi and Na'im, surely one of the most powerful, positive, and significant moments of connection in all of Yehoshua's fiction, as nothing more or less than a rape.

Anne Golomb Hoffman, a critic grounded in contemporary psycho-analytical and feminist theory, sees Yehoshua's subsequent two novels as profoundly subversive. In two essays, both published in 1992, she discusses Yehoshua's dissection of gender, body, and nationality in *Five Seasons* and *Mr. Mani*. In both essays she offers particularly exciting dissections of the body imagery in the novels.

In her essay on *Five Seasons* (1992b), she describes how Yehoshua subverts received values by "the feminization of the protagonist and dismantling of the plot of male desire." Using some of the details Domb used to make her case that the novel is an attack on Ashkenazi values, Hoffman argues that the "very texture of the narrative betrays a discomfort with gendered roles and the assumptions they produce." Like Morahg (1982), she believes that the "novels move toward closer attention to the individual psyche, while retaining their resonance on the level of the collective," and she argues that the novel "works against cultural binarisms," including male-female, Israel-Diaspora, and Ashkenazi-Sephardi. She traces the inward and regressive steps of Molkho's journey, which she links with infantile sexuality, death, and the "recovery of an archaic relationship to the maternal body" and shows how music and the Orpheus myth enrich the process. She is more interested in a thematic analysis of the way *Five Seasons* subverts gender roles and the male plot of desire than in a formal analysis that treats Molkho's immersion in regressive material as steps in a plot of liberation (or exorcism), which require Molkho to sift the spirit of his dead beloved wife through his living body to be free for new desire—because, for Molkho, desire requires being in love.

In her essay on *Mr. Mani* (1992a) Hoffman examines "the representation of sexuality and gender in relation to history and ideology" in *Mr. Mani* and characterizes the novel as an antifable of gender and nationalism. For instance, she analyzes Egon's narrative in the second conversation in the context of images of infantile sexuality, Freud's archaeological metaphor that compares Minoan-Mycenean civilization to preoedipal sexuality, and the nineteenth-century German ideology of nation, race, woman, and Jew. As in her essay on *Five Seasons,* her emphasis on theme leads to an anatomy of subversion: "the effect is to engage us in a demonstration . . . of the confusion, secrecy, and error that enters into constructions of the female body and sexuality and to bring us to an awareness of the function

of these confusions and errors to our reading of modern Jewish history."
She is more at home in uncertainty about "the source of the obscure
repetition buried within the generations of the Mani family" than in the
movement of the plot toward the possibility of a mythological comprehen-
sion of the roots of contemporary difficulties.

Nehama Aschkenasy (1988) analyzes the character Naomi of *A Late
Divorce* in a comparative study of women and the double in Berdichewsky,
Agnon, Oz, and Yehoshua. While she does not treat the extraordinary
pathos of Naomi's torment, she astutely shows how Naomi is endowed
"with an acute sensitivity, a larger than life vision, and near demonic
mental powers. These female qualities inevitably result in the creation of
doubles that estrange the woman from her environment but make her the
truthful mirror of our existential fears and social maladies."

A Late Divorce

A Late Divorce has to date received the most English commentary. The
earliest article is by Gershon Shaked (1982), the Israeli critic who first
characterized the "generation of the state" as a "new wave" in his
groundbreaking Hebrew book, *A New Wave in Hebrew Fiction* (Israel
1971; revised 1974). Shaked discussed the general features of the novel
more than a year before it was published in English. He emphasized the
comic elements of the novel and observes, "The tension between the
humorous details which shape this novel and the grave seriousness of its
overall scheme is perhaps its greatest artistic achievement." Two years
later, in a comparative study of *A Late Divorce* and Oz's *A Perfect Peace,*
Leon Yudkin (1984) concludes that "although the backdrop is characteristically Israeli, in both cases we witness a further movement away from
overt State concerns."

In 1987, in another comparative study, this one of *A Late Divorce*
and Heinrich Böll's *Billiards at Half Past Nine,* Leah Hadomi analyzes
the two works as family novels that reflect history and share three "leading
motifs: madness, murder, and adoption." She argues that *A Late Divorce*
tends "towards an acceptance of the inevitability of involvement in the
generational-historical process," while Böll's novel tends toward "dehis-
toricization." She effectively analyzes the allegorical elements of Kaminka's
relationship with Naomi in *Between Right and Right,* and is especially
valuable in her analysis of Asa's identity as historian, son, and husband
and her discussion of the Exodus story and the multiple Passover seders
as "quasi-archetypal elements" in the novel.

In a 1991 article, Aschkenasy explores in detail the powerful parallels between *A Late Divorce* and *The Sound and the Fury,* and appraises the differences between the two novels. Though she doesn't include Faulkner's use of Freud in her analysis and understates Dilsey's importance, she perceptively discusses many details of character and plot. She argues that Yehoshua divides elements of Quentin's monologue between Kaminka and Asa and elements of Jason's monologue between Kedmi and Tsvi and analyzes the consequences of Yehoshua's introduction of three feminine monologues.

Yehoshua's Shorter Works

A number of valuable individual analyses of Yehoshua's stories and novellas supplement the analyses that appeared as parts of broader discussions, notably Morahg's discussions of "Two Days and a Child" (1982) and "Early in the Summer of 1970" (1988) and Ramras-Rauch's dissection of "Facing the Forests" (1989). In a brief introduction to "Facing the Forests" in *Modern Hebrew Literature,* Robert Alter (1975) summarizes the psychological and existential strands of the story, particularly the narrator's gradual "disengagement from words" and the portrayal of "the balked consciousness of civilized man secretly longing for the cataclysm that will raze all the artificial hedging structures of human culture." Alter highlights Yehoshua's comic tone and the way he skillfully implicates the reader in the narrator's growing obsession with the forest. Bargad analyzes "The Last Commander," "Missile Base 612," and "Early in the Summer of 1970," as works "rooted in one, all-encompassing reality: war and its accompanying stresses on the human psyche." He singles out "Early in the Summer of 1970" for praise as a "technically dazzling work" in which it "becomes clear that the entire action of the story has taken place in the mind of the bereaved father." Mintz (1978) provides succinct analyses of "Missile Base 612" and "Early in the Summer of 1970" as stories of "loss of meaning, and the baffled search for a way to overcome that loss." He is among the many critics, including Wachtel (1979), Fuchs (1987), and Ramras-Rauch (1989), who discern the Binding of Isaac motif in Yehoshua's fiction.

In a more detailed study Naomi Sokoloff (1981) provides a close analysis of the opening strategies of "The Continuing Silence of a Poet," which "highlight the psychological impasse of one character in contrast with the growth of another." There is a side benefit in this article for readers who know little or no Hebrew. In a concrete and accessible way,

Sokoloff manages to give an intense and seductive taste of what is lost in the translation from Hebrew to English.

In another second close reading, Morahg (1988b) applies Roman Jakobson's model of metaphor to "Flood Tide," the most ambitious story in Yehoshua's first collection. He carefully traces the gradual accumulation of contrastive images in the story's binary system of metaphors and shows how significant meaning emerges from this metaphoric code. He locates the meaning in the story in the images of the storm, the prison, the sea, the plain, the dogs, the prisoners and the ideas of desire, control, death, freedom, and love. He demonstrates that the narrator does not desire death, but, on the contrary, in the concluding movement of the story, "reverses his priorities and affirms the passionate, erotic aspect of his inner self." This affirmation refutes "the existential code that attempts to confront the often absurd, and ultimately tragic, exigencies of human existence through repression and misdirection of human emotions."

Appendixes

Glossary

References

Index

Appendix A
Chronology

B.C.E.

1500	End of patriarchal period
1250	Exodus from Egypt
1200	Israelite conquest of Canaan
1200	Arrival of Philistines
950	King David
722	Northern Kingdom of Israel ended by Assyrians
587	Destruction of First Temple by Babylonians
515	Completion of Second Temple

C.E.

70	Destruction of Second Temple in Jerusalem by Romans
70s	Establishment of Yavneh by Yohanan ben Zakkai
135	End of Jewish revolt against Romans
632	Death of Muhammad
1028	Death of Gershom ben Judah of Mainz, the Light of the Exile
1095	First Crusade begins
1204	Death of Maimonides

1492	Jews expelled from Spain
1807	Napoleonic Sanhedrin in Paris
1811	Death of Nahman of Bratzlav
1848	European revolutions: "the springtime of nations"
1881	First *aliyah* from Russia begins
1894–99	Dreyfus affair in France
1896	Herzl publishes *Judenstaat*
1897	First Zionist Congress in Basel
1899	Third Zionist Congress in Basel
1917	British occupy Palestine
1917	November. Balfour Declaration
1922	League of Nations approves British Mandate
1933	Nazi Party comes to power
1939	World War II begins
1940–44	The Holocaust
1947	UN votes for partition of Palestine
1948	Declaration of Independence of the State of Israel
1948–49	Israel War of Independence
1949	Beginning of mass migration of Jews to Israel
1956	Sinai campaign
1961	Eichmann trial
1966	S. I. Agnon and Nelly Sachs receive Nobel Prize for literature
1967	June. Six-Day War
1969–70	War of Attrition between Egypt and Israel
1973	October. Yom Kippur War
1977	June. Menachem Begin becomes prime minister
1977	November. Anwar Sadat visits Jerusalem
1978	Camp David negotiations between Begin, Sadat, and Jimmy Carter
1978	Peace Now founded
1979	Signing of Israeli-Egyptian peace agreement
1981	Sadat assassinated
1982	June. Lebanon War
1983	Yitzhak Shamir becomes prime minister

1987	December 8. Intifada begins
1991	January. Gulf War begins
1991	December. Madrid Conference
1992	June. Yitzhak Rabin becomes prime minister
1993	"Oslo I" and "Oslo II" negotiated
1993	September. Israel-PLO accord
1994–96	"Oslo I" in effect
1994	Goldstein's terrorism at Hebron's Ibrahami Mosque
1995	November 4. Rabin assassinated
1996	February, March: suicide bombings
1996	May. Benjamin Netanyahu elected prime minister
1996	May. "Oslo II" final status negotiations scheduled to begin (according to 1993 accord)
1999	May. "Oslo II" to go into effect

Appendix B
Works by A. B. Yehoshua

Novels

The Lover (U.S. 1978; Israel 1977)
A Late Divorce (U.S. 1984; Israel 1982)
Five Seasons (U.S. 1989; *Molkho,* Israel 1987)
Mr. Mani (U.S. 1992; Israel 1990)
Open Heart (U.S. 1996; *The Return from India,* Israel 1994)
Voyage to the End of the Millennium (Israel 1997)

Story Collections and Plays

Death of the Old Man (Israel 1963)
Three Days and a Child (U.S. 1970; *Facing the Forests,* Israel 1968)
Early in the Summer of 1970 (Israel 1972)
A Night in May (U.S. 1974, Israel 1969)
The Continuing Silence of a Poet (U.S. 1988)
Possessions (U.S. 1993). In *Modern Israeli Drama in Translation,* edited by Michael Carasik. Portsmouth, N.H.: Heineman.

Essays

Between Right and Right (U.S. 1981; *In Defense of Normality,* Israel 1980)
The Wall and the Mountain (Israel 1989)
"Brenner's Wife—As Metaphor." *Modern Hebrew Literature* 8 (spring/summer 1983): 5–12.

"The Injustice of Death." *Modern Hebrew Literature* 3 (fall 1989): 8–10.
"Sleeping Beauty." *The Jewish Monthly* (Dec. 1990): 32–7.
"The Other Power." *Modern Hebrew Literature* 7 (fall/winter 1991): 9–10.
"Israeli Identity in a Time of Peace: Prospects and Perils." *Tikkun* 10 (Nov./Dec. 1995): 34–40, 94.
"The Power of Tikkun:" Translated by Daphna Poskanzer. *Tikkun* 11 (Jan./Feb. 1996): 39–40.
"Democracy and the Novel." Translated by Dan Schlossberg. unpublished lecture.

Interviews

"Let U.S. Not Betray Zionism." In *Unease in Zion,* by Ehud Ben Ezer, 321–39. New York: Quadrangle/New York *Times,* 1974.
"Interview 2: A. B. Yehoshua. March 7, 1985." In *Voices of Israel,* by Joseph Cohen, 69–79. Albany: State Univ. of New York Press, 1990.
"One Has to Fall in Love." Shmuel Huppert, interviewer. *Modern Hebrew Literature* 13 (fall/winter 1987) 7–11.

Glossary

akedat yitzhak: the Binding of Isaac.

aliyah: "going up," immigration to Israel.

am yisrael: the nation of Israel.

Ashkenaz, Ashkenazi: Germany, German; later, the general name for the Jews of northern and eastern Europe and of Western Jews, in general.

balagan: chaos.

eretz yisrael: the Land of Israel.

eretz yisrael ha'gedolah: the "Greater Land of Israel," all the land from the Jordan River east to the Mediterranean Sea.

et sha'arei ratzon le'hippate'ah: "To Open the Gates of Favor," a **piyut** by Judah Samuel Abbas (d. 1167).

even shetiyyah: the "rock from which the world was woven," "the foundation rock" of the whole world, where Mohammed rose to heaven during his Night Journey and where Isaac was bound for the slaughter.

gal hadash: the "new wave" in literature, the generation that came of age too late to have fought in the War of Independence.

golah: Diaspora, exile.

goyim: Gentiles.

hagim: festivals.

halachah: the traditional body of Jewish law.

halutz: pioneer.

haredim: ultraorthodox; usually, anti-Zionist Israelis.

haver: friend, comrade, lover.

havurah, havurot: group, groups; also refers to the special decentralized religious groups that have become an important movement within contemporary American liberal Judaism.

herem: ban, excommunication.

kever rahel: Rachel's Tomb, outside Bethlehem.

kivan negdi: opposite direction, countermove.

kotel: the Western wall of the site of the ancient temple in Jerusalem.

l'chaded et asurov: to strengthen his bonds, to sharpen his bonds.

Me'ah She'arim: (literally, "a hundred fold") an ultraorthodox neighborhood in Jerusalem.

Me'or ha-Golah: the Light (or the Luminary) of the Diaspora, the title of Rabbi Gershom ben Yehudah of Mainz (c. 960–1028), one of the first great German talmudic scholars.

me'orat ha-machpelah: the Machpelah Cave in Hebron, the traditional burial place of Abraham and Sarah, Isaac and Rebecca, and Jacob and Leah.

mitnahalim: West Bank settlers.

nigunim: traditional, usually Hasidic, melodies, which are chanted communally.

oleh (masculine), **olah** (feminine): "one who goes up," an immigrant to Israel.

pesukim: biblical verses.

piyut: liturgical poem, usually from the Middle Ages.

p'lishtim: the Philistines.

Rosh Hashanah: Jewish New Year in the fall, which begins the ten days of repentance, which culminate in Yom Kippur, the Day of Atonement.

Sepharad, Sephardi: Spain, Spanish; later, the term for the Jews of the Mediterranean Sea, Africa, and Asia.

shabbas goy: Yiddish term for a Gentile hired to do activities prohibited to the Jews on Sabbath.

shiva: return (when spelled with the Hebrew letter *vet*); Shiva, the Indian god (when spelled with two *vavs*).

shofar: the ram's horn, blown during the synagogue service on Rosh Hanshanah.

siddurim: prayer books.

teku: a stalemate, an unresolved question; traditionally, an acronym **TYKU** for "Elijah (the Tishbite) will answer the questions and problems."

tikkun olam: the repair or restoration of the world, often with religious kabbalistic connotations.

torah: the Pentateuch, the Five Books of Moses.

yahrzeit: Yiddish term for the anniversary of someone's death, traditionally marked by lighting a *yahrzeit* candle, which burns for twenty-four hours, and reciting a special prayer, the mourner's *kaddish*.

yeridah: "going down," emigration from Israel.

yeshivot: orthodox religious academies.

yored, yoredet: "one who goes down," an émigré from Israel.

References

Alter, Robert, ed. 1975. *Modern Hebrew Literature*, 353–56. New York: Behrman House.

———. 1977a. "Fiction in a State of Siege." In *Defenses of the Imagination: Jewish Writers and Modern Historical Crisis*, 213–32. Philadelphia: Jewish Publication Society.

———. 1977b. "Images of the Arab in Israeli Fiction." *Hebrew Studies* 18: 61–55.

———. 1991. "The Reception of Hebrew Literature Abroad: The Rise and the Rise in the United States." *Modern Hebrew Literature* 7 (fall/winter) 5–7.

Aschkenasy, Nehama. 1988. "Women and the Double in Modern Hebrew Literature: Berdichewsky/Agnon, Oz/Yehoshua." *Prooftexts* 8: 245–63.

———. 1991. "Yehoshua's 'Sound and Fury': *A Late Divorce* and Its Faulknerian Model." *Modern Language Studies* 21: 92–104.

Band, Arnold J. 1992. "*Mar Mani:* The Archeology of Self-Deception." *Prooftexts* 12: 231–44.

Bargad, Warren. 1977. "The Image of the Arab in Israeli Literature." *Hebrew Annual Review* 1: 53–65. Reprinted in *From Agnon to Oz*, 28–40. Atlanta: Scholars Press, 1996.

———. 1978. "War, Allegory, and Psyche." *Midstream* 24 (Oct. 1978): 76–78. Reprinted in *From Agnon to Oz*, 159–63. Atlanta: Scholars Press, 1996.

———. 1979. "Private Testimonies, Public Issues." *Midstream* 25 (Aug.-Sept.): 55–56. Reprinted in *From Agnon to Oz*, 164–71. Atlanta: Scholars Press, 1996.

Bloom, Harold. 1984. "Domestic Arrangements." *New York Times Book Review* (Feb. 19): 1,3.

Cohen, Joseph. 1990. "A. B. Yehoshua." In *Voices of Israel*, 45–80. Albany: State Univ. of New York Press.

189

Domb, Risa. 1995. *"Molcho* by A. B. Yehoshua." In *Home Thoughts from Abroad,* 36–60. London: Valentine Mitchell.

Feinberg, Anat. 1975. "A. B. Yehoshua as Playwright." *Modern Hebrew Literature* 1 (spring): 43–47.

Feldman, Yael. 1987. "Zionism on the Analyst's Couch in Contemporary Israeli Literature." *Tikkun* 2 (May): 31–34, 91–96.

Frieden, Ken. 1993. "A. B. Yehoshua: Arab Dissent in His Early Fiction." In *Israeli Writers Consider the Outsider,* edited by Leon I. Yudkin, 112–23. Rutherford, N.J.: Farleigh Dickinson Univ. Press.

Fuchs, Esther. 1984. "The Sleepy Wife: A Feminist Consideration of A. B. Yehoshua's Fiction." *Hebrew Annual Review* 8: 71–81.

———. 1987 "A. B. Yehoshua: The Lack of Consciousness." In *Israeli Mythogynies,* 35–57. Albany: State Univ. of New York Press.

Hadomi, Leah. 1987. "The Family Novel as a Reflection of History: *Billiards at Half Past Nine* (H. Böll) and *A Late Divorce* (A. B. Yehoshua)." *Hebrew Annual Review* 11: 105–27.

Hakak, Lev. 1993. "Israeli Society as Depicted in the Novels of A. B. Yehoshua." In *Equivocal Dreams: Studies in Modern Hebrew Literature,* 79–143. New York: Ktav.

Hoffman, Anne Golomb. 1992a. "Fictions of Identity and Their Undoing in Yehoshua's *Mr. Mani." Prooftexts* 12: 245–63.

———. 1992b. "Oedipal Narrative and Its Discontents: A. B. Yehoshua's *Molkho (Five Seasons)."* In *Gender and Text in Modern Hebrew and Yiddish Literature,* edited by Naomi B. Sokoloff, Anne Lapidus Lerner, and Anita Norich, 195–211. New York: Jewish Theological Seminary.

Kazin, Alfred. 1978. "Missing Connections." *New York Review of Books* (Dec. 21): 25.

Kurzweil, Baruch. 1970. "An Appraisal of the Stories of Abraham B. Yehoshua." *Literature East and West* 14:60–72.

Megged, Aharon. 1971. "Some Problems of New Israeli Writing." *Midstream* 17 (Mar.): 21–28.

Mintz, Alan. 1978. "New Israeli Writing." *Commentary* 65 (Jan.): 64–67.

———. 1992. "The Counterlives." *New Republic* (June 29): 41–45.

Morahg, Gilead. 1979. "Outraged Humanism: The Fiction of A. B. Yehoshua." *Hebrew Annual Review* 3: 141–55.

———. 1979–80. "Affirmative Structure in A. B. Yehoshua's *The Lover." Hebrew Studies* 20–21: 98–106.

———. 1982. "Reality and Symbol in the Fiction of A. B. Yehoshua." *Prooftexts* 2: 179–96.

———. 1986. "New Images of Arabs in Israeli Fiction." *Prooftexts* 6: 147–62.

———. 1988a. "Facing the Wilderness: God and Country in the Fiction of A. B. Yehoshua." *Prooftexts* 8: 311–31.

———. 1988b. "A Symbolic Psyche: The Structure of Meaning in A. B. Yehoshua's Flood Tide." *Hebrew Studies* 29: 81–100.

———. 1992. "From Madness on to Sanity: A. B. Yehoshua's Shifting Perspective on the Diaspora." *Shofar* 11 (fall): 50–60.

———. 1993. "A. B. Yehoshua: Fictions of Zion and Diaspora." In *Israeli Writers Consider the Outsider,* edited by Leon I. Yudkin, 124–37. Rutherford, N.J.: Farleigh Dickinson Univ. Press.

Novak, William. 1977. "Terrible Events Are Imminent." *Village Voice* 22 (Apr. 25):72.

Ofrat, Gideon. 1986. *"Possessions* as a Death Wish." *Modern Hebrew Literature* 12 (fall/winter) 40–42.

Ramras-Rauch, Gila. 1989. *The Arab in Israeli Literature,* 125–47. Bloomington: Indiana Univ. Press.

———. 1991. "A. B. Yehoshua and the Sephardic Experience." *World Literature Today* 65 (winter): 8–13.

Shaked, Gershon. 1982–83. "A Great Madness Hides Behind All This." *Modern Hebrew Literature* 8 (fall/winter): 14–26.

Siddiq, Muhammad. 1992. "The Making of a Counter-Narrative: Two Examples from Contemporary Arabic and Hebrew Fiction." *Michigan Quarterly Review* 31 (fall): 649–62.

Sokoloff, Naomi. 1981. "Contrast, Continuity, and Contradiction: Opening Signals in A. B. Yehoshua's 'A Poet's Continuing Silence.' " *Hebrew Annual Review* 5: 115–35.

Solotaroff, Ted. 1992. "Strange Jews." *The Nation* (June 15): 826–29.

Wachtel, Nili. 1979. "A. B. Yehoshua: Between the Dream and the Reality." *Midstream* 25 (Aug.-Sept.): 48–54.

Weseltier, Leon. 1984. "The Fall of a Family." *New Republic* (Mar. 12): 38–40.

Yudkin, Leon I. 1977. "Multiple Focus and Mystery: *The Lover* by A. B. Yehoshua." *Modern Hebrew Literature* 3 (autumn): 38–41.

———. 1984. *1948 and After: Aspects of Israeli Fiction,* 167–73. Manchester Eng.: Univ. of Manchester.

Index

Orpaz, Yitzhak, 78
Oslo Accords, 1, 5, 11–12, 35–37, 150
Oz, Amos, 3, 12, 35, 49, 78, 161, 176;
  politics of, 35, 41, 43, 135; *works: The
  Black Box,* 52, 161; *In the Land of
  Israel,* 71; *A Perfect Peace,* 59

Palestine Liberation Organization (PLO),
  10–11, 35
Palestinian identity, 2, 12, 48, 116; *See
  also* Palestinians
Palestinians, 1, 7–8, 17–18, 49, 115,
  138; dreams of, 9; elections of, 1, 36;
  in "Facing the Forests," 48, 141;
  fundamentalists and, 18, 38; Gulf War
  and, 40; internecine violence among,
  7–8; negotiations with, 8, 30, 38;
  origins of, 138; Oslo agreement with,
  11; peace and, 145; PLO and, 10;
  recognition of, 35–36, 105; right to
  self-determination of, 9–10, 35, 38,
  73, 116. *See also* Intifada; Palestine
  Liberation Organization; Palestinian
  identity
Paley, Grace, 84, 96
Peace, 39, 143–48
Peace Now, 34–35
Peace process. *See* Madrid Conference;
  Oslo Accords; Palestinians
Peres, Shimon, 11, 38, 147, 151
Philistines, 115
Pinter, Harold, 51
Possessions, 45–47
Pound, Ezra, 65
Proust, Marcel, 69, 162
Psychoanalysis, 14, 15–16, 63, 87, 110,
  169–70, 172, 175

Rabin, Yitzhak 8, 10–11, 35, 37–38, 39;
  assassination of, 1, 17, 36–37, 124,
  150, 156–57
Ramras-Rauch, Gila, 171–72, 173, 177
Readers, 8–9, 123–25, 156, 189–90,
  192–93, 207–8, 269, 336

Reagan, Ronald, 34, 36
"Remembrance of Sephardic Things
  Past," 79
*Return from India, The. See Open
  Heart*
Roth, Philip, 71, 126

Sadan, Dov, 144–45
Sadat, Anwar, 35
Shabtai, Yaakov, 78
Shaked, Gershom, 176
Shalev, Meir, 78, 174
Shamir, Moshe, 44
Shamir, Yitzhak, 8, 10, 39, 74, 154
Shammas, Anton, 48–49, 73, 74,
  78
Shamosh, Amnon, 78
Shoah. *See* Holocaust
Shoah (film), 123
Siddiq, Muhammed, 75, 172
Sinyavsky, Andrei, 34
Six-Day War, 9, 35–36, 38, 43, 46, 77,
  105, 111
Sokoloff, Naomi, 177–78
Solotaroff, Ted, 19
Suicide, 70, 83–85, 130
Suicide bombings, 11, 17, 100

Tammuz, Benjamin, 44, 52
Territories. *See* West Bank and Gaza
Terrorism, 1, 8, 14, 40, 142, 151
Tikkun olam (repair of the universe),
  137
Tolstoy, Leo, 2, 4–5, 19, 58, 81, 84, 95,
  140, 173

United States: assassinations in, 36–37;
  culture of, 2, 34, 40, 135, 144;
  individualism in, 131, 155–56, 158–
  59; literature of, 57, 76, 141; politics
  of, 34, 37, 41, 42, 105; and the power
  of language, 77; reception of
  Yehoshua's work, 12–13; role in